POSTCARD HISTORY SERIES

Southeast Georgia

in Vintage Postcards

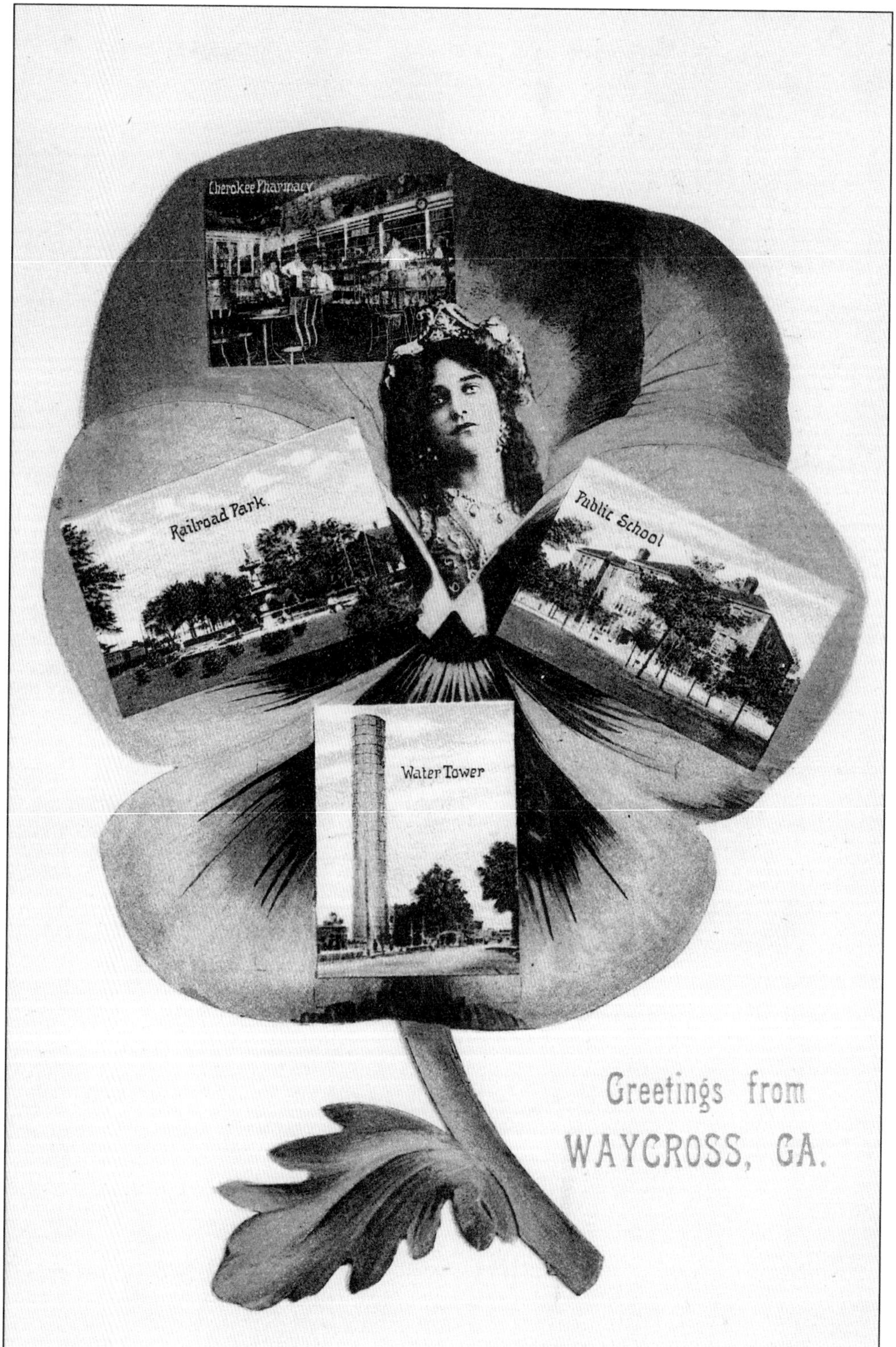

Cherokee Pharmacy
Railroad Park.
Public School
Water Tower
Greetings from
WAYCROSS, GA.

POSTCARD HISTORY SERIES

Southeast Georgia in Vintage Postcards

Gary L. Doster

ARCADIA PUBLISHING

ISBN 978-0-7385-6891-1

Published by Arcadia Publishing
Charleston, South Carolina

Printed in the United States of America

Library of Congress Catalog Card Number: Applied for

For all general information contact Arcadia Publishing at:
Telephone 843-853-2070
Fax 843-853-0044
E-mail sales@arcadiapublishing.com
For customer service and orders:
Toll-Free 1-888-313-2665

Visit us on the Internet at www.arcadiapublishing.com

For Faye Thomas Doster,
The Best Helpmate a Man Ever Had

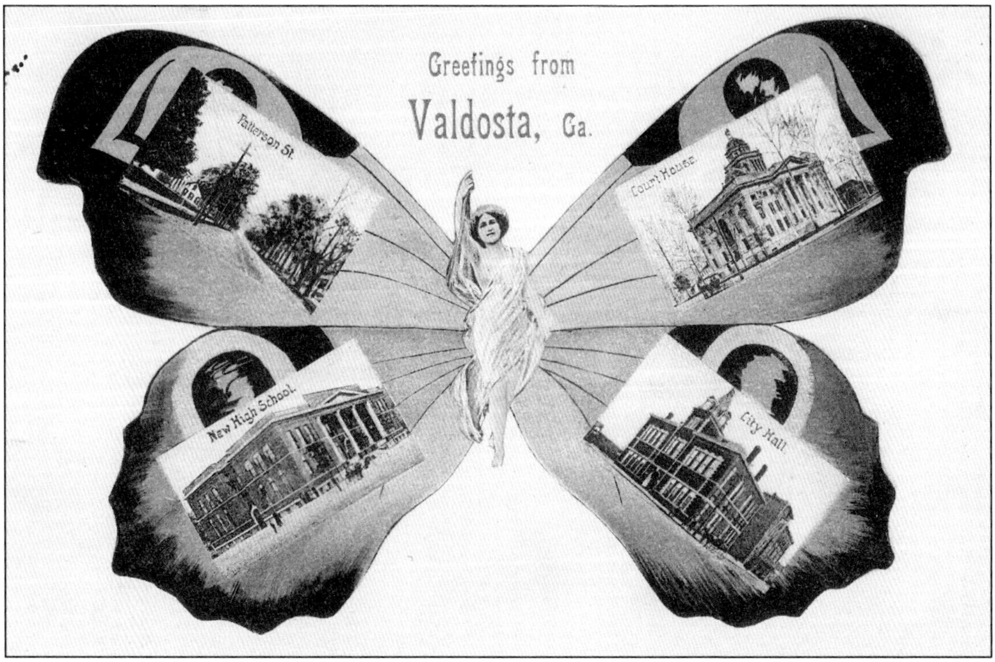

Contents

Acknowledgments

For help in various ways, including advice, information, and post cards, I wish to thank the following people:

Carl Anderson
Jim Dunn
Nell Dunn
John Kovalski
Jerald Ledbetter
Ernest Malcom
Charlotte Marshall
Dan Marshall
George Marshall
Bill Moffat
Edwin Oldham
Hershel Reeves
Gordon Sanford
Sue Fan Tate
Jeff West
Bill Wheless

Introduction

We are indeed fortunate that post cards* were invented and were so popular during the first several years of this century. In the clamor to satisfy the almost overwhelming demand for more and more post cards by the public, literally thousands of scenes were photographed that were never captured on film for any other reason. Over time, many of the homes, depots, courthouses, stores, and other buildings so pictured have disappeared and these early post card views are the only images that remain. Two particularly interesting facts that were discovered while selecting and compiling the cards for these books concerned Georgia's Confederate monuments. A great many monuments were unveiled or dedicated on Confederate Memorial Day, April 26, and few of them remain on their original sites. The ladies of the United Daughters of the Confederacy and the old veterans themselves usually selected some prominent spot in the middle of town, almost always at the intersection of two main streets. Invariably, as automobile use increased over years, the monuments became traffic hazards and were moved to another part of town. Consequently, many of these post card views are the only pictures of them in their original locations.

Also of great interest are the views showing the intrusion of the automobile onto the scene. It is fun to note that the earlier post card views, those before 1907 or 1908, usually have horse- or mule-drawn wagons, buggies, or carriages in the street scenes (a few even show mule-powered streetcars!). Then, from that time to about 1912 or 1914, these views will typically show a mix of the animal-drawn vehicles and early automobiles. After this time, a wagon or buggy is only rarely seen, and the number of automobiles on the streets increased rapidly.

*Throughout the book, I have chosen to use the older spelling of the word, i.e. "post card" versus "postcard."

The collecting frenzy that swept the world began in Europe in the 1890s, crept into this country before the turn of the century, and erupted a few years later. Many of the better quality post cards were produced in Europe, particularly Germany. Some of the post card factories in Germany were the size of cotton mills in this country, and they employed hundreds of people. For example, one German plant in 1909 had 112 cylinder printing presses and employed 1,500 workers. During the peak years of the post card collecting fad, more than a million people in Germany were employed in the post card business. In the three-year period from 1907 to 1909, more than 85,000 tons of post cards were imported into the United States from Germany.

In the Images of America book series published by Arcadia, the major effort has been to render pictorial books on individual towns or counties. And these are wonderful. Those of us who have an interest in preserving whatever we can of our past are hungry for books like this and they serve a valuable purpose. However, there are hundreds of smaller communities across every state that offer only a limited number of views of life of yesteryear that also are striking and important. Some medium-sized towns may have a handful of good views that show what their community and its people looked like nearly one hundred years ago. Many of the very small towns may have only one or two representative views. All of these are important, but none of them can support a book alone. Hence, this series of six volumes was conceived to provide a vehicle whereby a collection of early Georgia post cards from numerous small communities could be exhibited.

It is important to note here that this set of books is not intended to be any sort of scholarly work. It is merely an attempt to provide access to a selection of early views of Georgia that are not available in any other form, most of which have not been reprinted since their original publication. Many of the captions we provide in these books are no more than the caption printed on the cards when they were produced. Some additions have been made to some cards when the author had knowledge of some facts regarding the view in question. Other information came from the few reference books listed in the bibliography. To have researched each view and provided a comprehensive caption for each would have taken a lifetime of research, and then would still have been incomplete.

The author is a lifelong Georgian and has collected all manner of Georgiana for most of his life. Some of his other collecting interests are obsolete currency from the Colonial period through the War between the States, early letters and other documents, slave bills of sale and other items pertaining to slavery, Confederate letters and documents, old photographs, trade tokens, and Native-American relics.

One

Appling, Evans, Jeff Davis, Montgomery, Telfair, and Toombs Counties

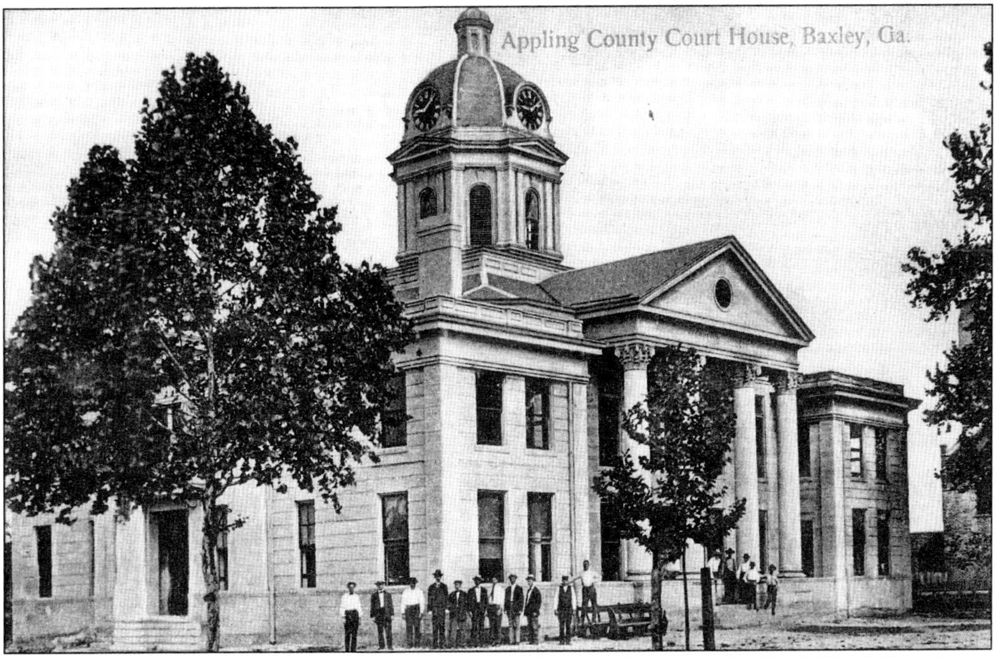

The Appling County Courthouse at Baxley. The courthouse was built 1907–1908 and cost $20,000. The design was by M.T. Lewman and construction was by Falls City Construction. Major renovations and additions were made in 1967.

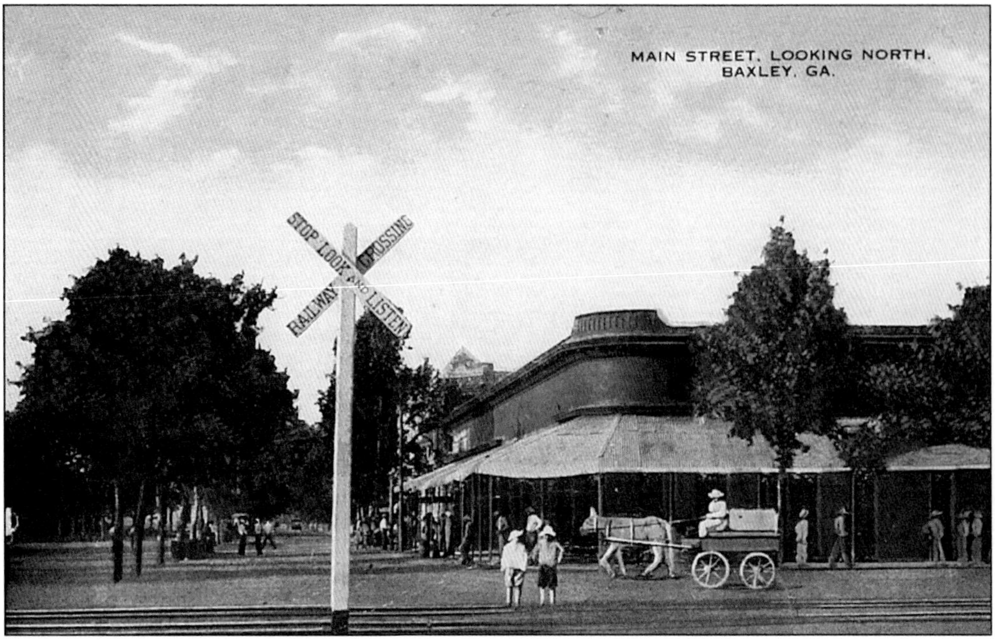

MAIN STREET LOOKING NORTH IN BAXLEY, C. 1917.

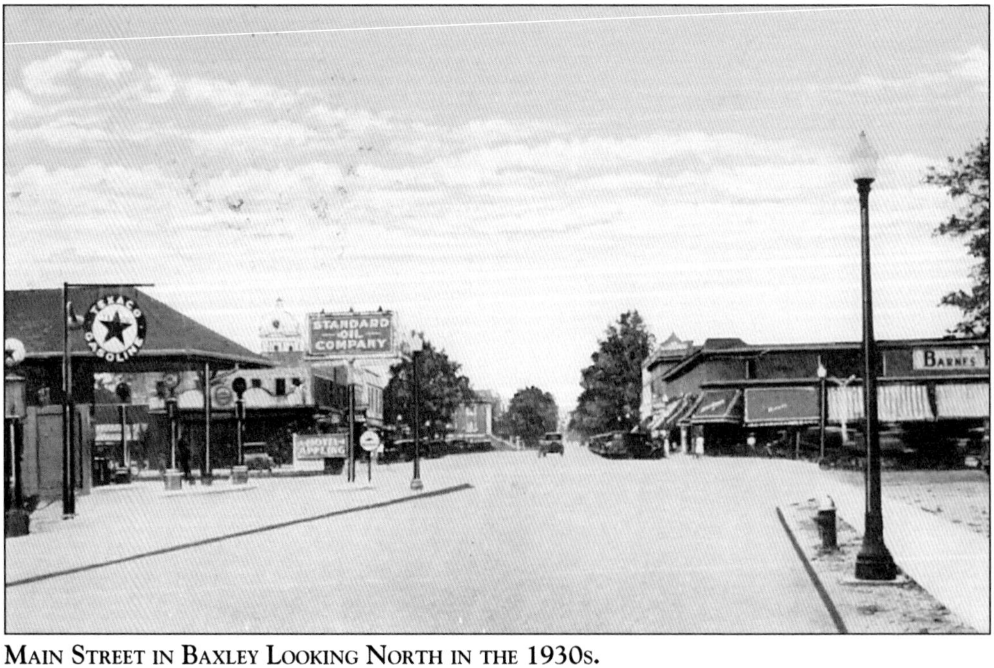

MAIN STREET IN BAXLEY LOOKING NORTH IN THE 1930S.

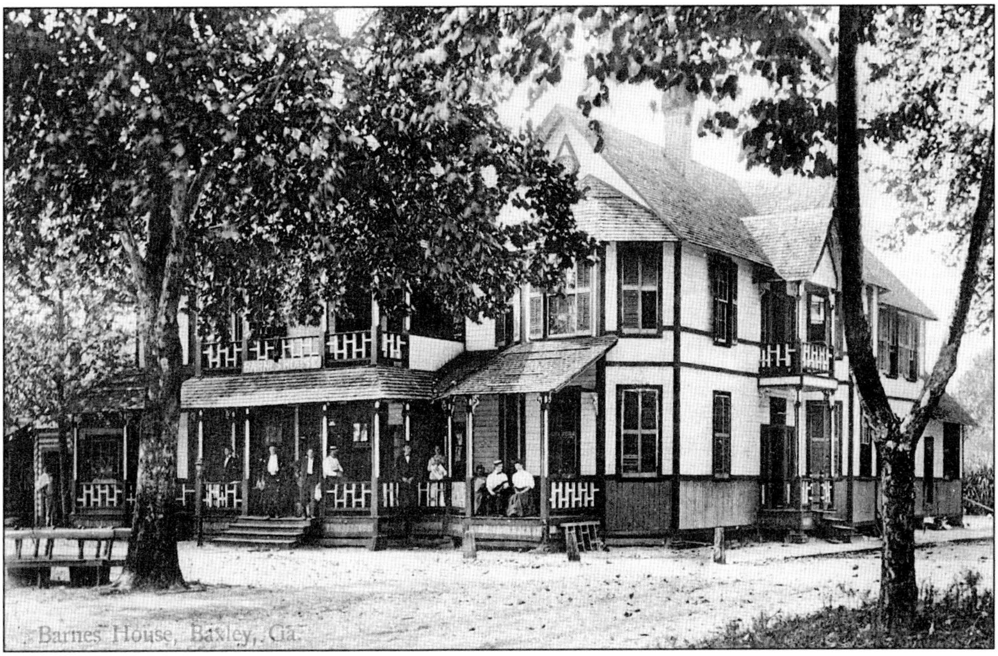

THE BARNES HOUSE FOR BOARDERS IN BAXLEY, C. 1910.

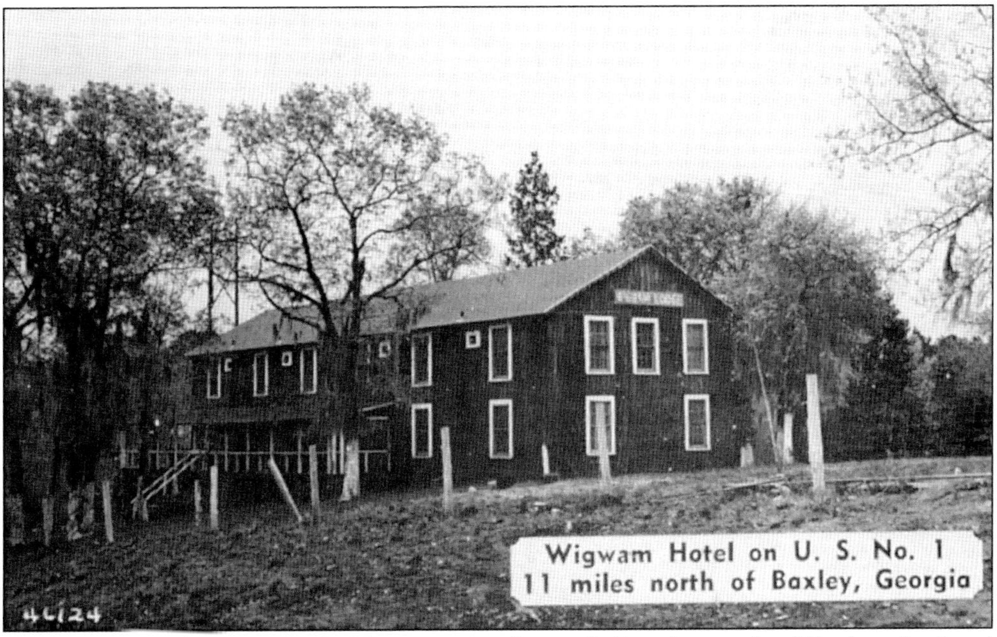

THE WIGWAM HOTEL ON U.S. HIGHWAY #1. Located 11 miles north of Baxley, the hotel provided accommodations for travelers in the 1930s.

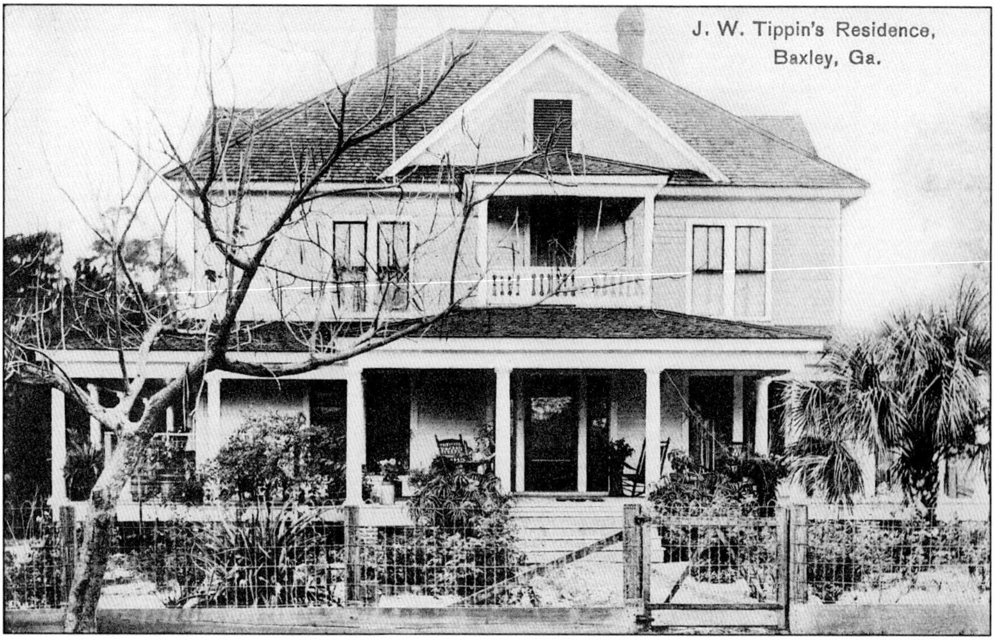

THE 1910 HOME OF J.W. TIPPINS, A BAXLEY GROCER, C. 1910.

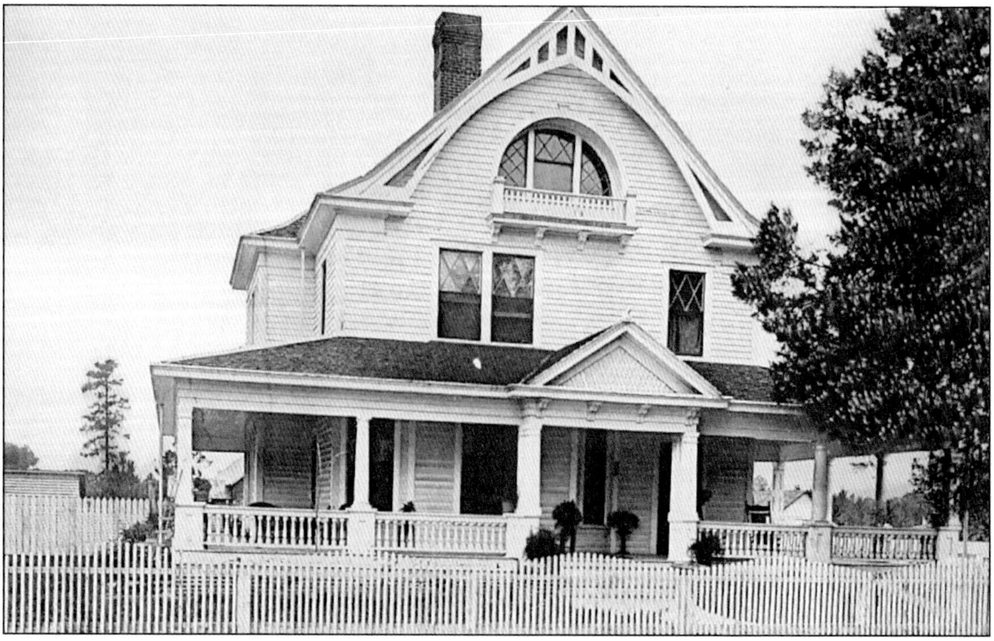

D.D. GILMORE'S RESIDENCE IN BAXLEY, C. 1910.

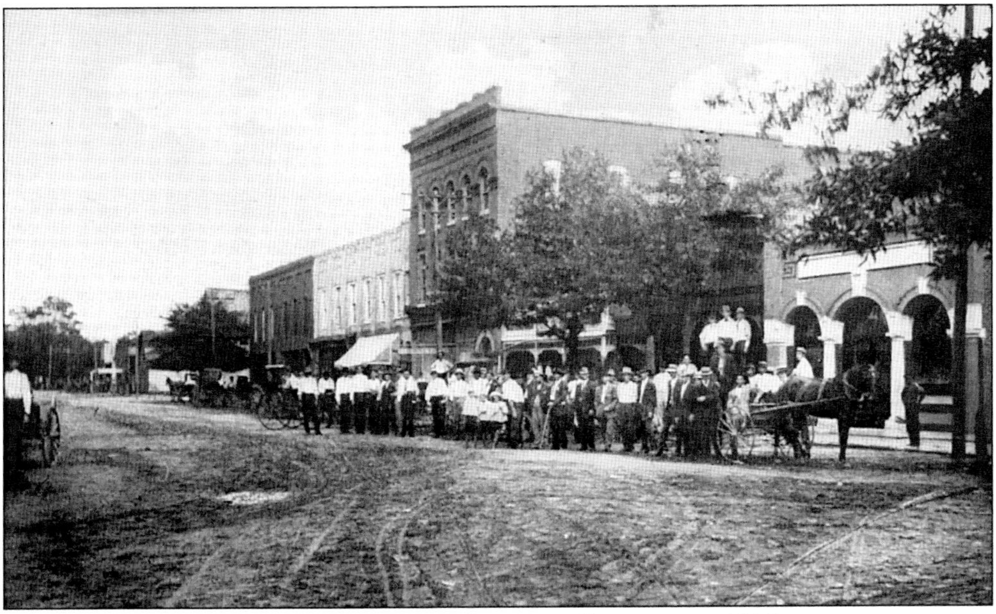

A Large Gathering on South Railroad Street in Claxton, c. 1907.

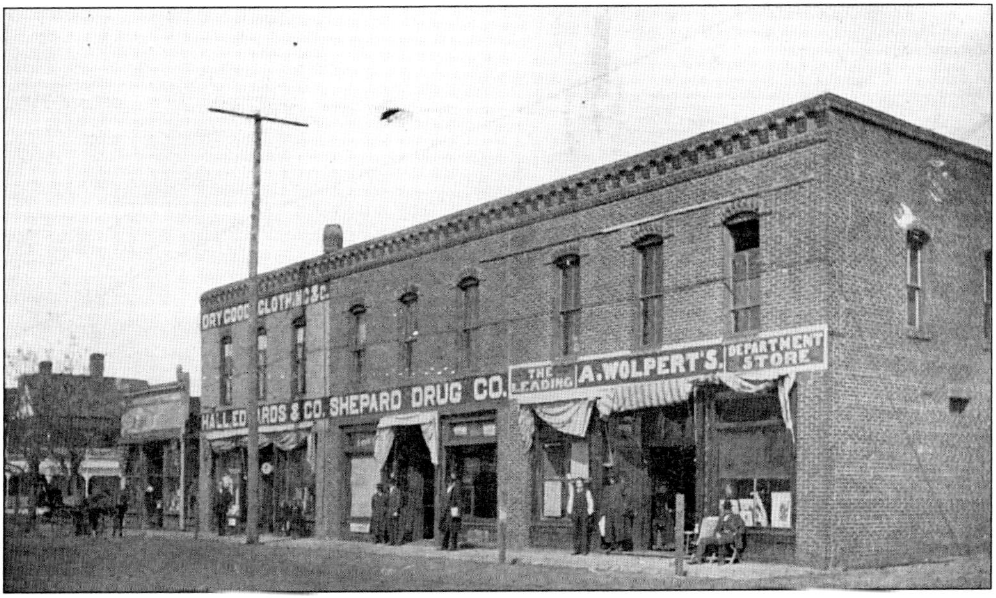

Several Claxton Businesses, c. 1910, Looking West on Railroad Street.

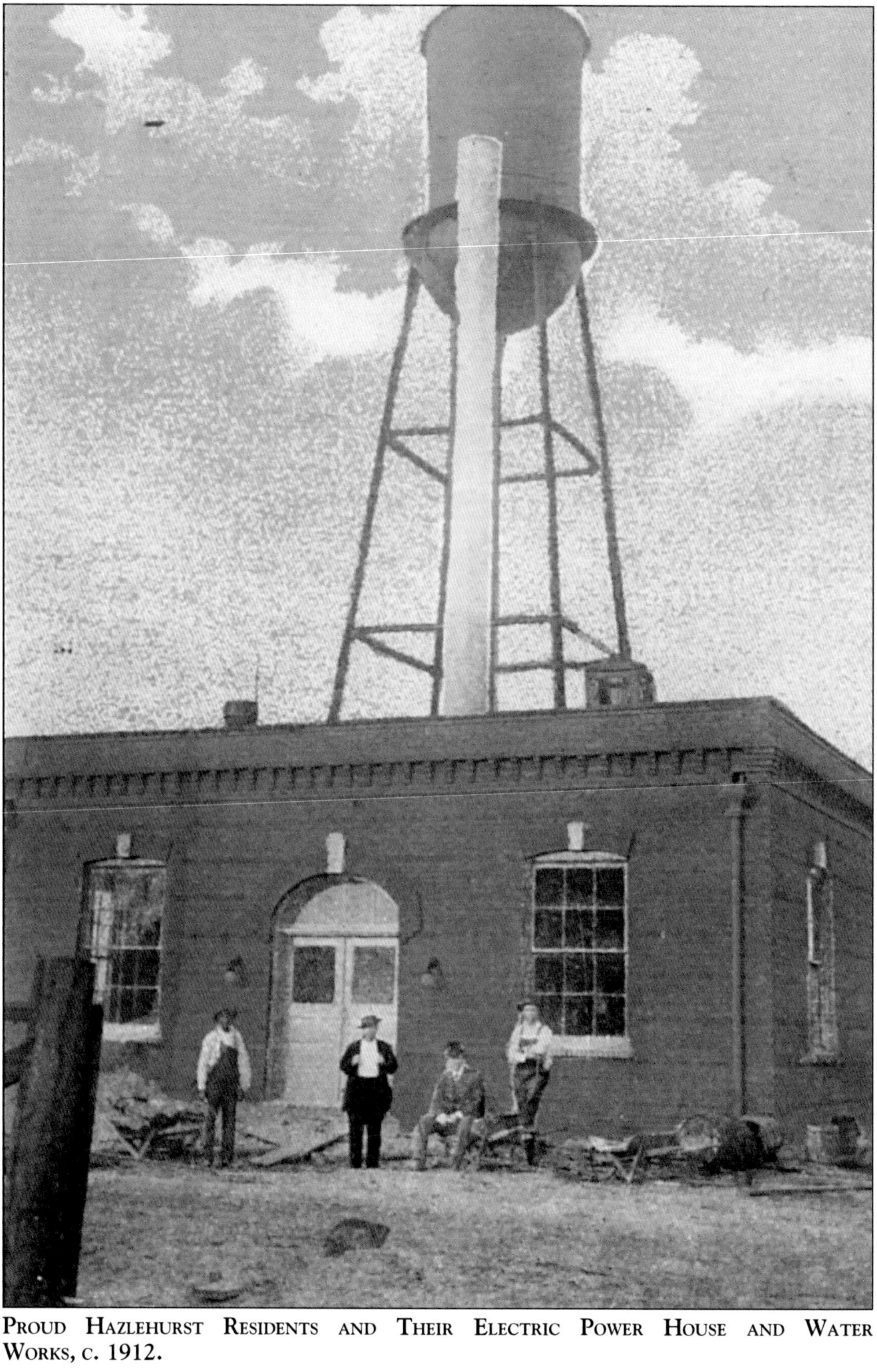

PROUD HAZLEHURST RESIDENTS AND THEIR ELECTRIC POWER HOUSE AND WATER WORKS, C. 1912.

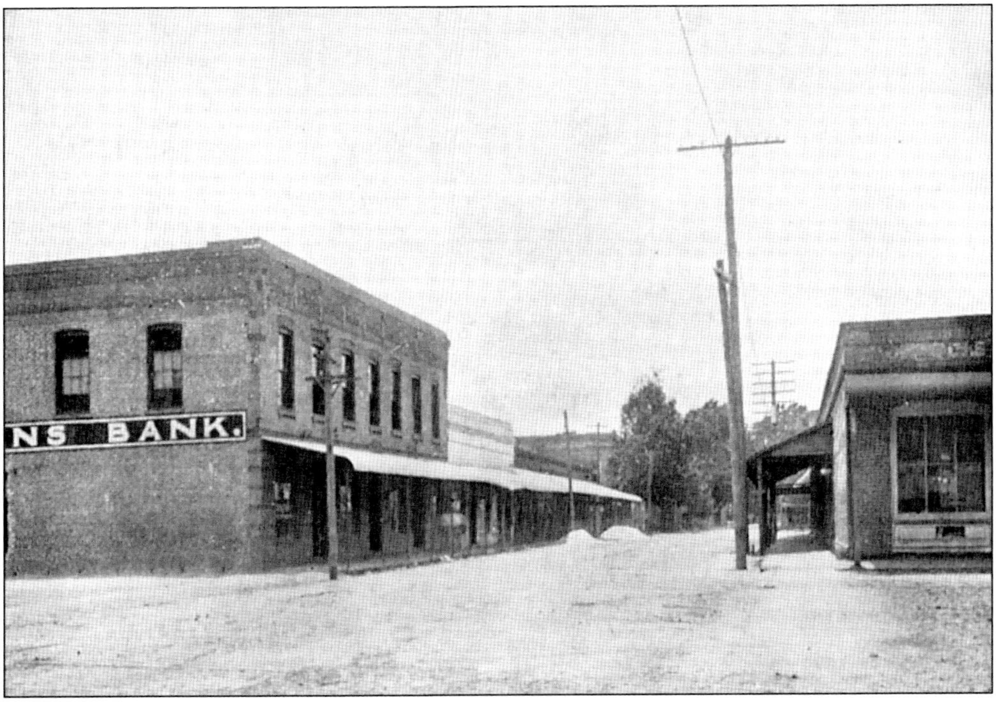

A c. 1910 View of Downtown Hazlehurst. The Citizens Bank on the corner was prominent.

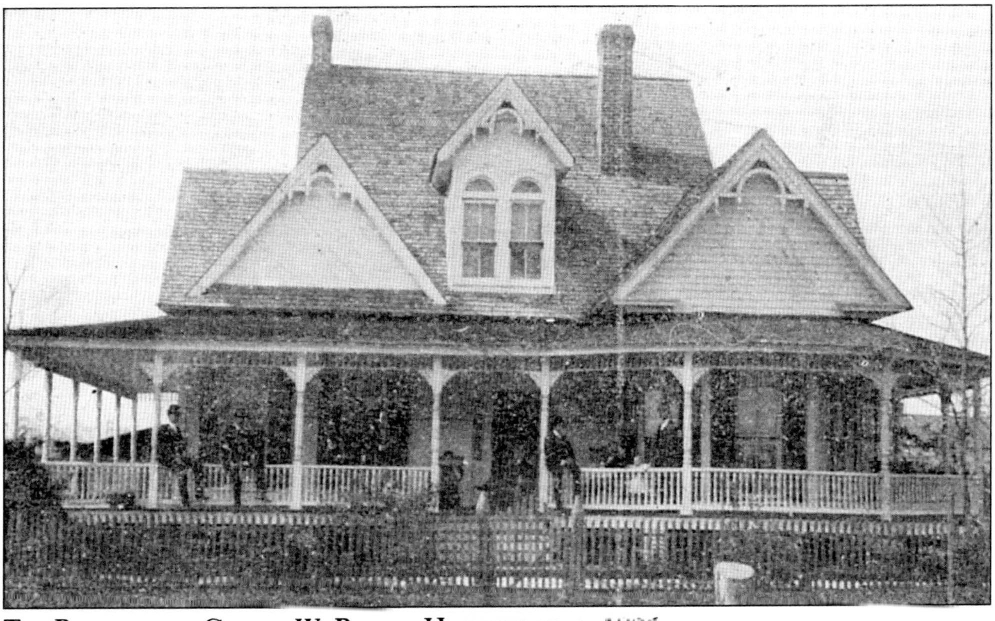

The Residence of George W. Best in Hazlehurst, c. 1906.

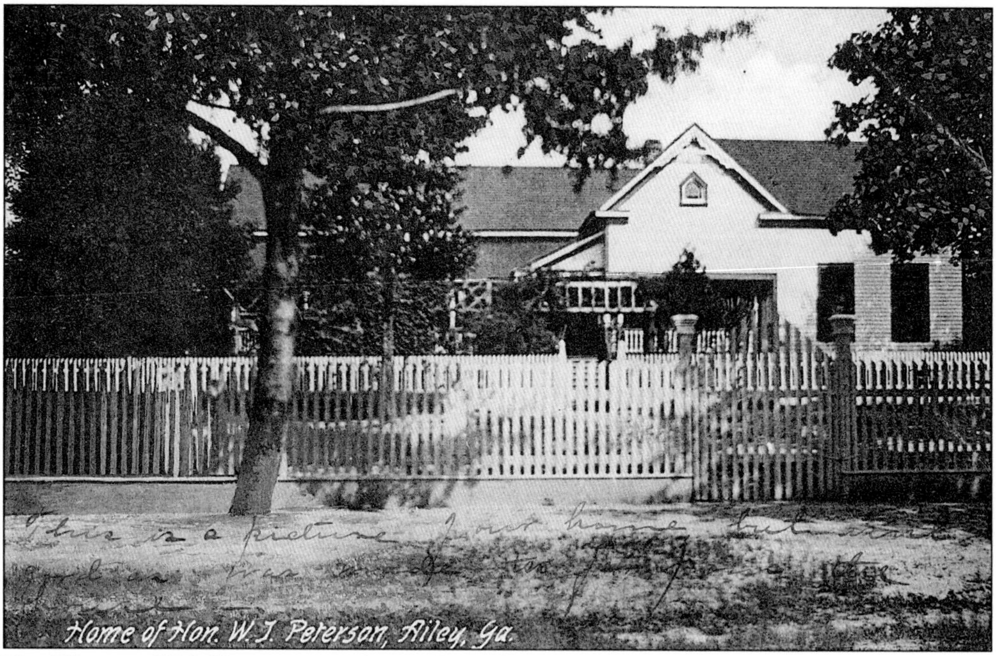

THE HOME OF W.J. PETERSON OF AILEY, WHO OPERATED A GENERAL STORE.

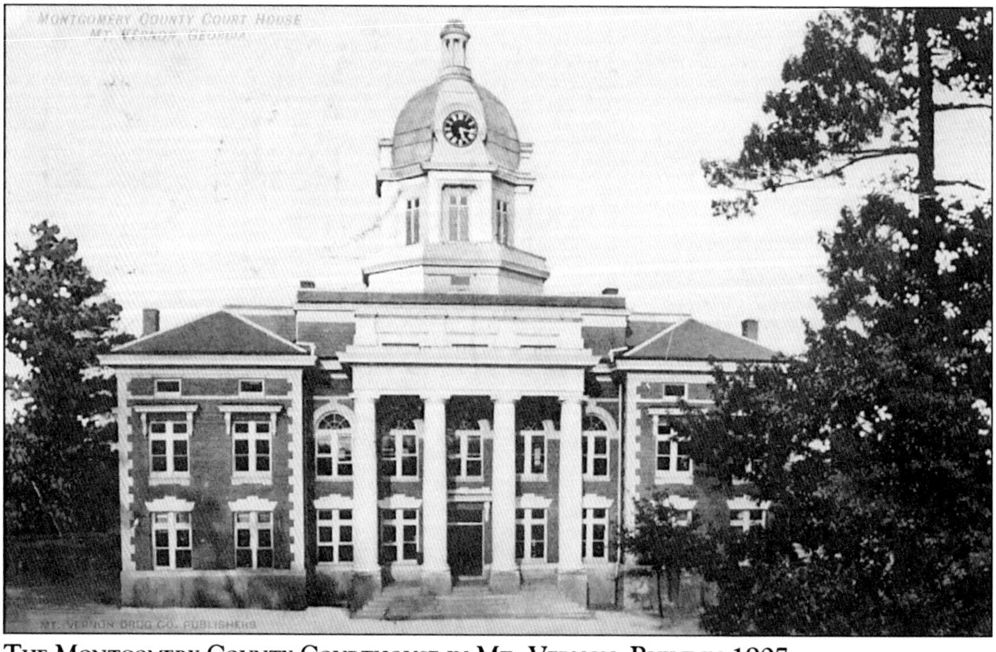

THE MONTGOMERY COUNTY COURTHOUSE IN MT. VERNON, BUILT IN 1907.

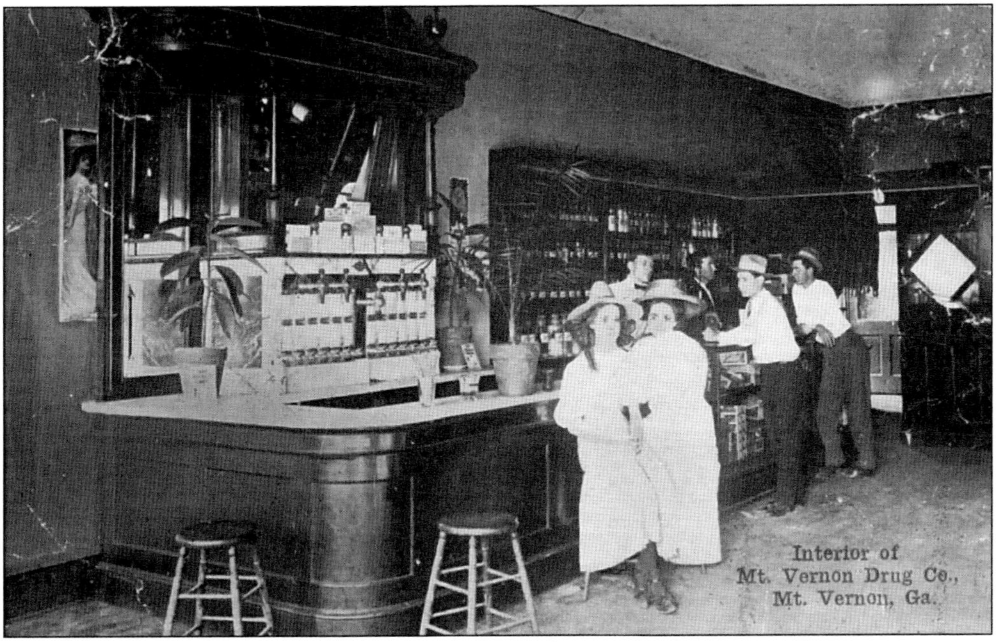

An Interior View of the Mount Vernon Drug Company.

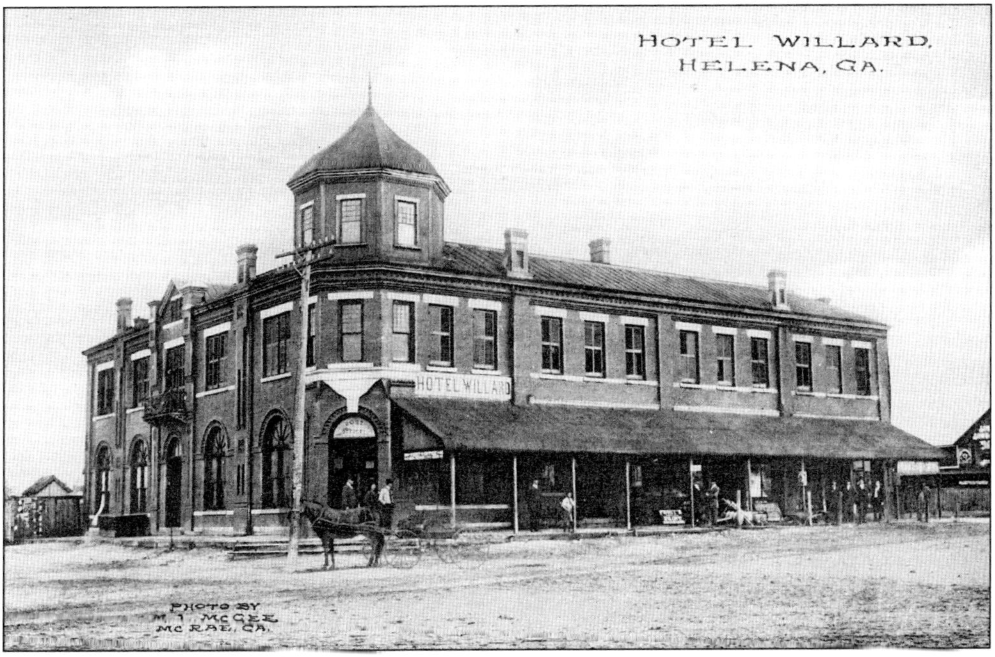

The Hotel Willard in Helena, c. 1912.

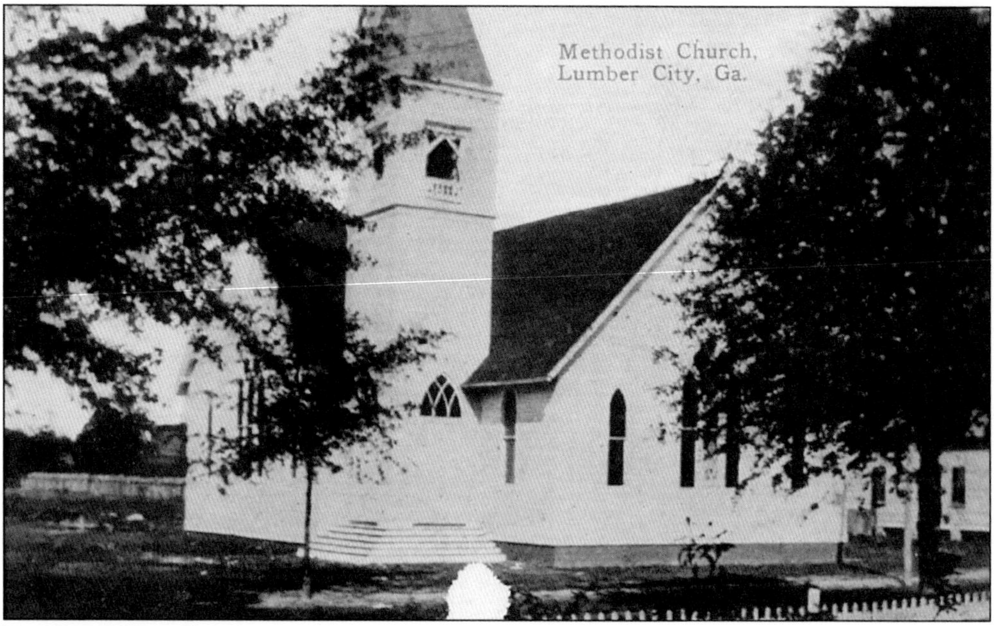

THE METHODIST CHURCH IN LUMBER CITY, c. 1910.

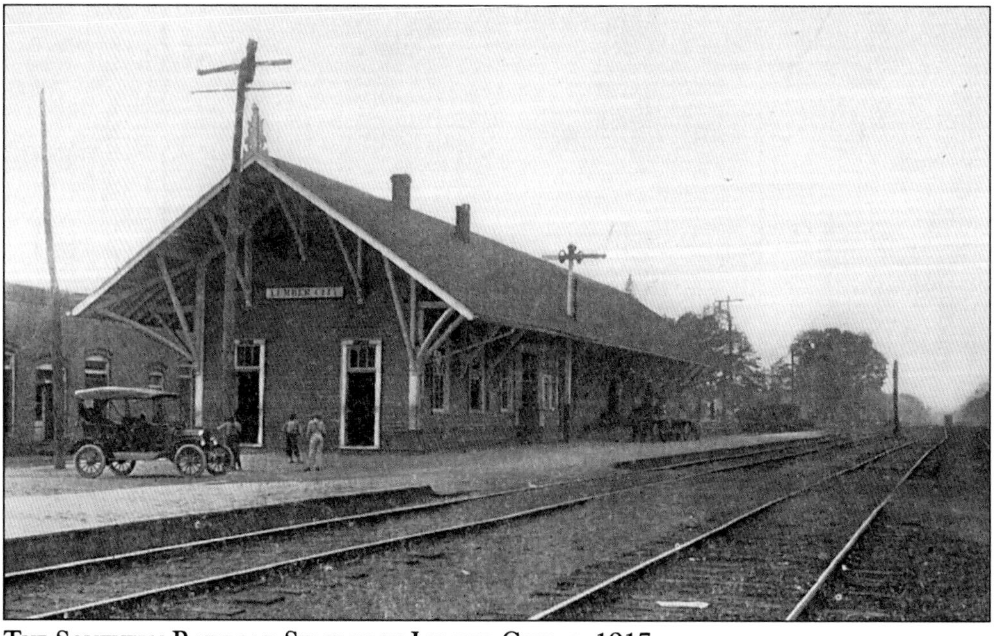

THE SOUTHERN RAILROAD STATION IN LUMBER CITY, c. 1917.

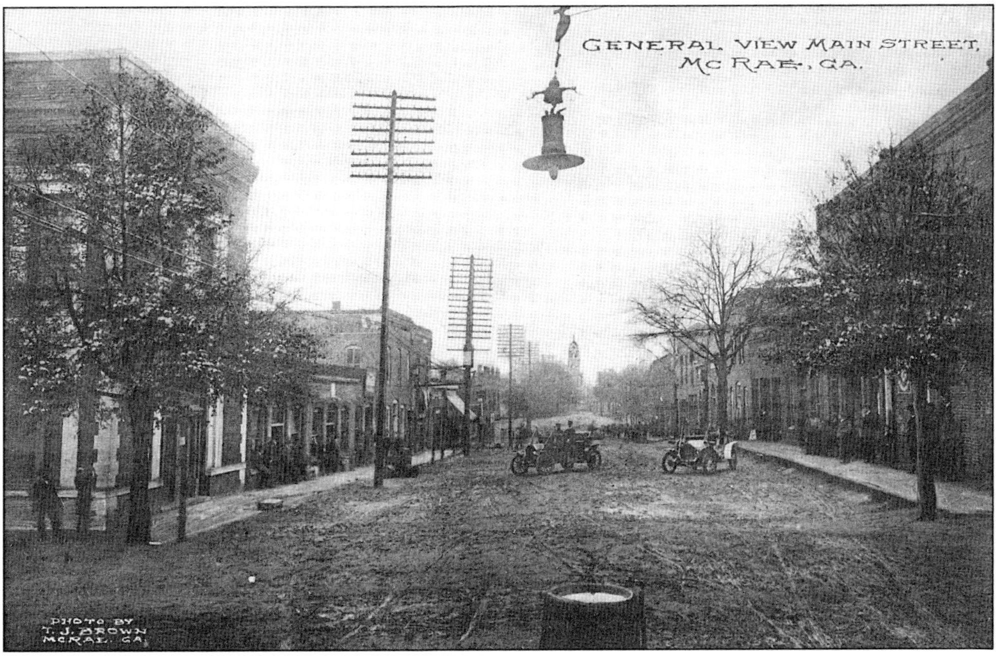

Main Street in McRae, c. 1912. This view shows such "modern conveniences" as automobiles, utility poles, and a street light, but a watering trough remains in the middle of the street for those who still used horses and mules.

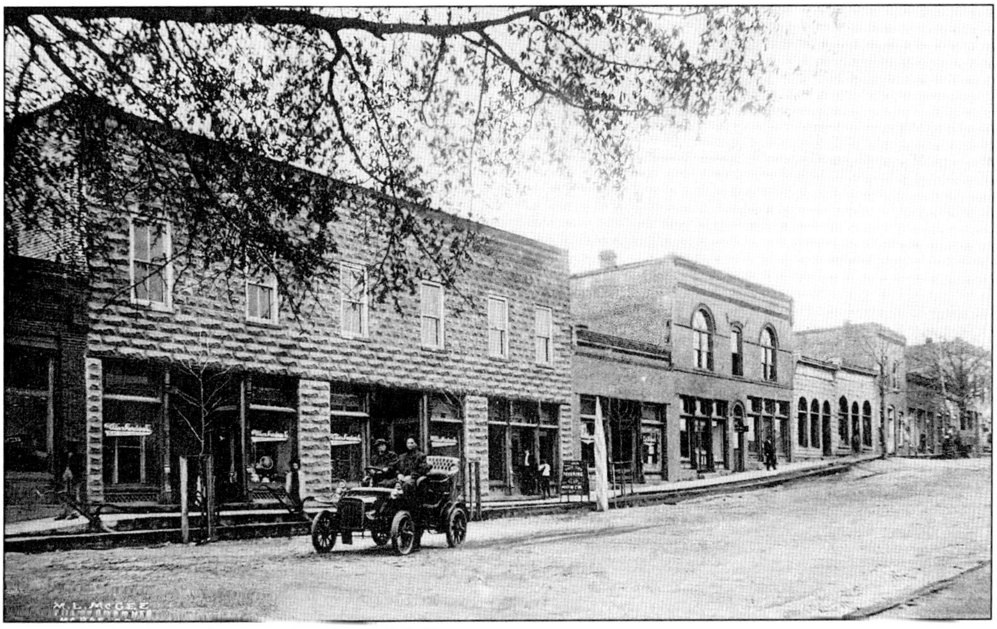

Another c. 1912 Street Scene in McRae.

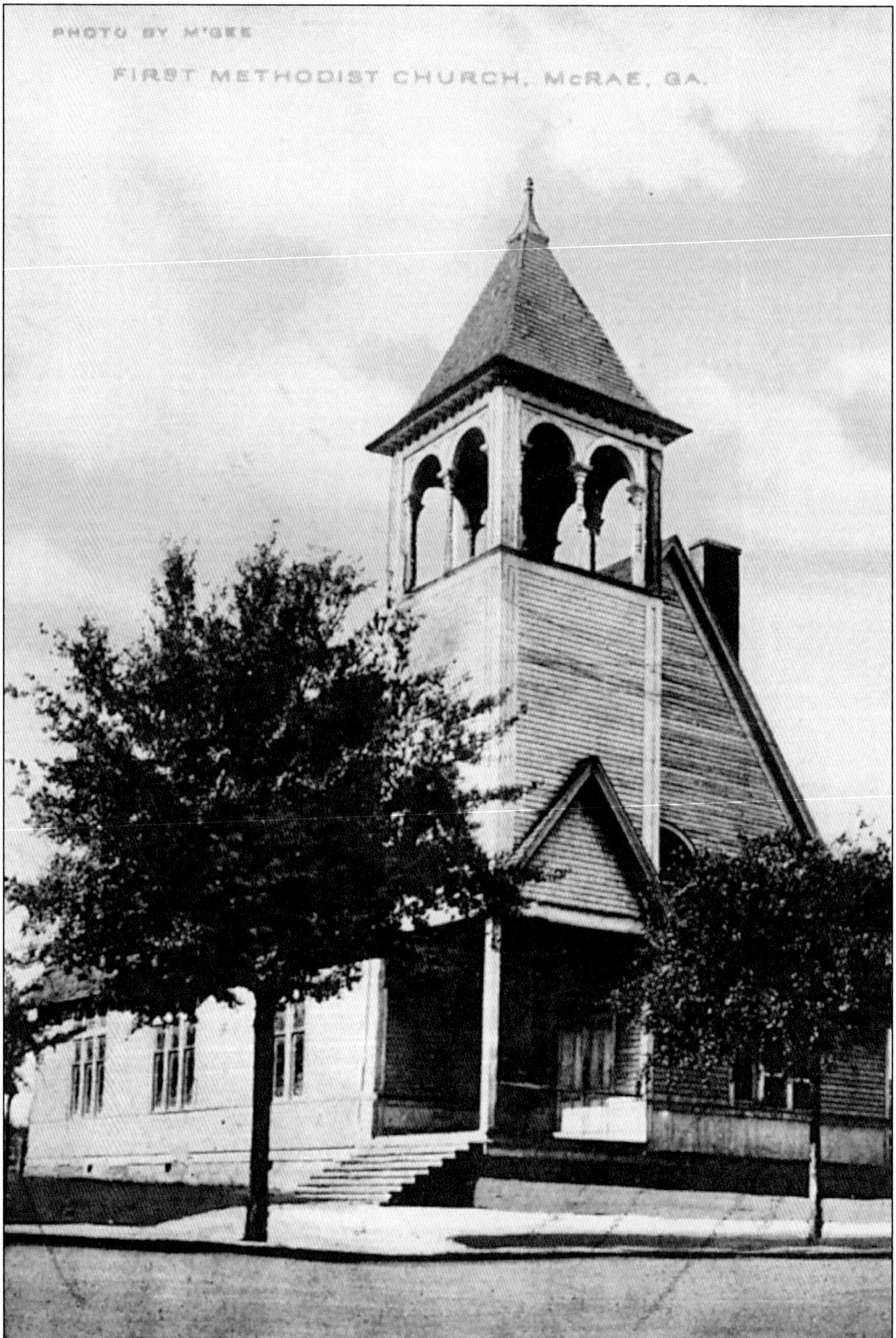

THE OLD WOODEN METHODIST CHURCH AND ITS HUGE BELFRY, LOCATED IN MCRAE.

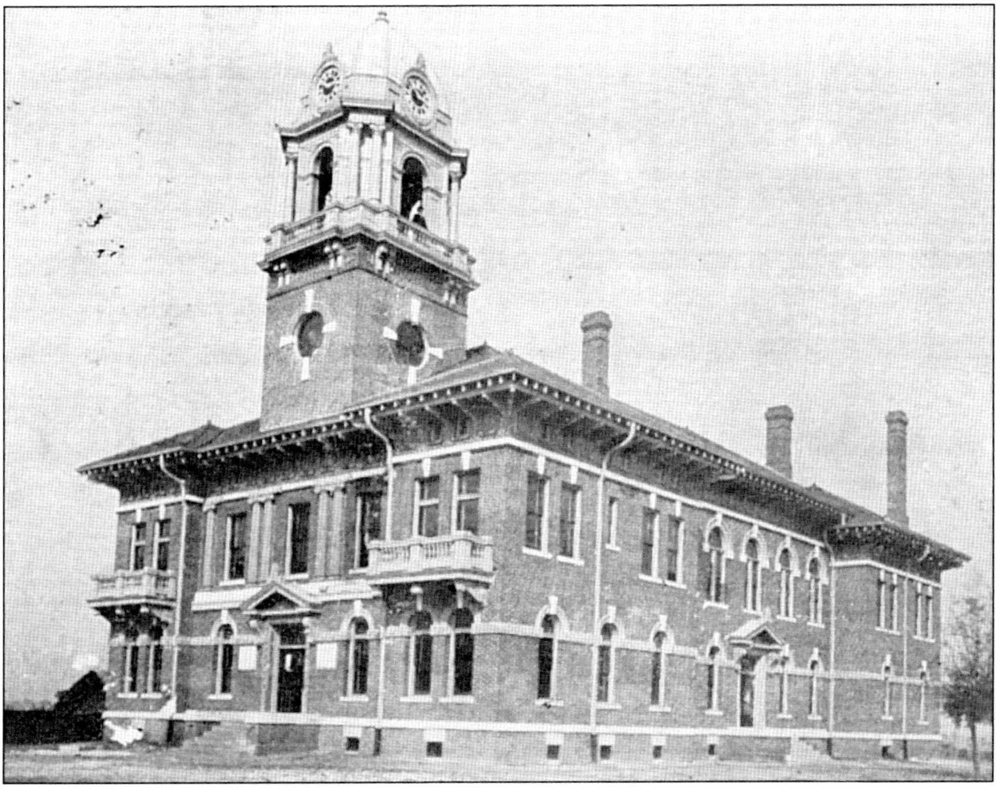

The Old Telfair County Courthouse. This old building in McRae was constructed in the 1870s and was destroyed by fire in the early 1900s.

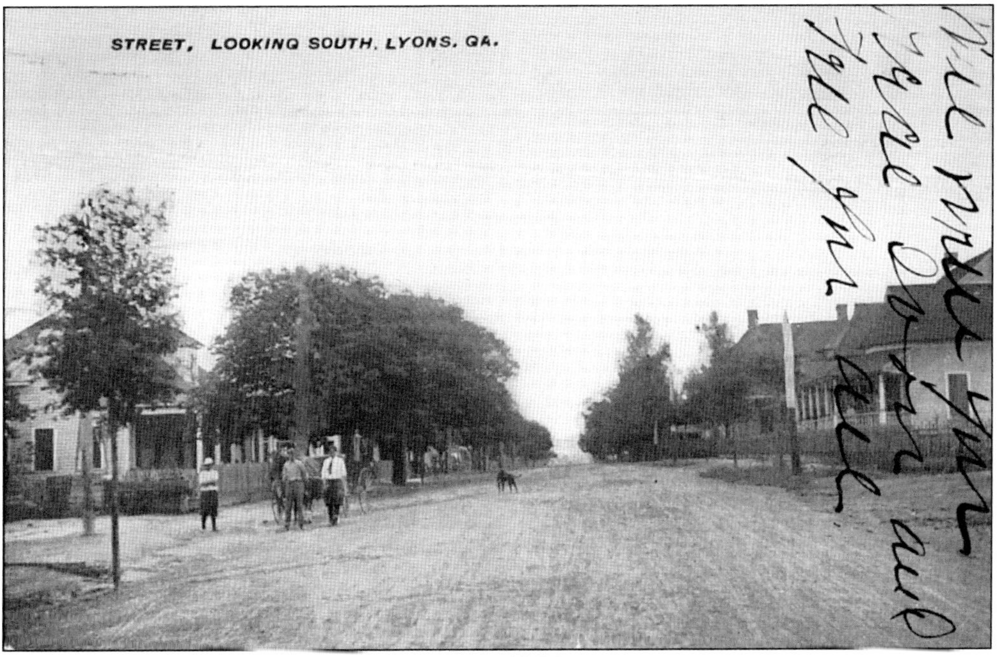

A Street Scene Looking South in Lyons, c. 1912.

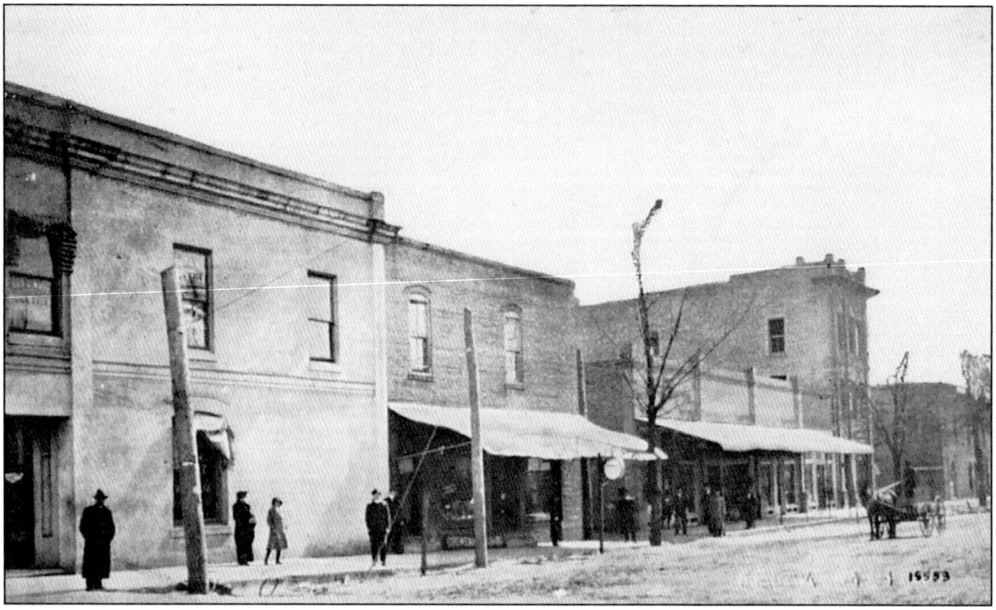

Looking South from Walker's Jewelry Store in Vidalia, c. 1908.

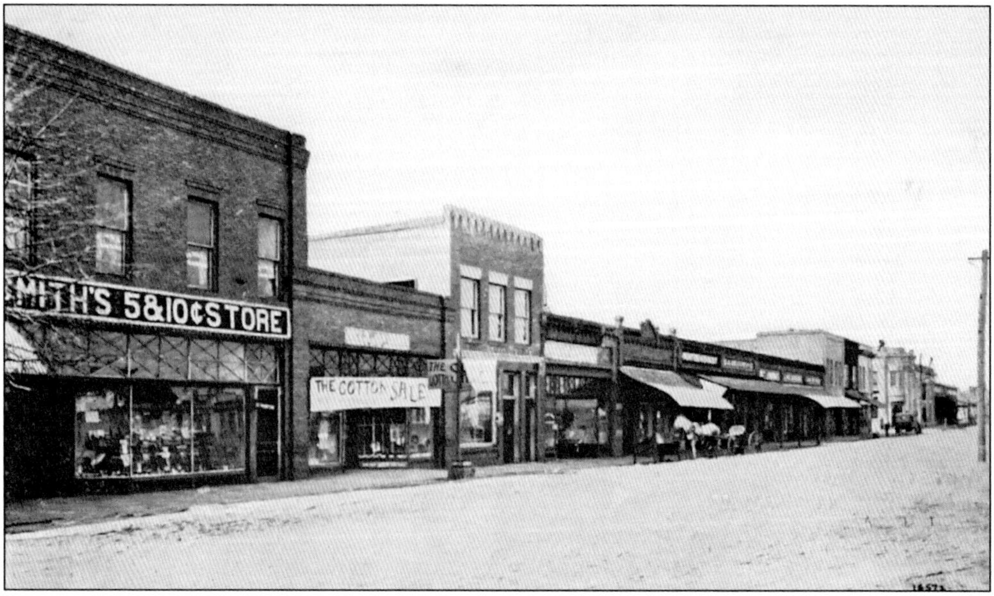

Looking West on Railroad Avenue in Vidalia, c. 1908.

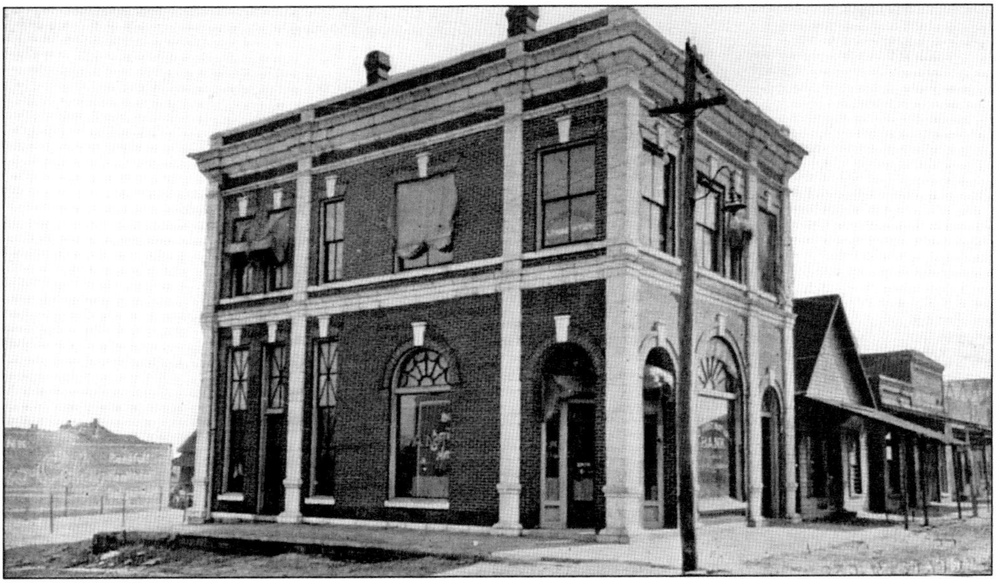

THE FIRST NATIONAL BANK IN VIDALIA, C. 1908.

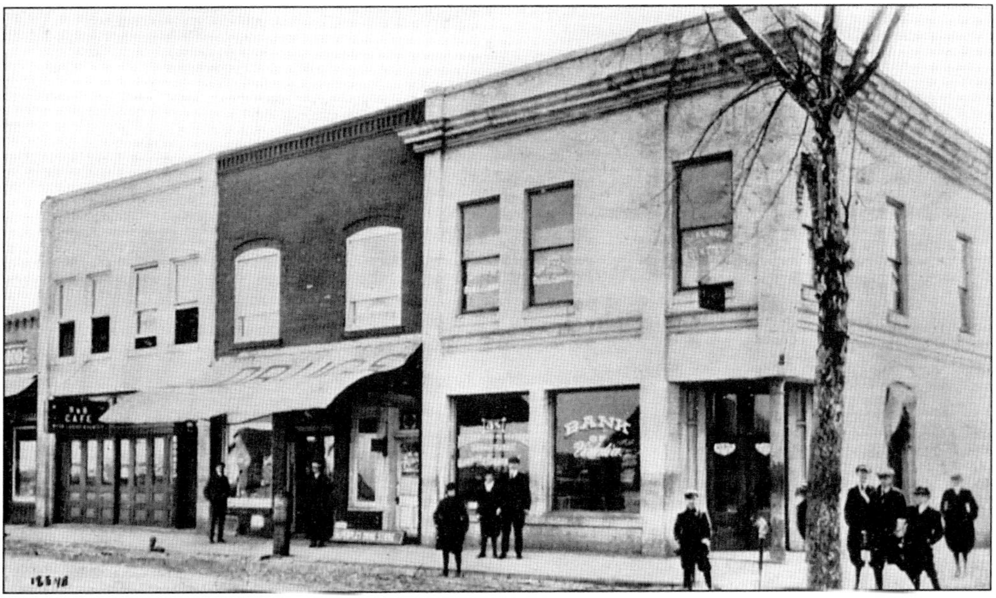

THE BANK OF VIDALIA, C. 1908.

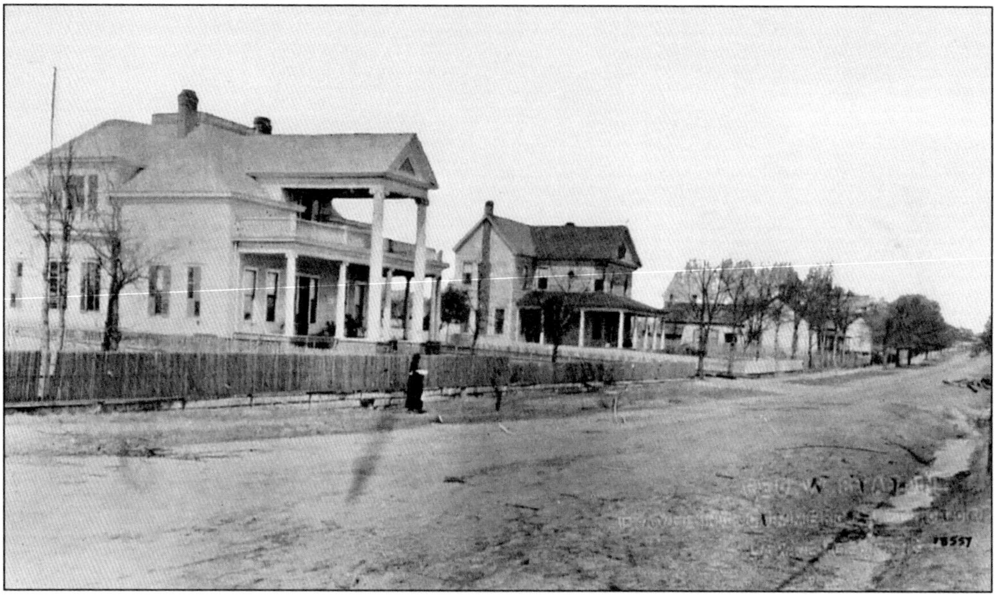

SOME FINE HOMES ON MCINTOSH STREET IN VIDALIA, C. 1908.

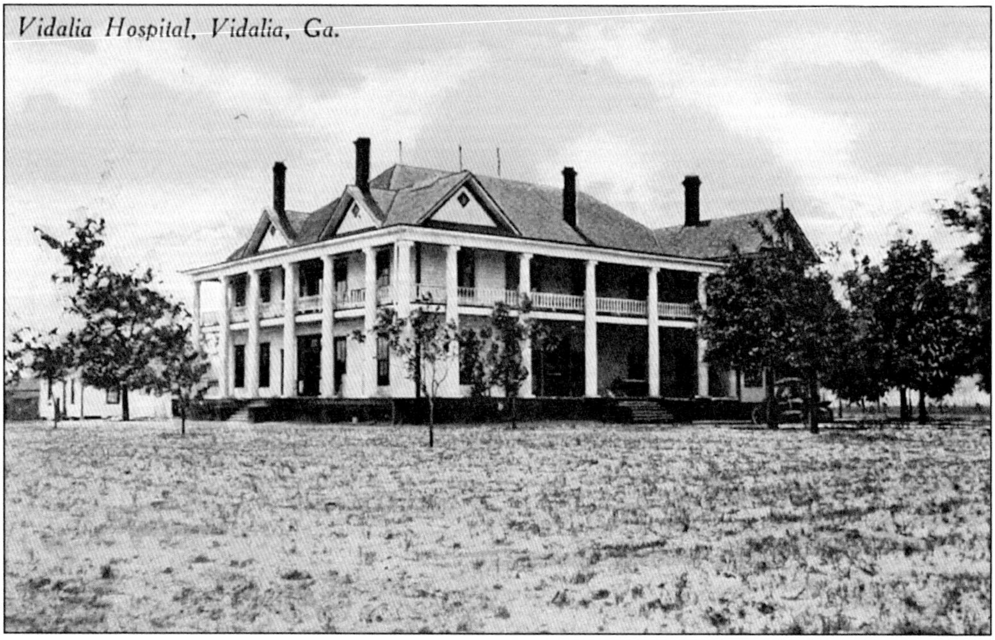

VIDALIA HOSPITAL, C. 1914.

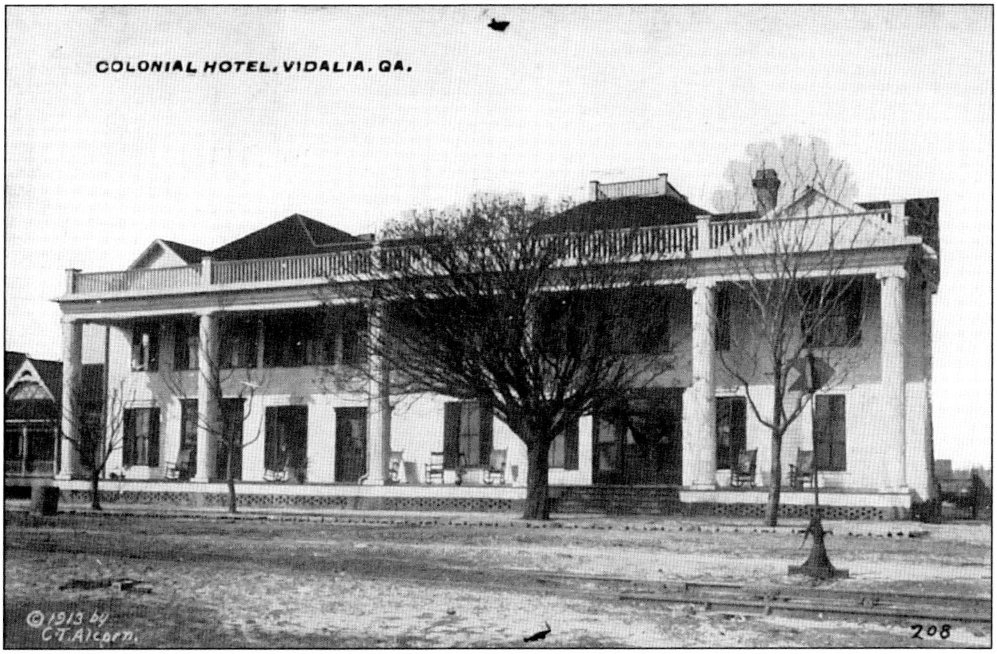

THE COLONIAL HOTEL IN VIDALIA, OPERATED BY MRS. R.L. KING.

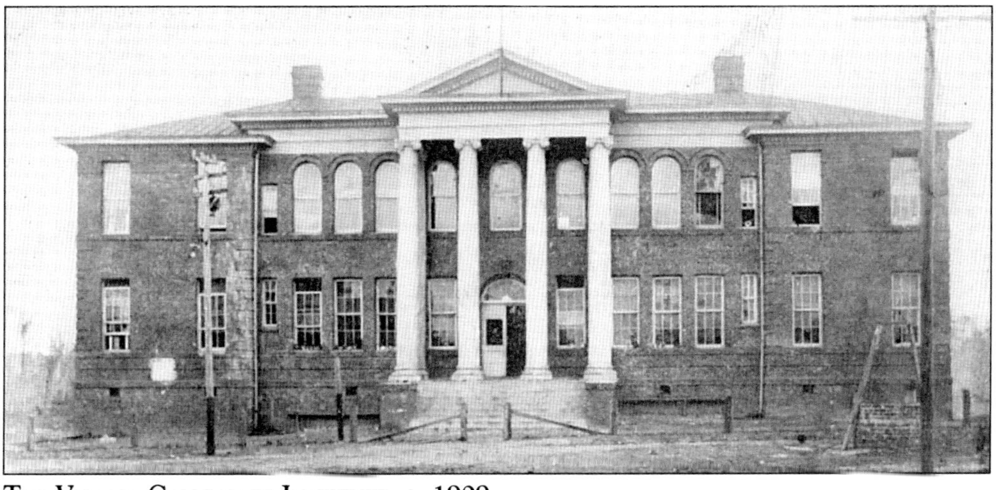

THE VIDALIA COLLEGIATE INSTITUTE, C. 1909.

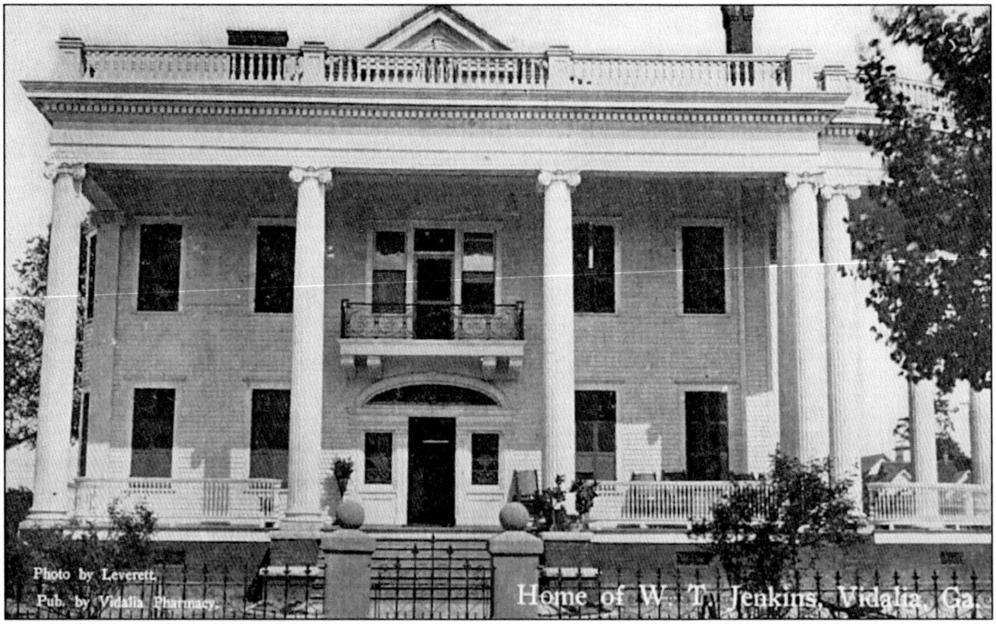

THE HOME OF W.T. JENKINS IN VIDALIA, C. 1909.

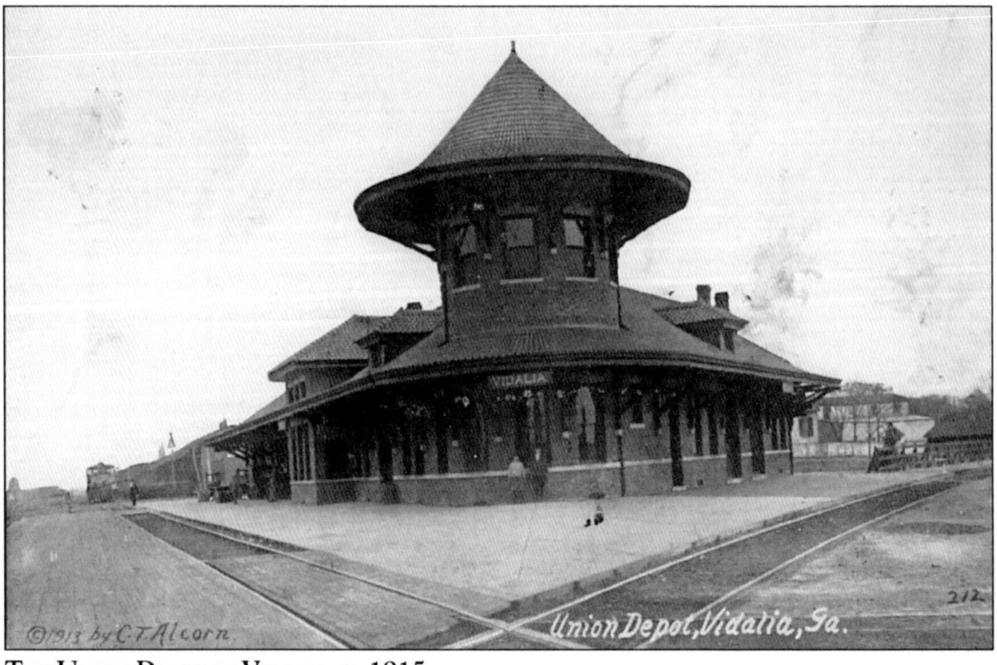

THE UNION DEPOT IN VIDALIA, C. 1915.

Two

Atkinson, Berrien, Coffee, Cook, Echols, Irwin, and Lowndes Counties

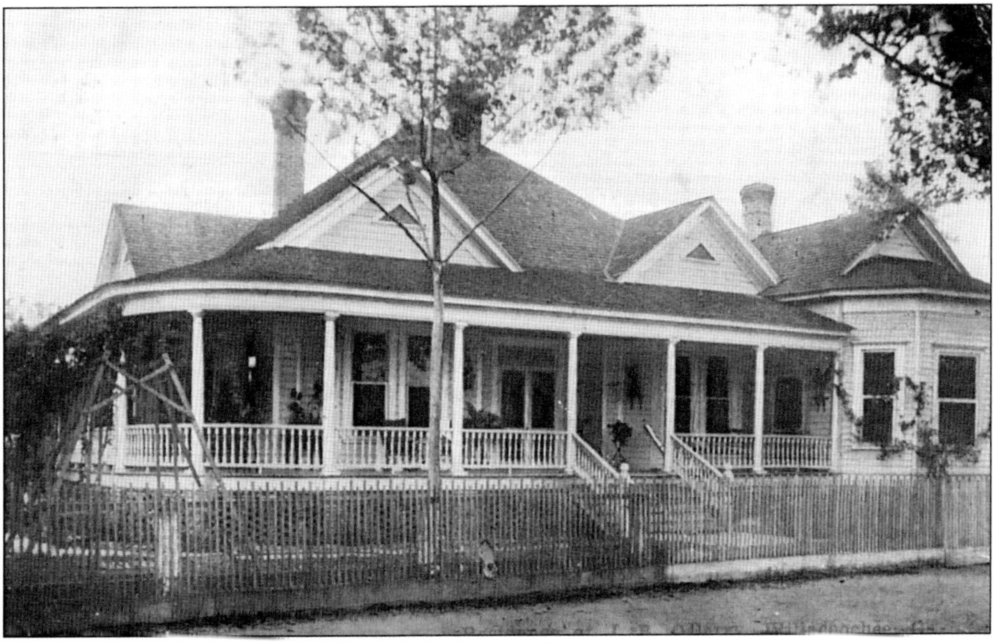

THE HOME OF J.B. OBERRY IN WILLACOOCHEE, C. 1912.

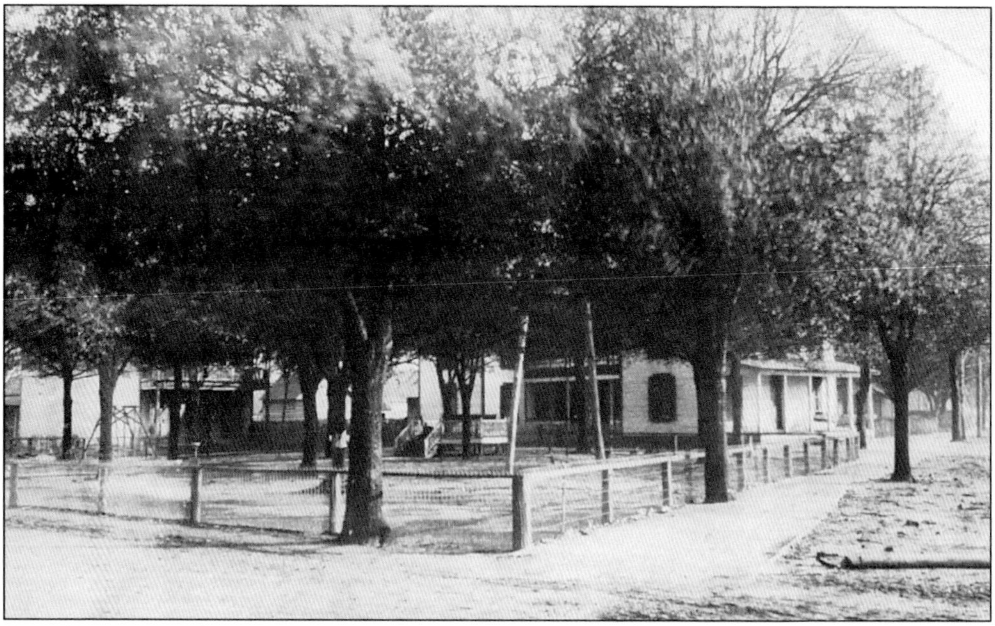

City Park and Oak View Hotel in Willacoochee. The card was mailed to Wilmore, Kentucky, and reads in part: "Dear Minnie: You see I still think about you if it has been seven years since you have been to see me. We are getting along fine. Hope you are all well. You have been having *some* winter up there. Your cuz Sallie."

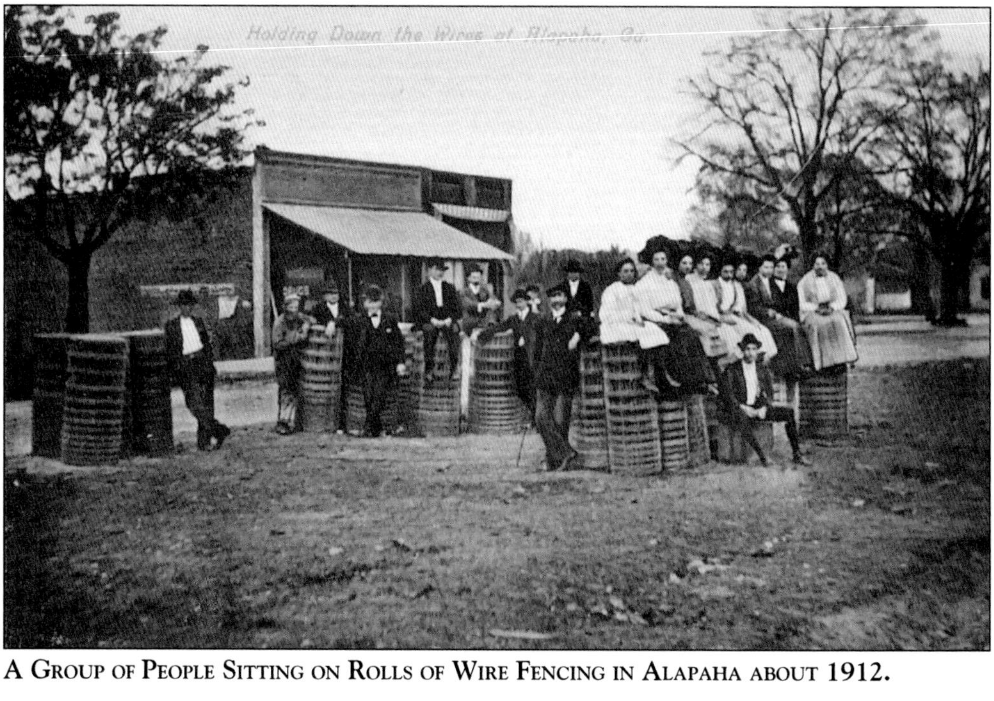

A Group of People Sitting on Rolls of Wire Fencing in Alapaha about 1912.

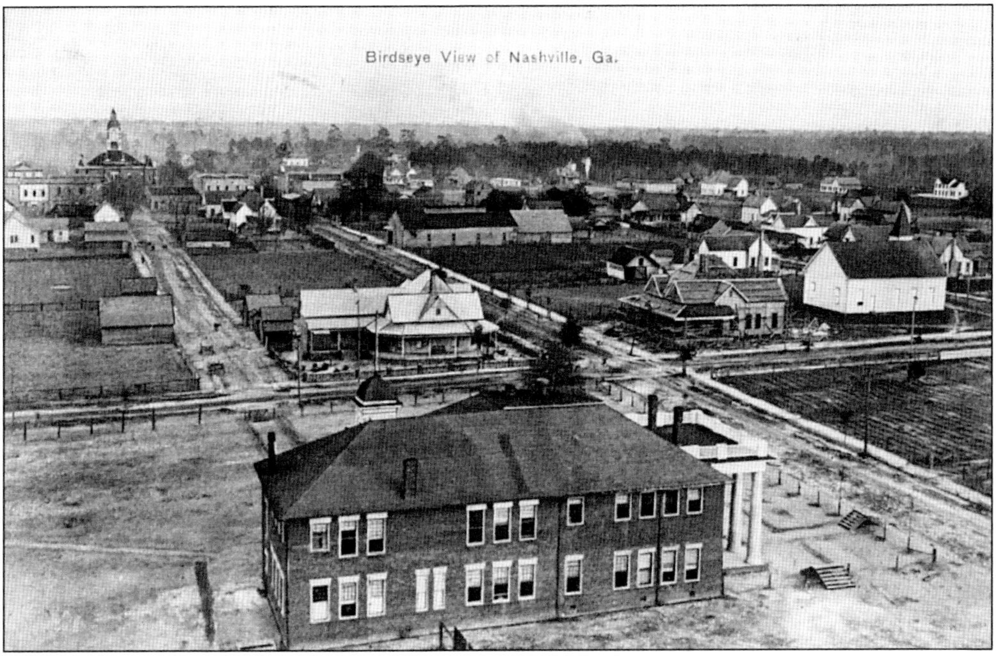

A BIRD'S-EYE VIEW OF NASHVILLE IN 1909.

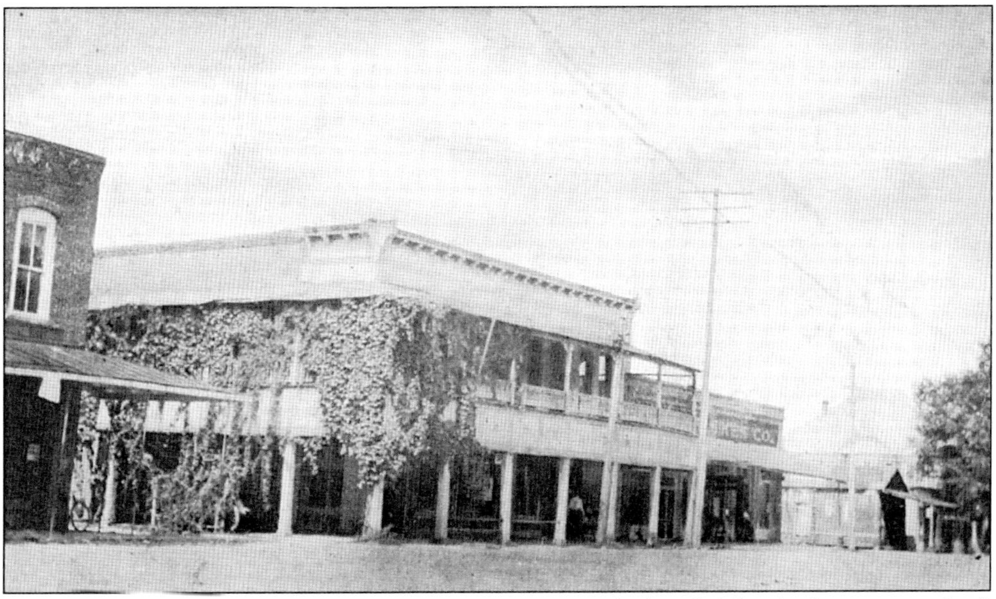

THE NEW MARION HOTEL IN NASHVILLE ABOUT 1917. The hotel didn't look so new with all the vines growing on the front.

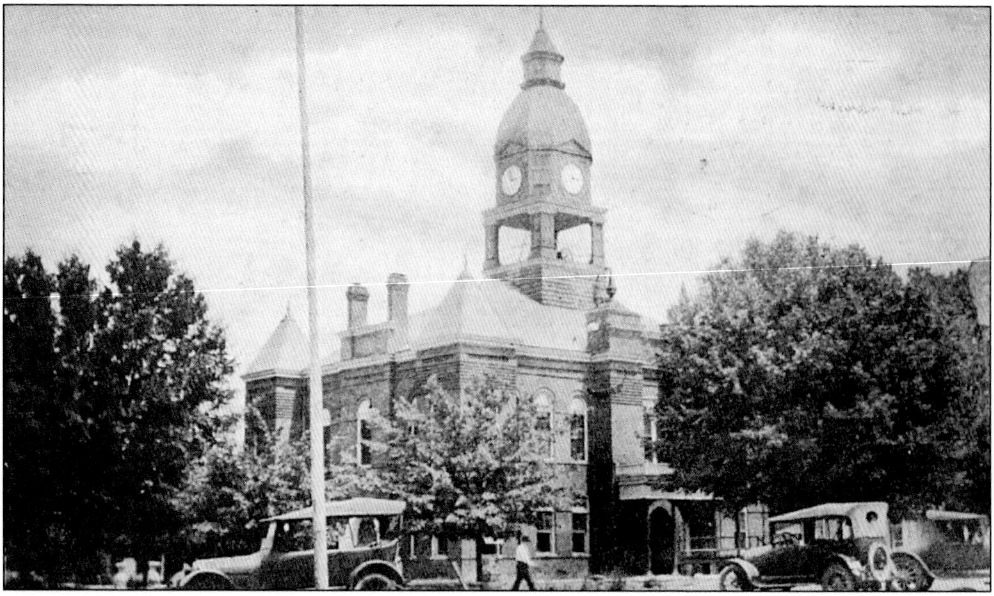

THE BERRIEN COUNTY COURTHOUSE AT NASHVILLE, BUILT IN 1898 AT A COST OF $24,980.

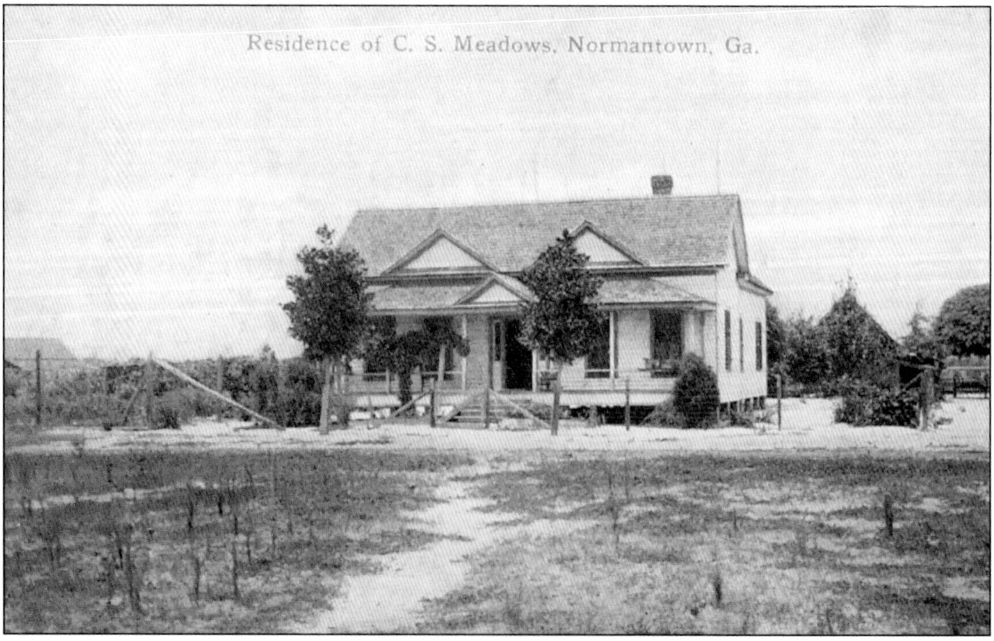

THE RESIDENCE OF C.S. MEADOWS AT NORMANTOWN.

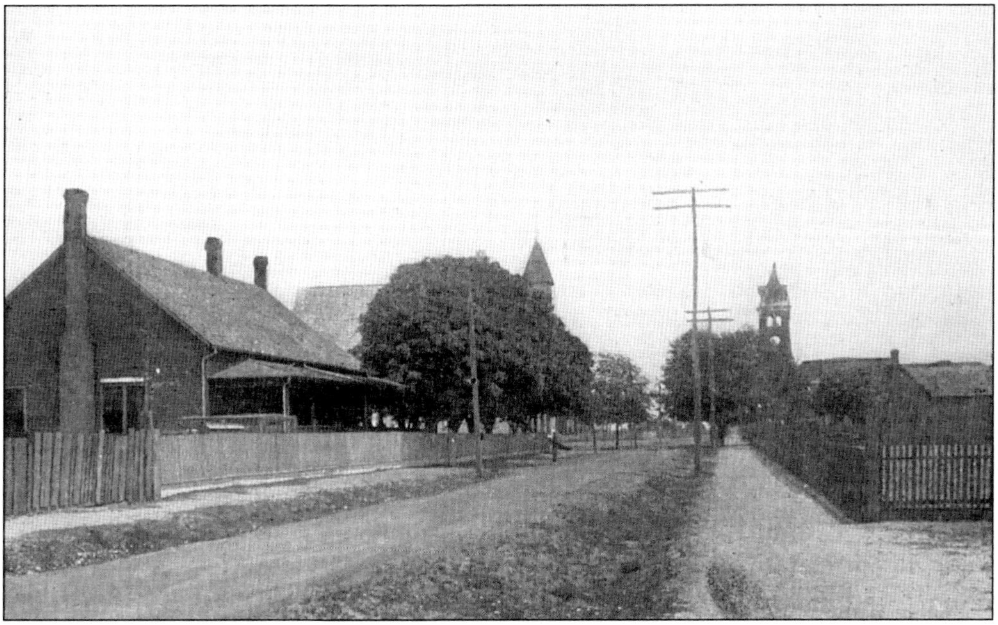

A Street Scene at Broxton, c. 1910.

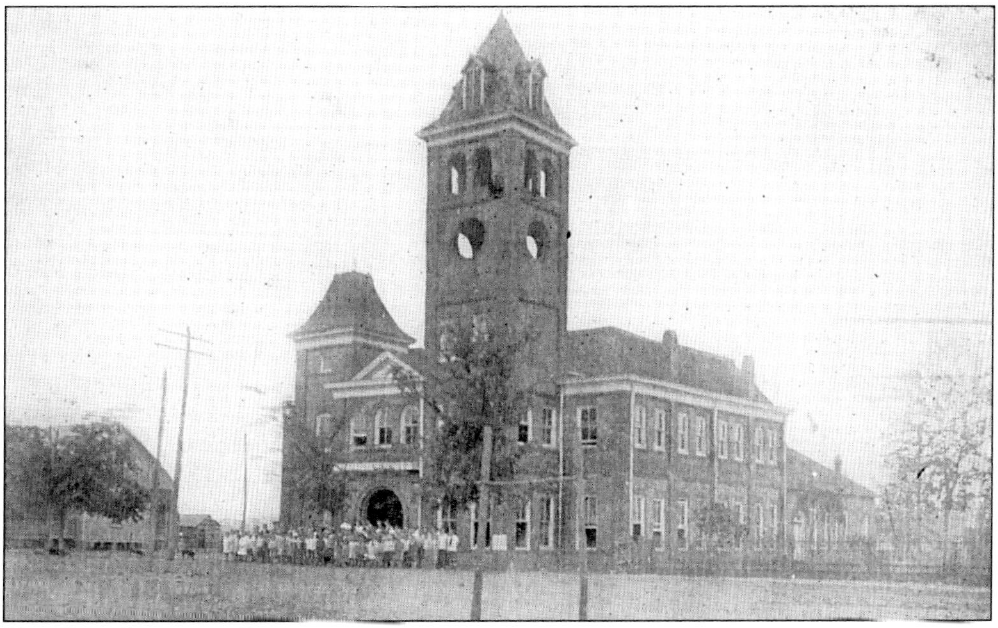

The High School at Broxton, c. 1910.

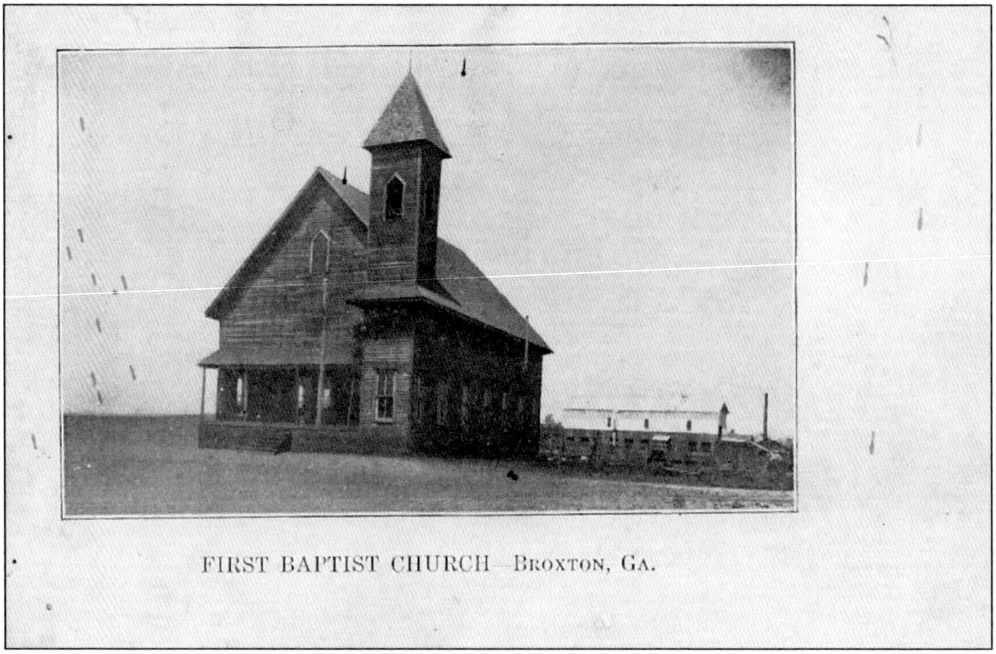

THE FIRST BAPTIST CHURCH AT BROXTON IN 1907.

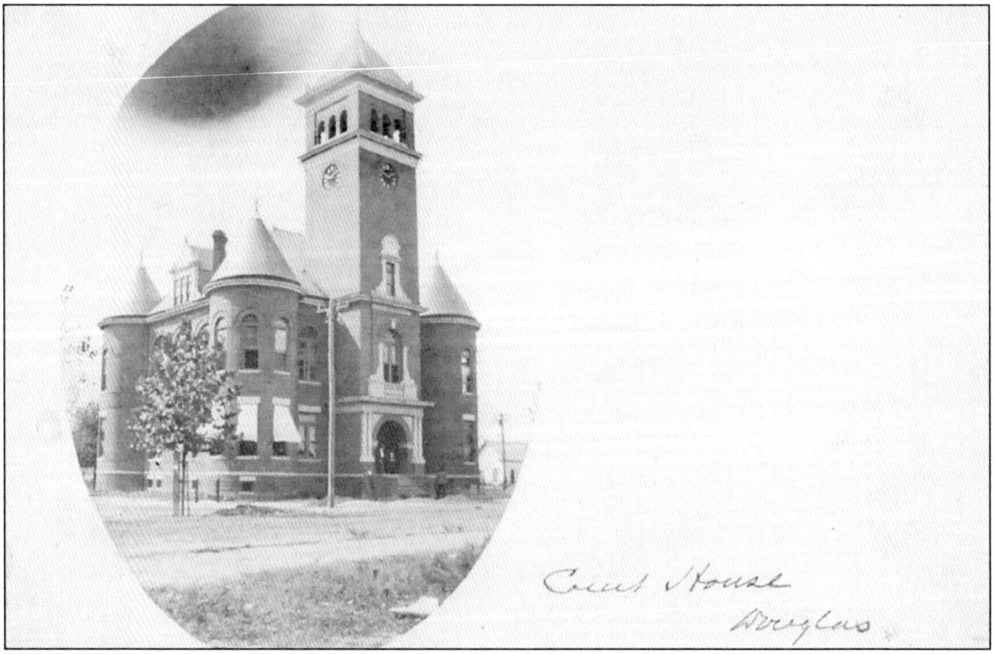

THE DOUGLAS COUNTY COURTHOUSE BUILDING IN DOUGLAS. This building was constructed in 1902 and burned down in 1930.

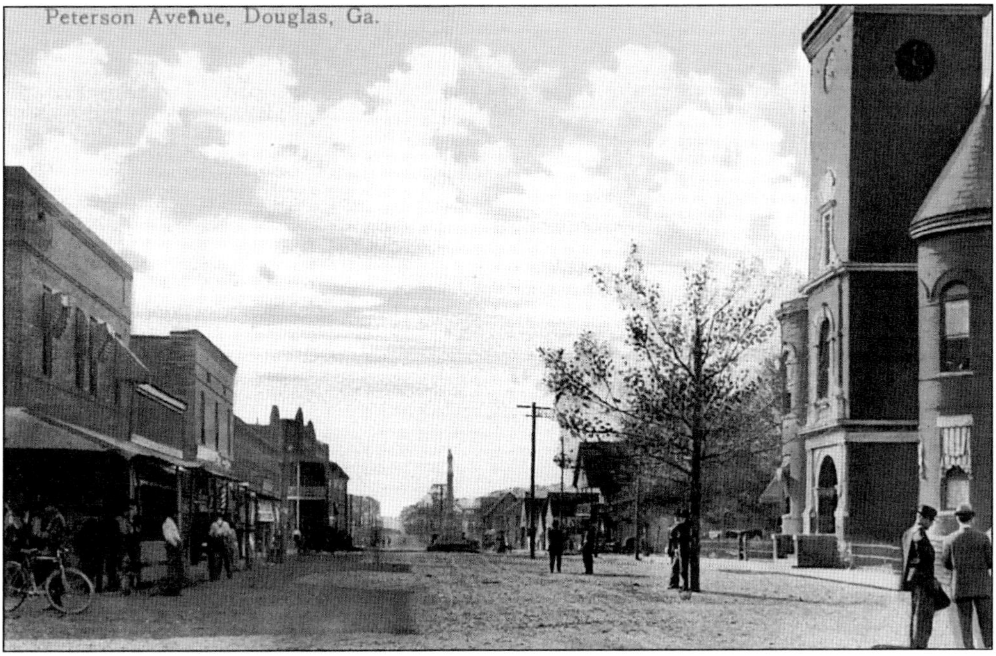

PETERSON AVENUE IN DOUGLAS, C. 1908.

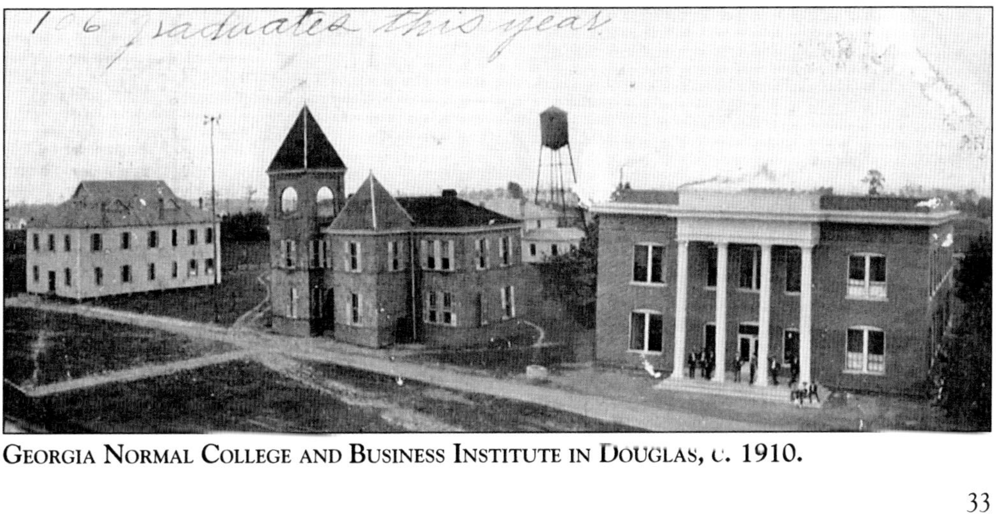

GEORGIA NORMAL COLLEGE AND BUSINESS INSTITUTE IN DOUGLAS, C. 1910.

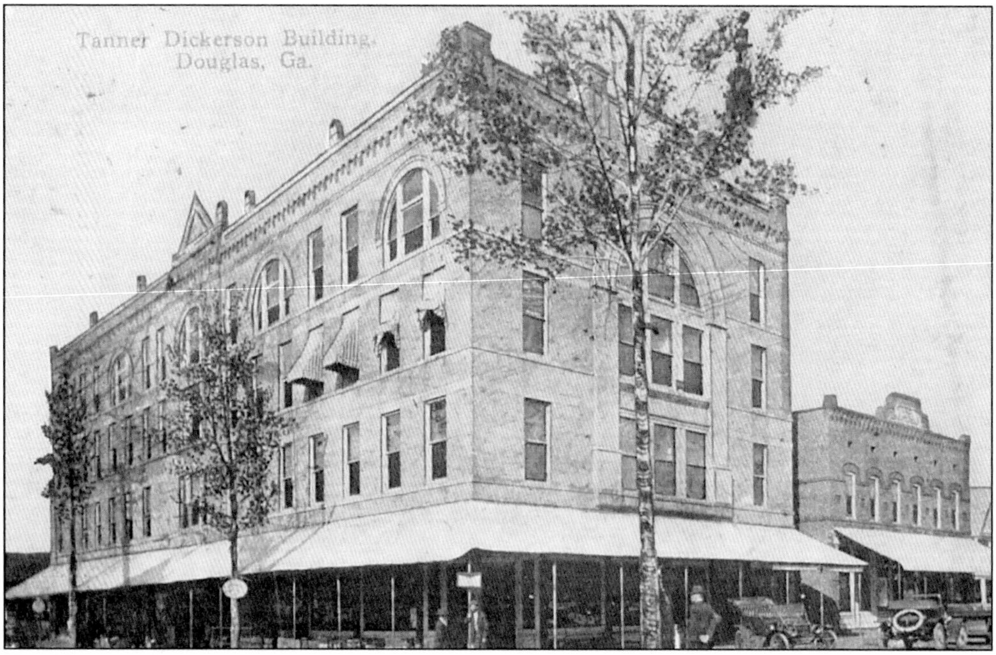

THE TANNER-DICKERSON BUILDING IN DOUGLAS IN THE MID-1910S.

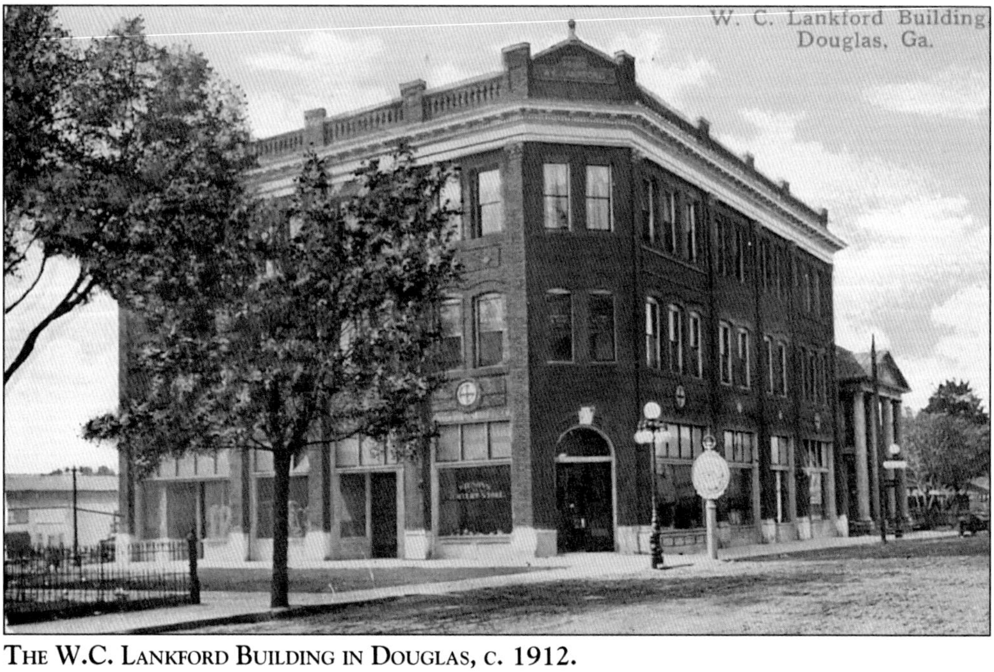

THE W.C. LANKFORD BUILDING IN DOUGLAS, C. 1912.

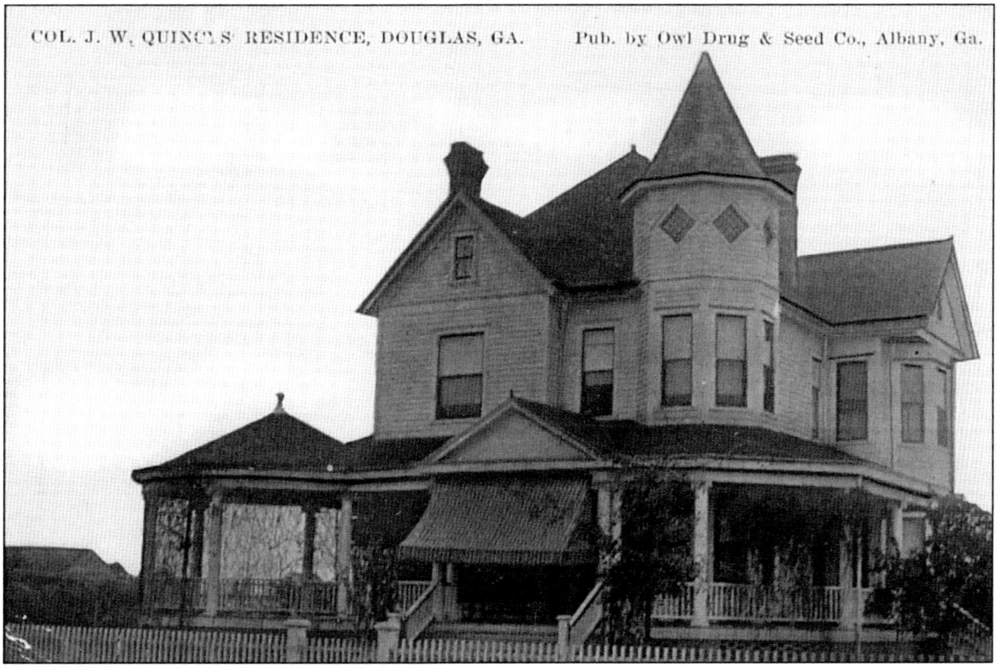

The Residence of J.W. Quincy in Douglas, c. 1910. Quincy was a lawyer in Douglas.

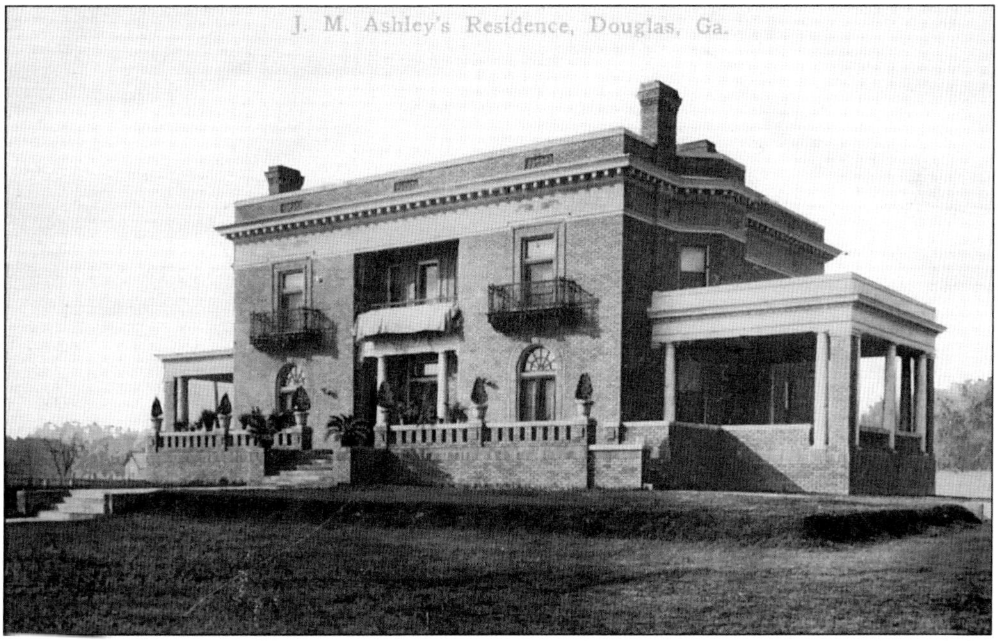

J.M. Ashley's Home in Douglas. Ashley ran a general merchandise store in Douglas and also dealt in turpentine.

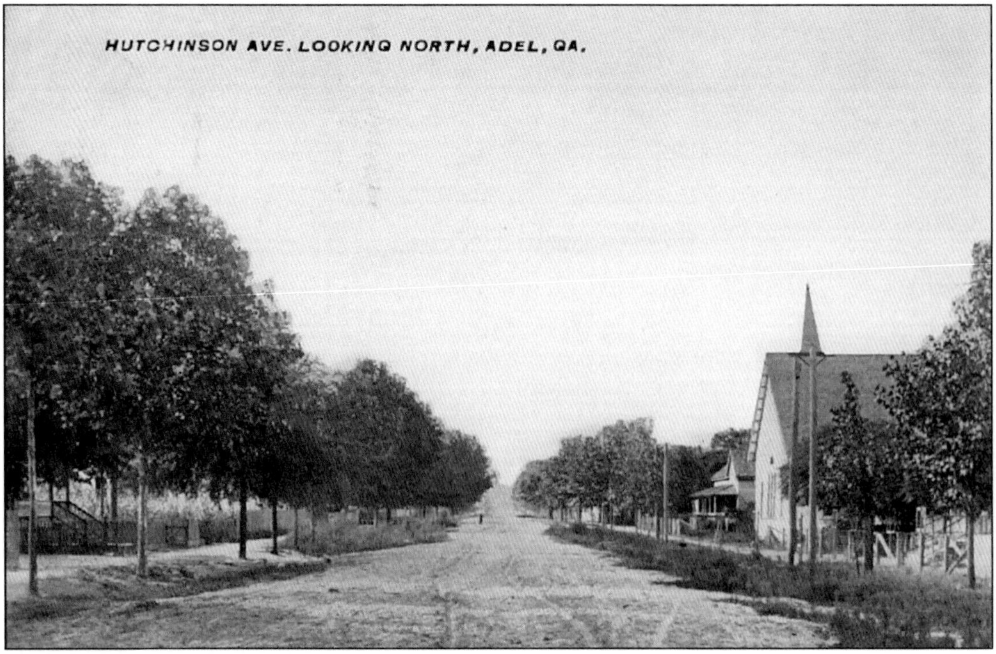

HUTCHINSON AVENUE LOOKING NORTH IN ADEL, C. 1910.

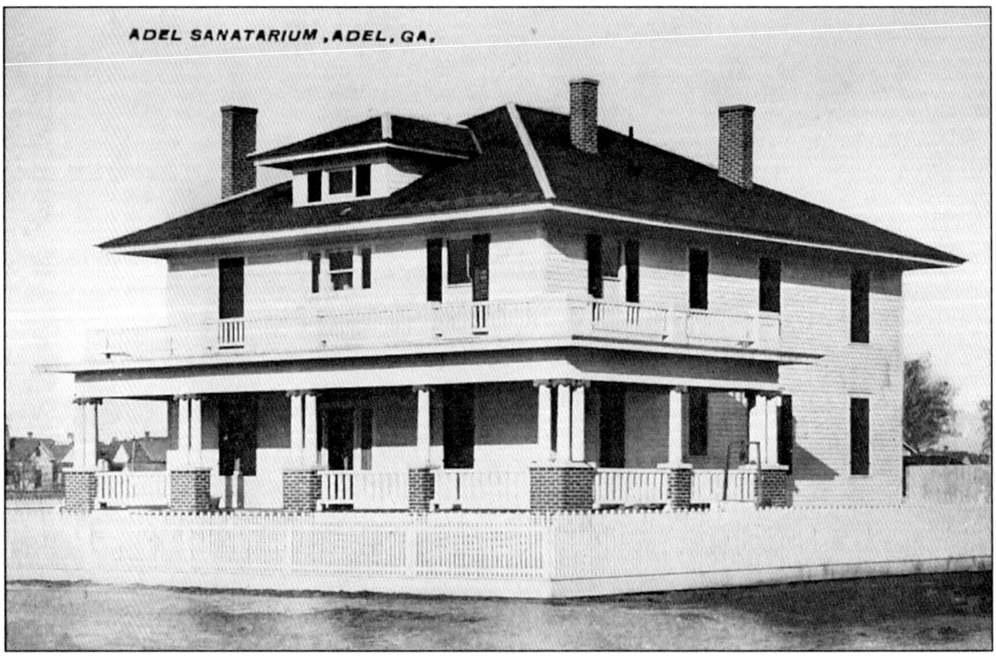

THE SANATARIUM IN ADEL, C. 1910.

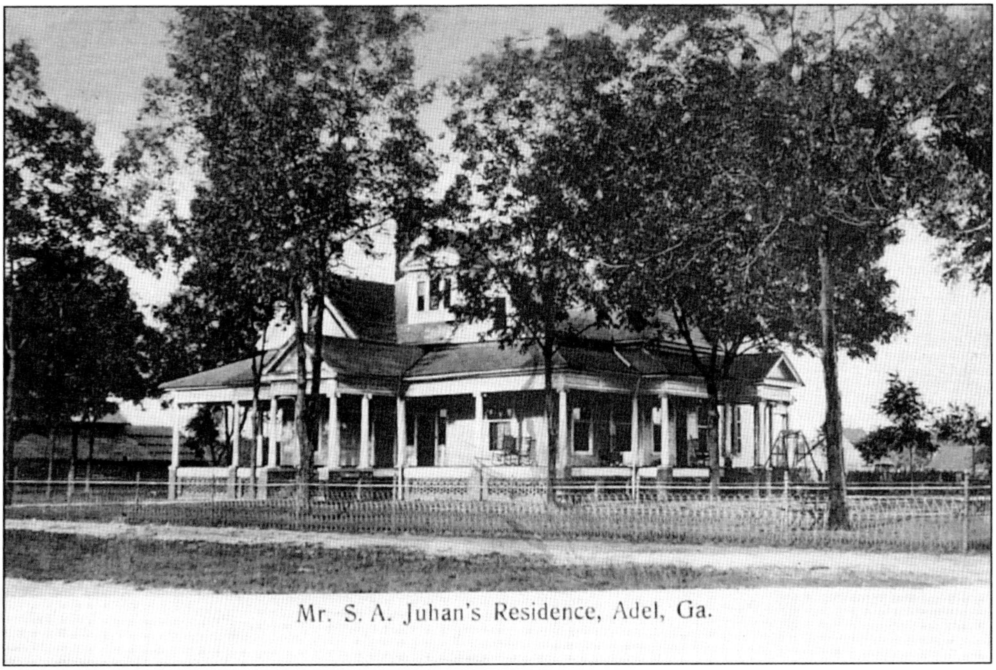

MR. S.A. JUHAN'S HOME IN ADEL, C. 1908.

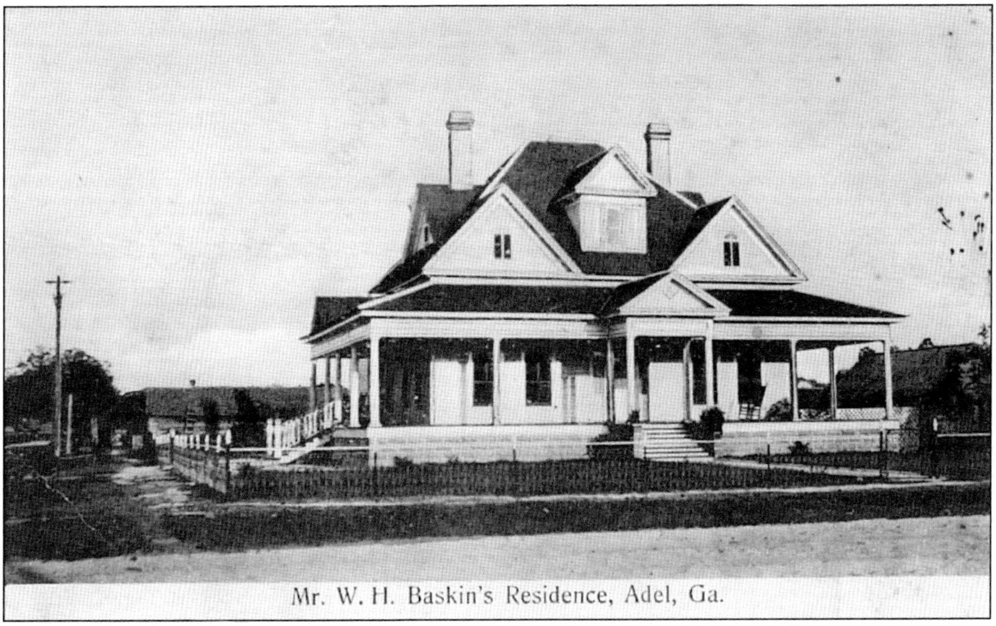

THE HOME OF MR. W.H. BASKIN IN ADEL, C. 1908. This card was mailed to Chula and part of the message reads: "Hello! Davie, how are you all these days. Davie we are going to have a pound party at Toms next Sat. night. You and Lila must be sure and come. There are also a big singing convention on Sun. Be sure and come. we will take it all in. we are looking for our relatives from Hahira. If you dont come this time we will not write you no more."

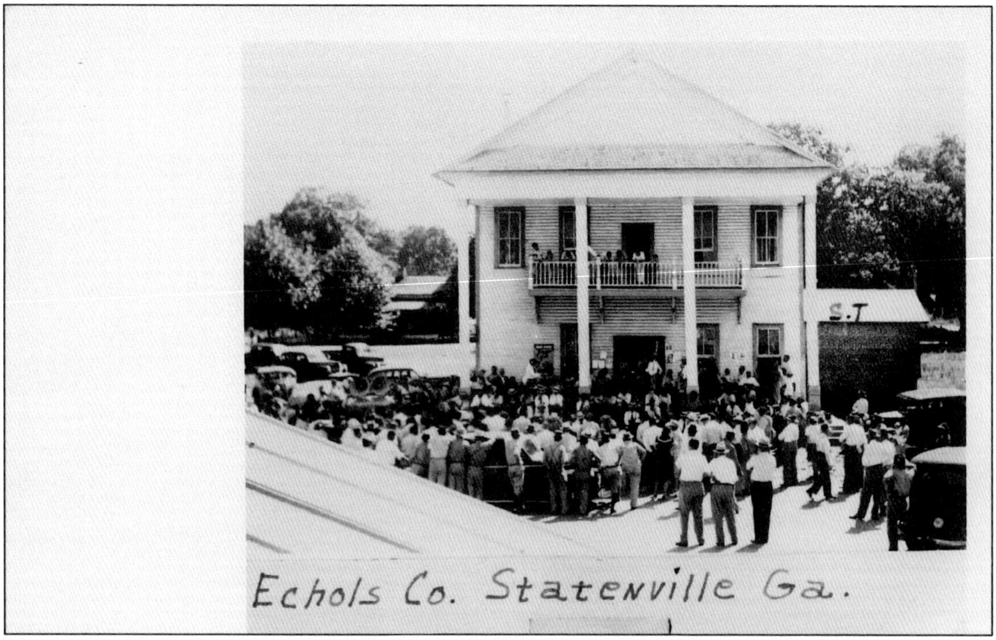

The Echols County Courthouse. The courthouse was completed in 1899 and was used until the new courthouse was built in 1956.

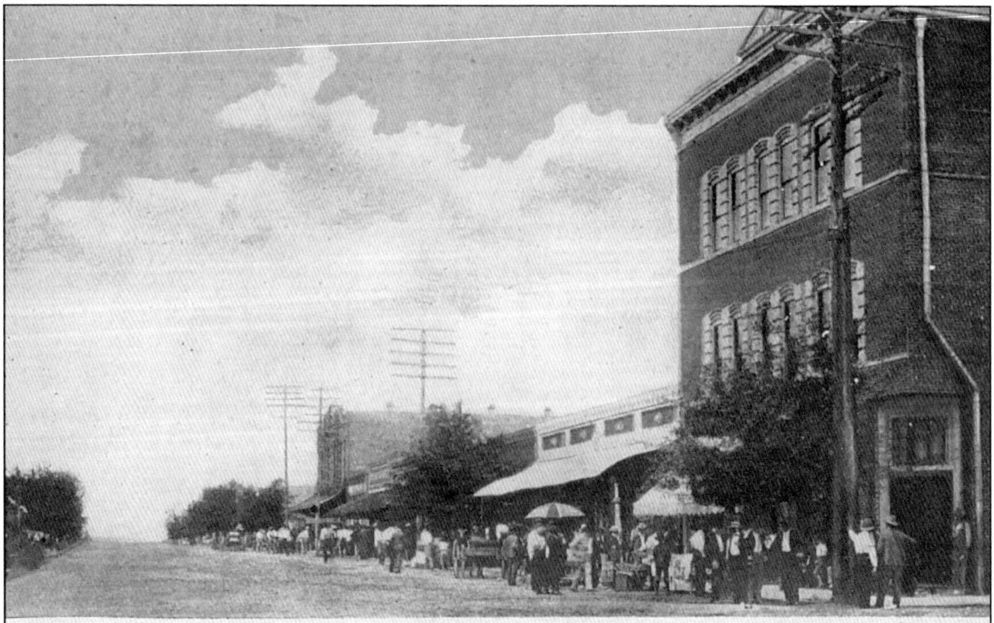

A Busy Fourth Street in Ocilla in 1909.

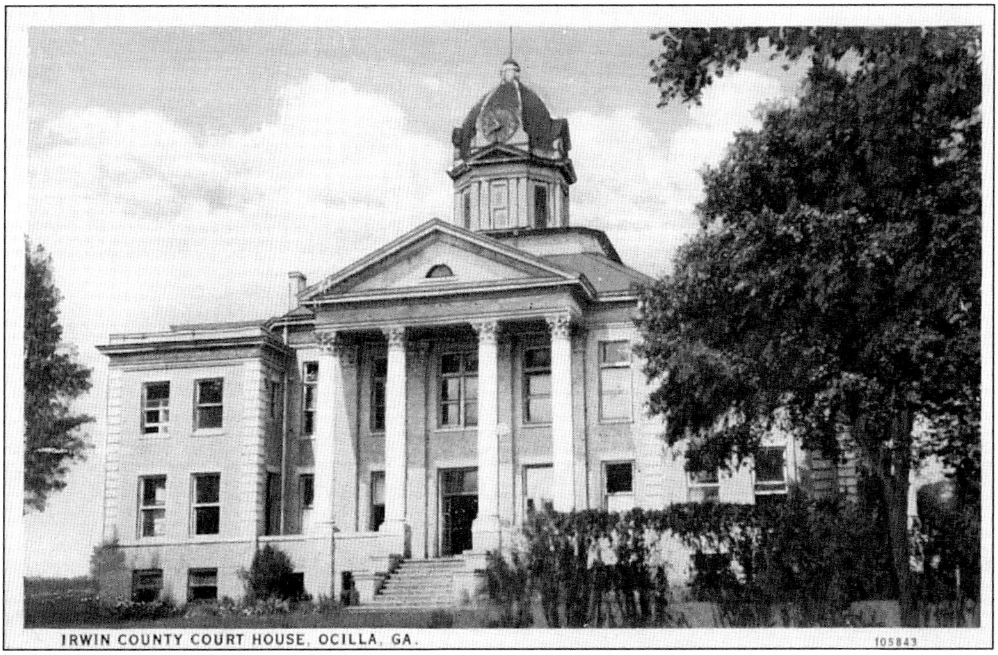

THE IRWIN COUNTY COURTHOUSE, COMPLETED IN 1910 AT A COST OF $52,642. The building was completely renovated in 1972.

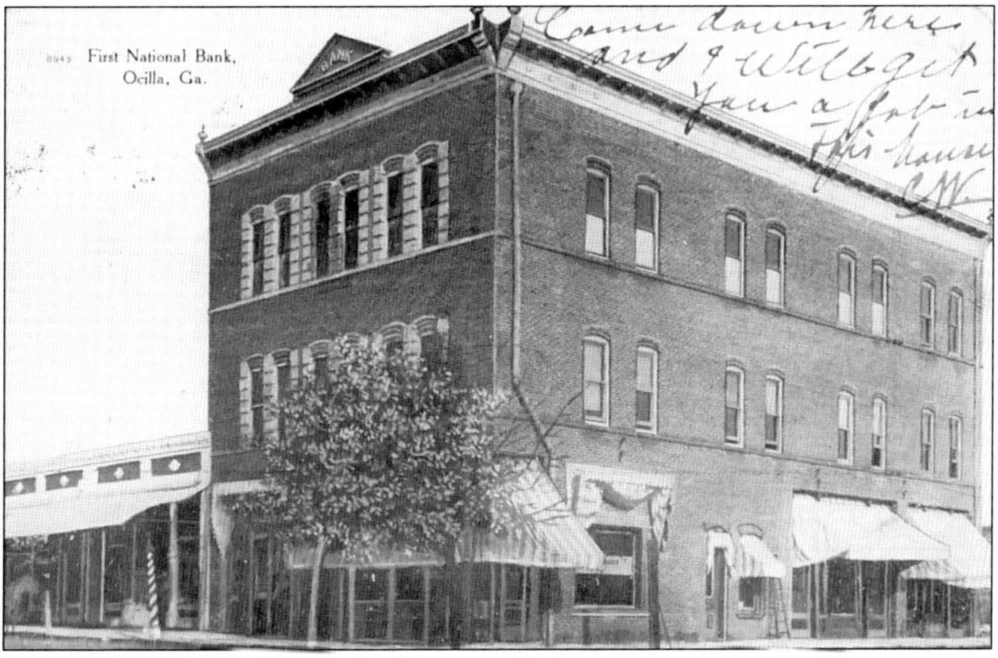

THE OLD FIRST NATIONAL BANK IN OCILLA, C. 1909.

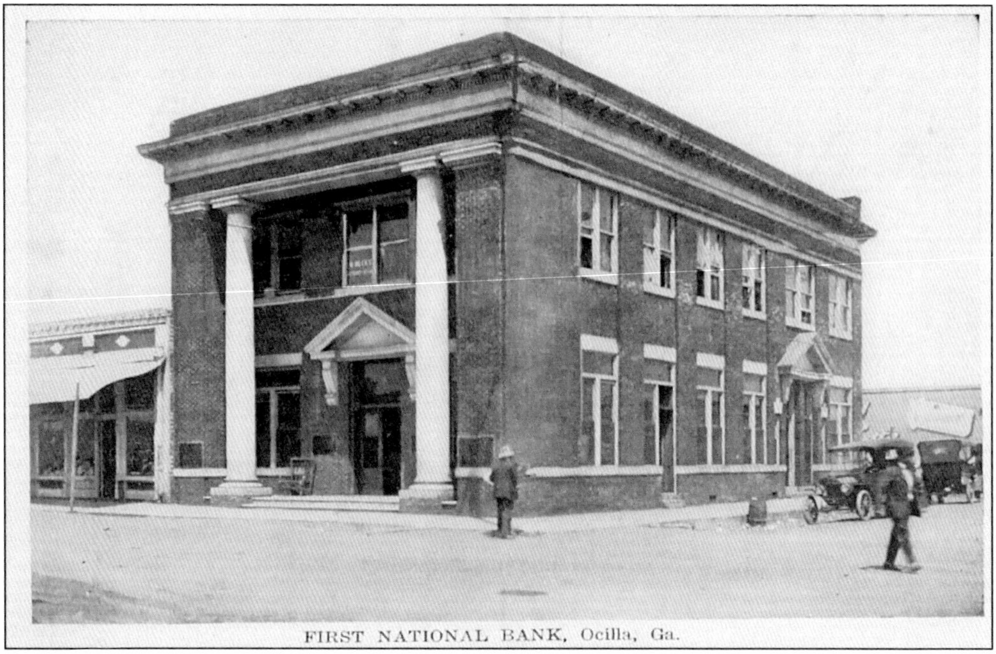

THE FIRST NATIONAL BANK IN OCILLA, C. 1917.

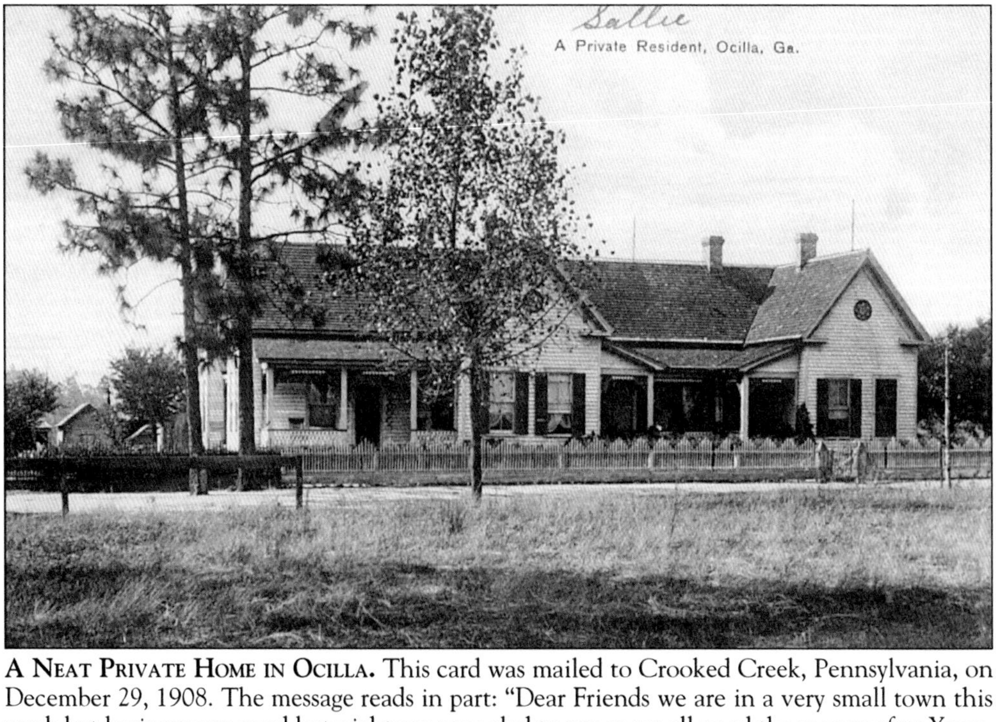

A NEAT PRIVATE HOME IN OCILLA. This card was mailed to Crooked Creek, Pennsylvania, on December 29, 1908. The message reads in part: "Dear Friends we are in a very small town this week but business was good last night am very glad to say as we all need the money after Xmas. Next week Adel, Ga., next Tallahassee, Fla. Good by love to all. S."

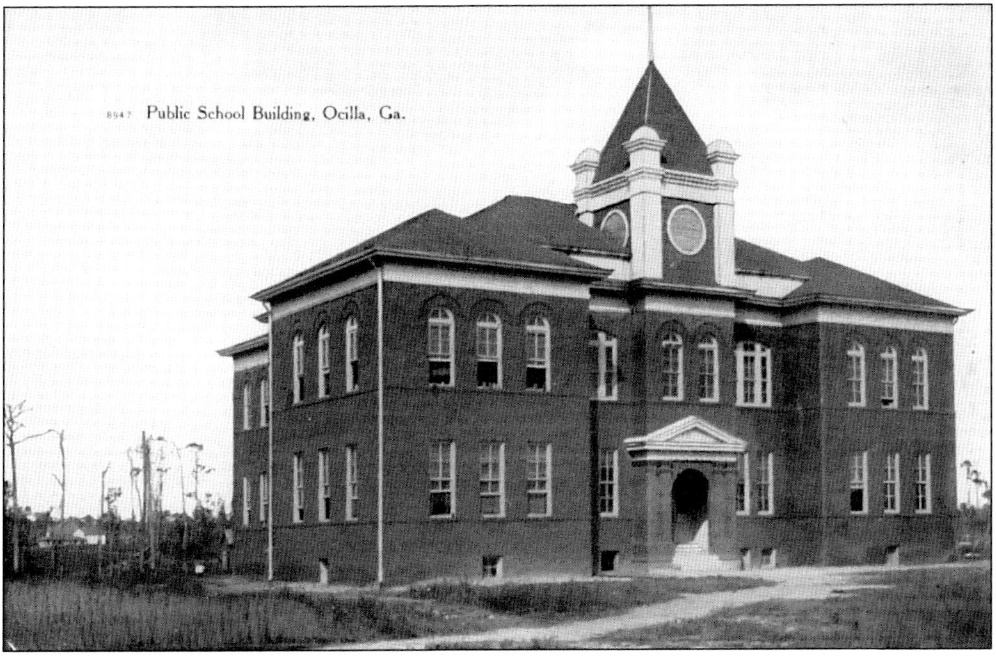

THE PUBLIC SCHOOL BUILDING IN OCILLA, C. 1910.

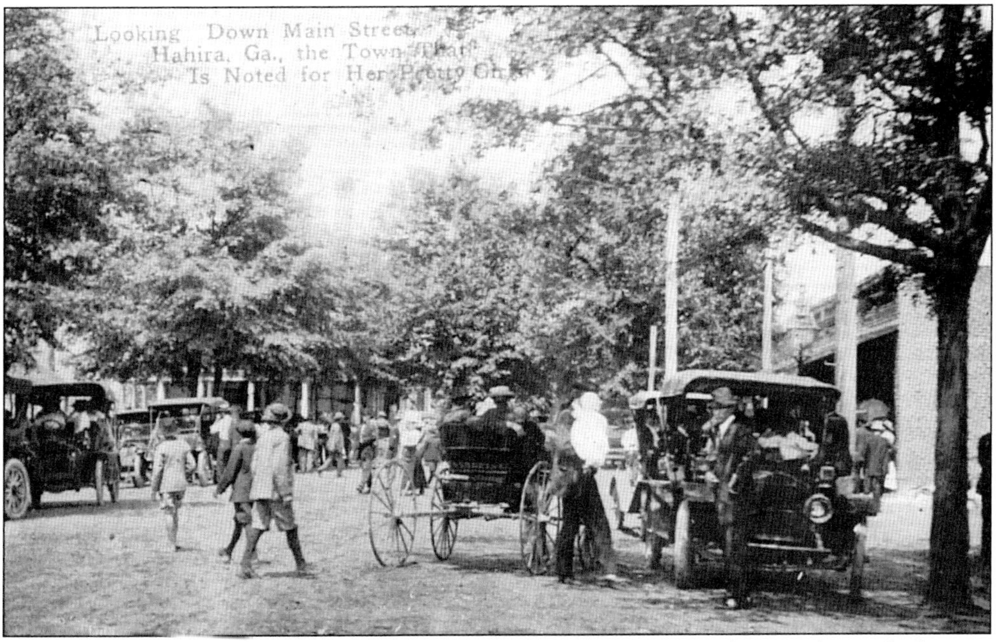

LOOKING DOWN A BUSY MAIN STREET IN HAHIRA, C. 1912. According to the card, this was "The town that is noted for her pretty girls."

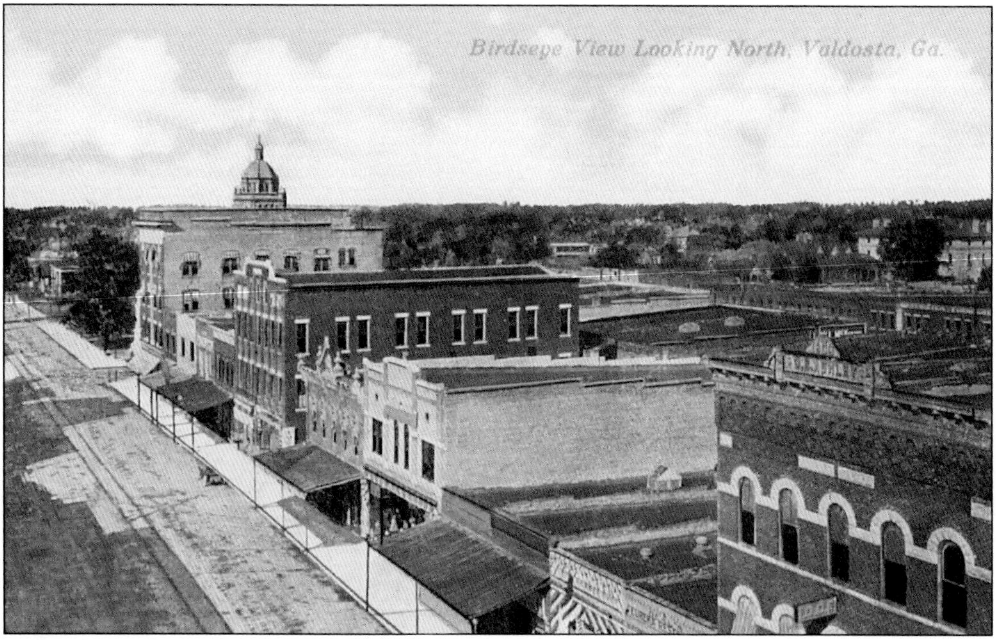

A Bird's-eye View Looking North in Valdosta, c. 1910.

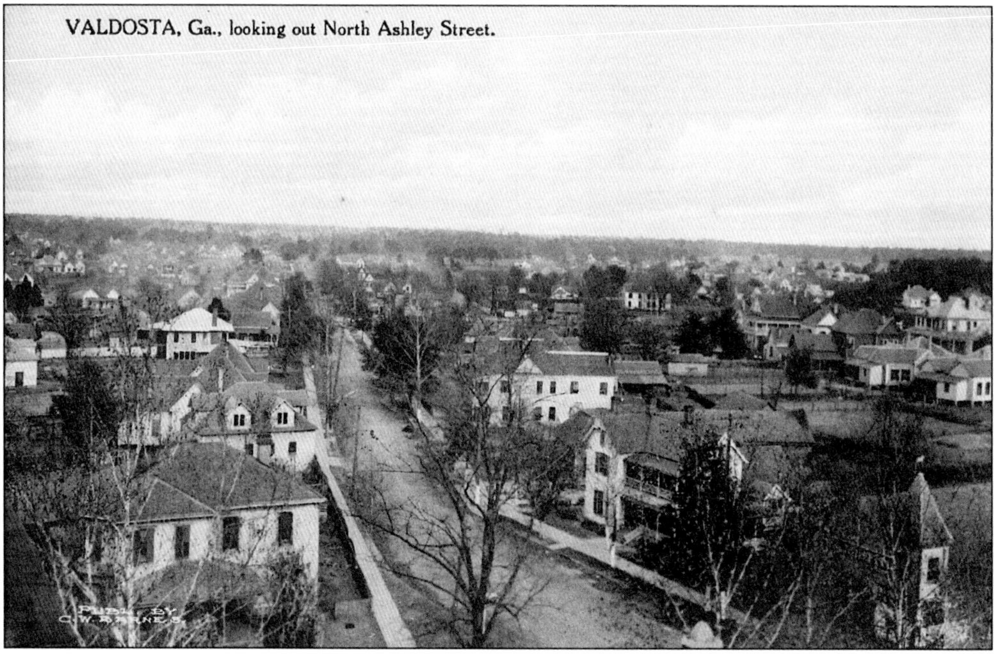

Another Bird's-eye View of Valdosta, Looking out North Ashley Street.

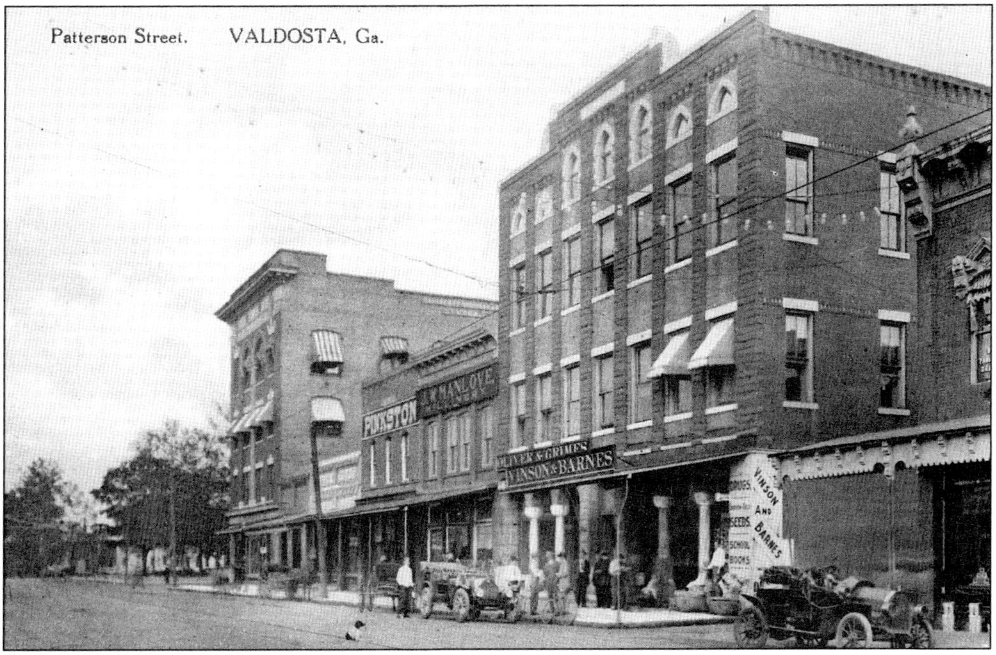

PATTERSON STREET IN VALDOSTA, C. 1912, SHOWING SEVERAL PROMINENT BUSINESSES.

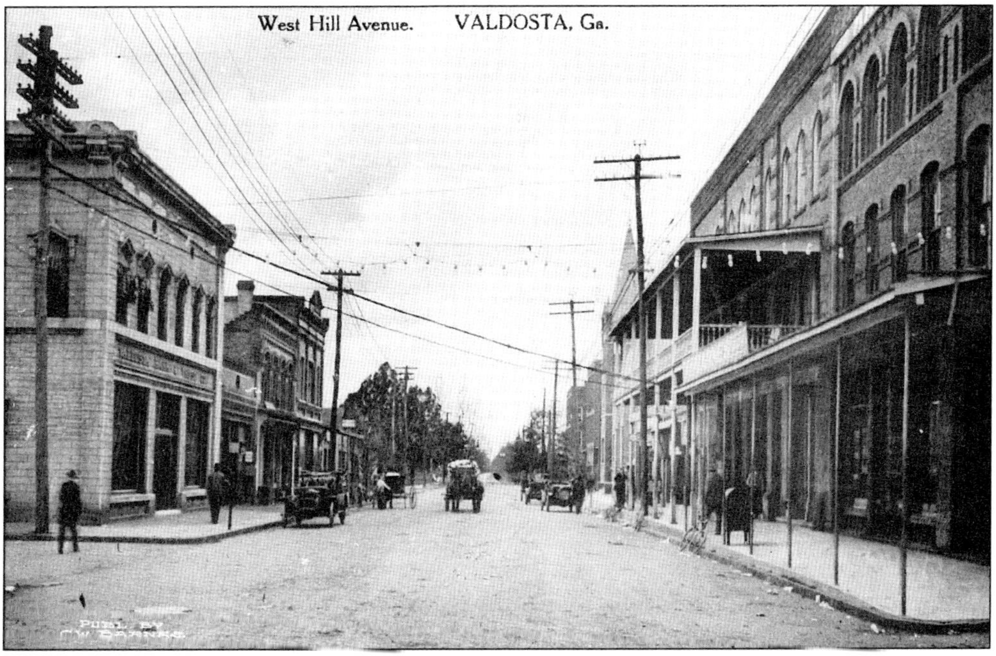

WEST HILL AVENUE IN VALDOSTA, C. 1912.

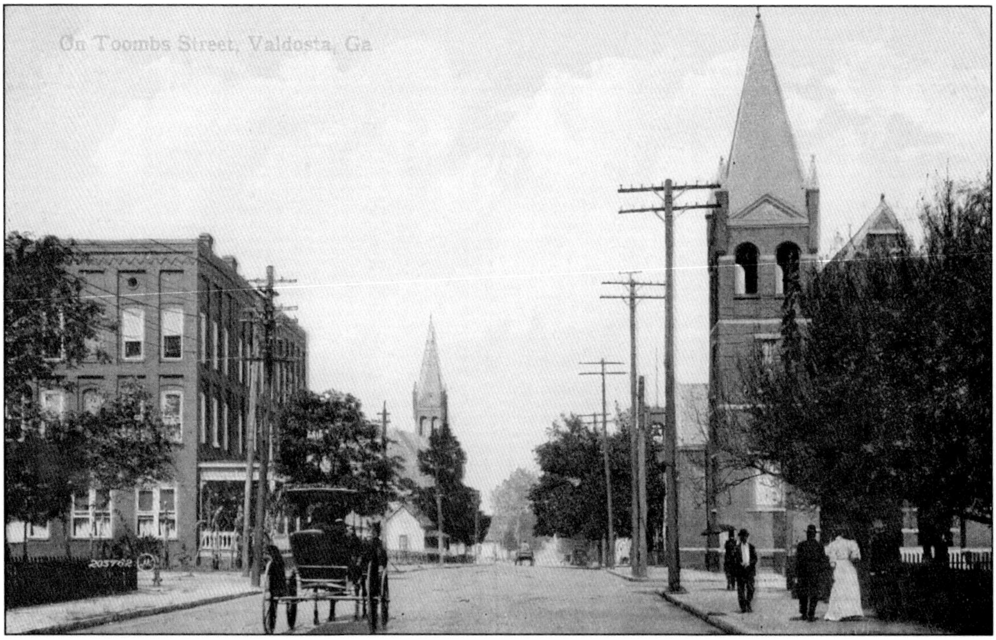

TOOMBS STREET IN VALDOSTA, C. 1908.

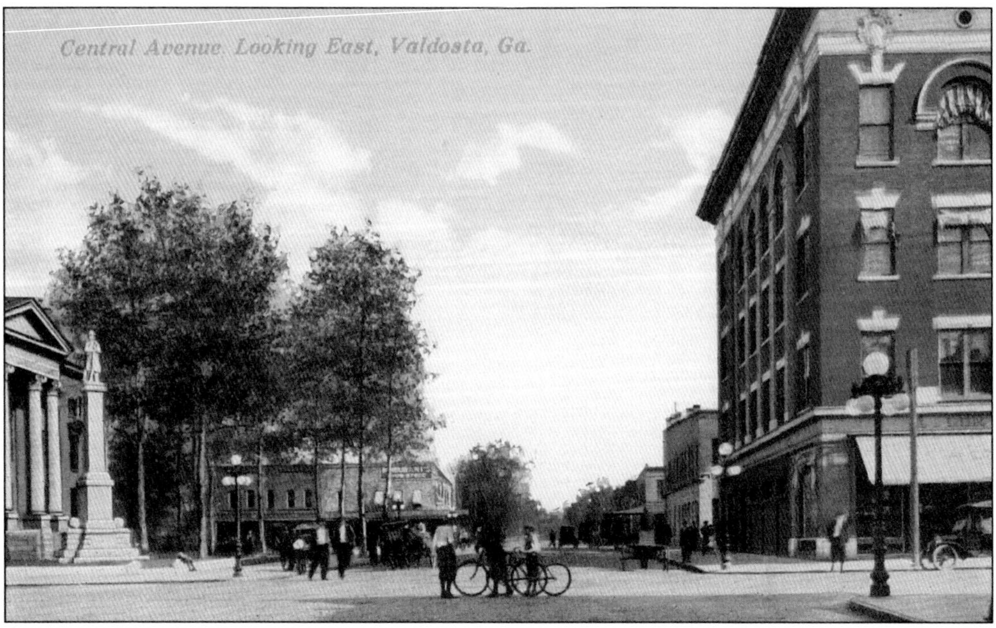

CENTRAL AVENUE LOOKING EAST IN VALDOSTA, C. 1910.

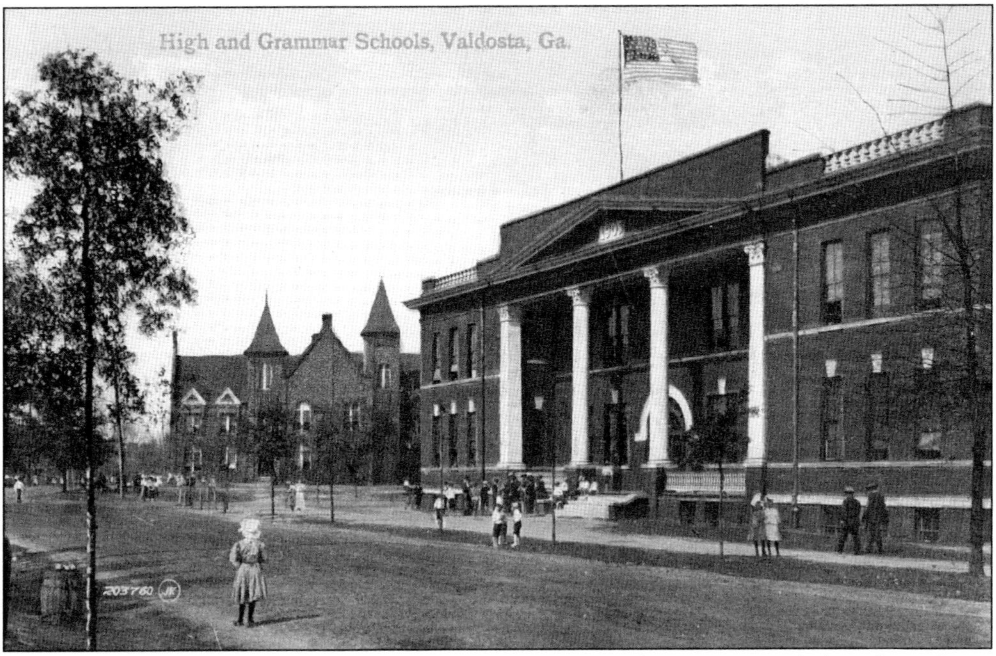

THE HIGH SCHOOL AND GRAMMAR SCHOOL IN VALDOSTA. The two were side by side in this *c.* 1910 view.

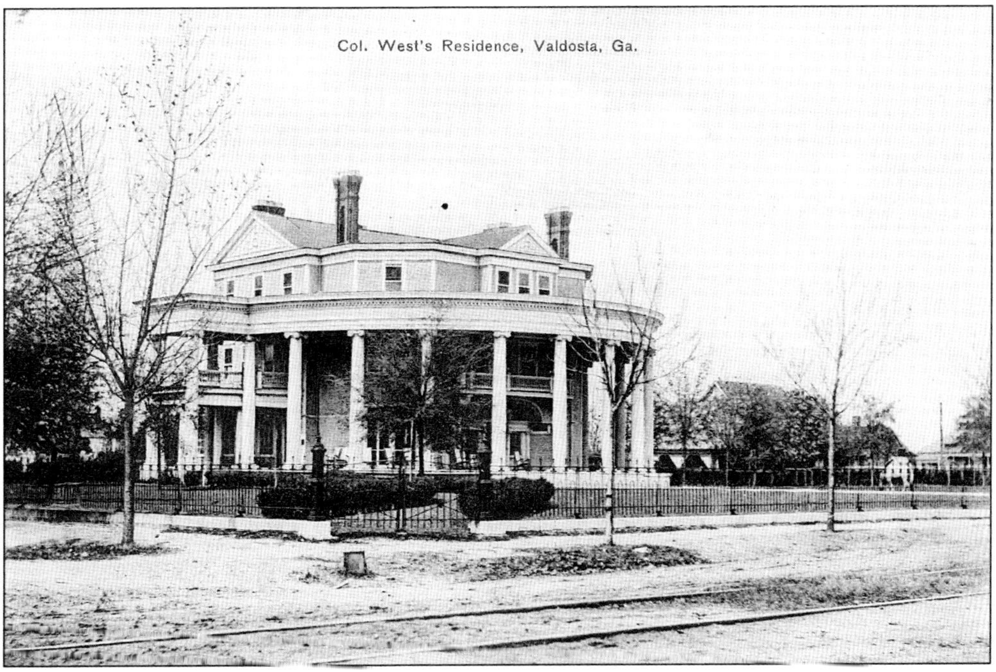

THE HOME OF COLONEL WEST IN VALDOSTA ABOUT 1908.

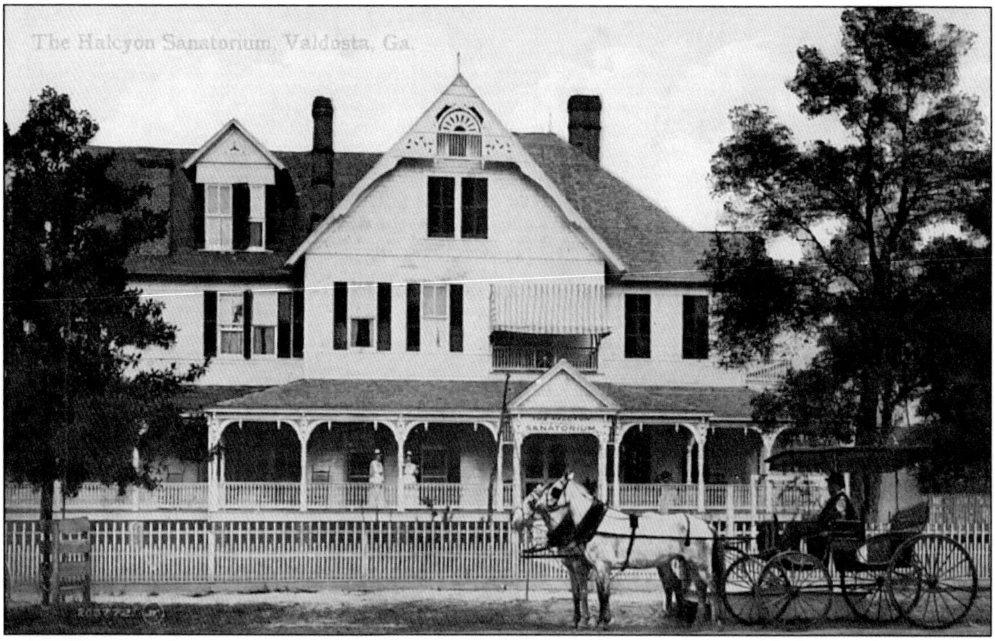

The Halcyon Sanatorium in Valdosta, c. 1909. A matched pair of gray mules is hitched to a surrey out front.

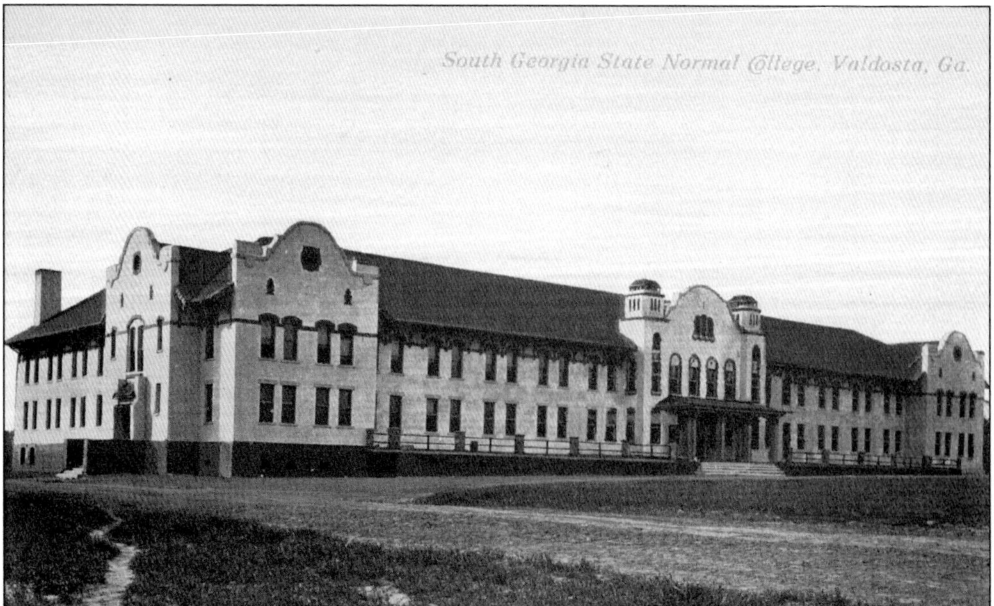

South Georgia State Normal College at Valdosta.

Three

Ben Hill, Dodge, Pulaski, and Wilcox Counties

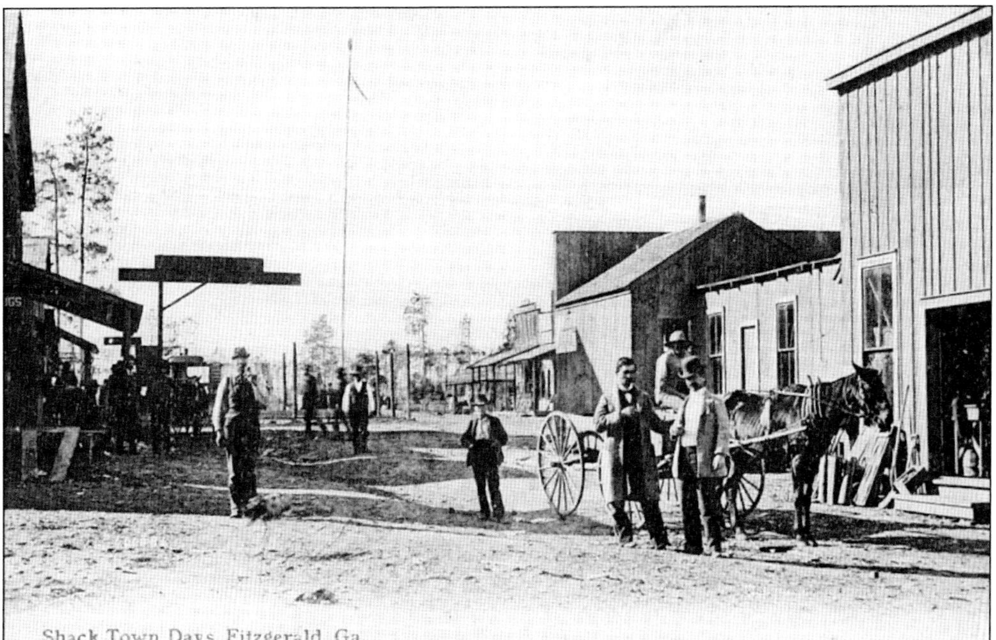

A Post Card View of a Street Scene in Fitzgerald. The card was produced about 1907, but a photograph from the 1890s may have been used.

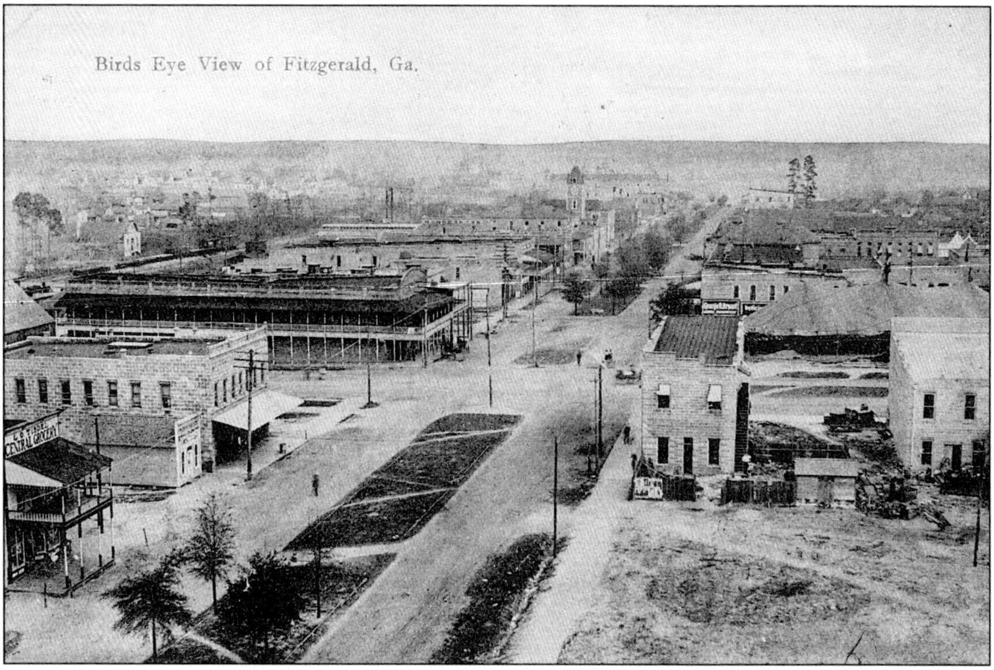

A Bird's-eye View of Central Avenue in Fitzgerald, c. 1910. This view shows a lot of the town. Note the huge canvas tent on the right.

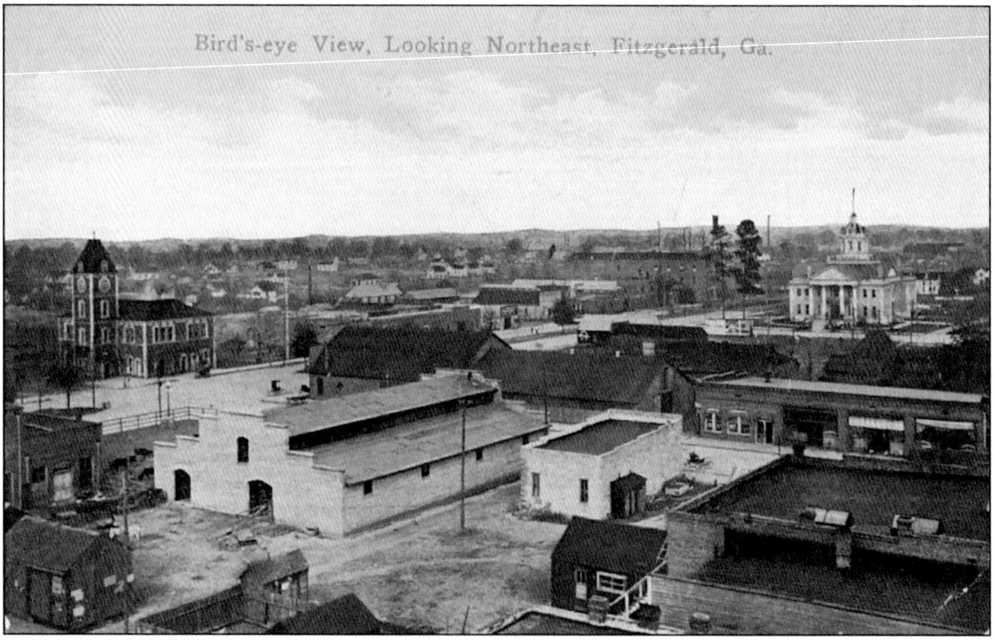

Another Bird's-eye View of Fitzgerald Looking Northeast, c. 1908. The Ben Hill County Courthouse can be seen at the upper right.

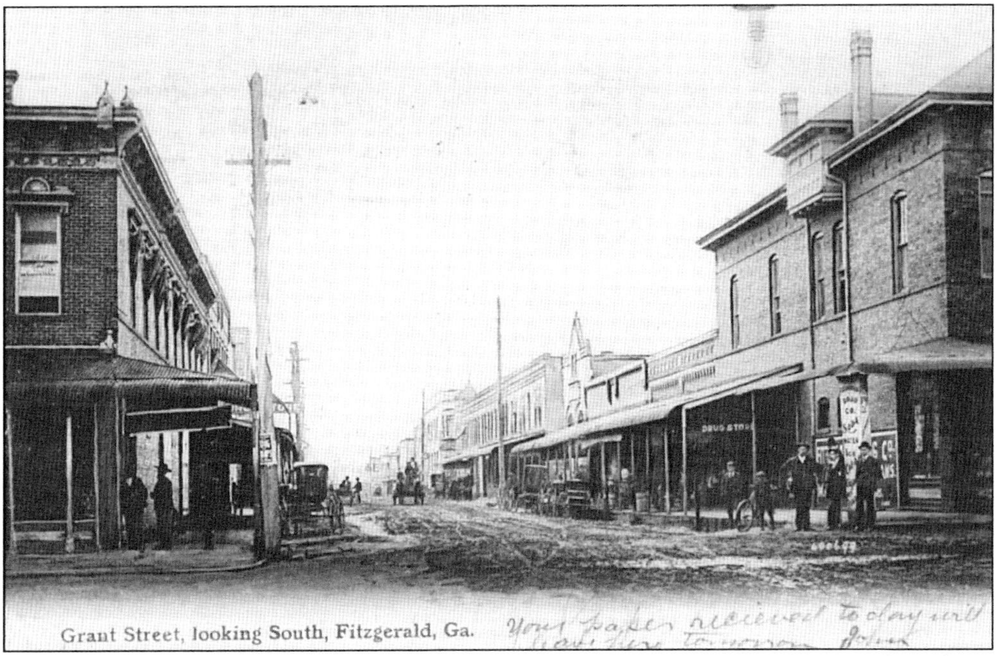

A Street Scene in Fitzgerald. This is another *c.* 1907 post card view that may have been made from an earlier photograph. The view is of Grant Street, looking south.

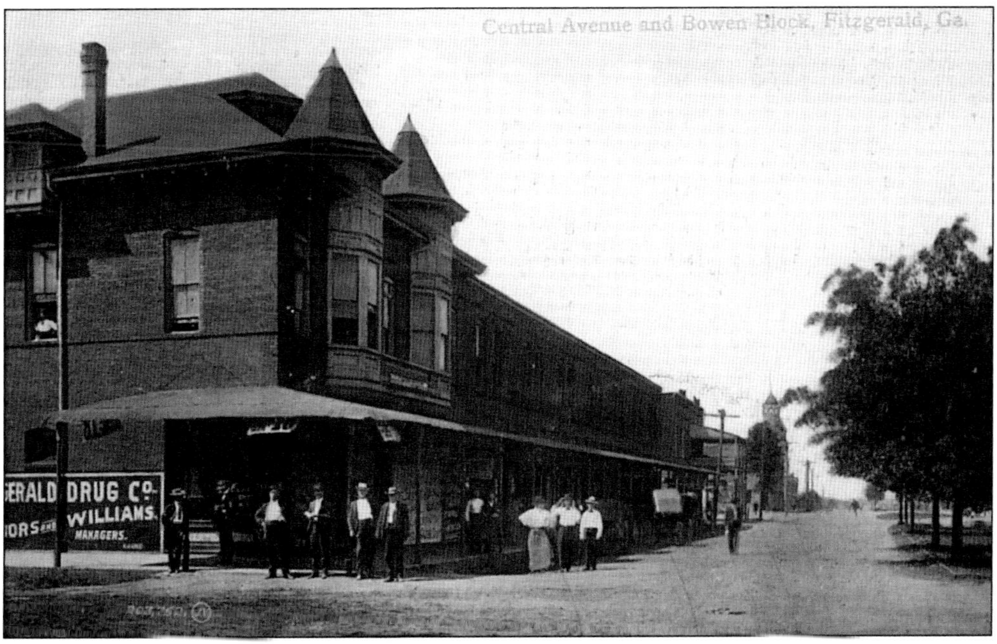

Central Avenue and the Bowen Block in Fitzgerald, *c.* 1908.

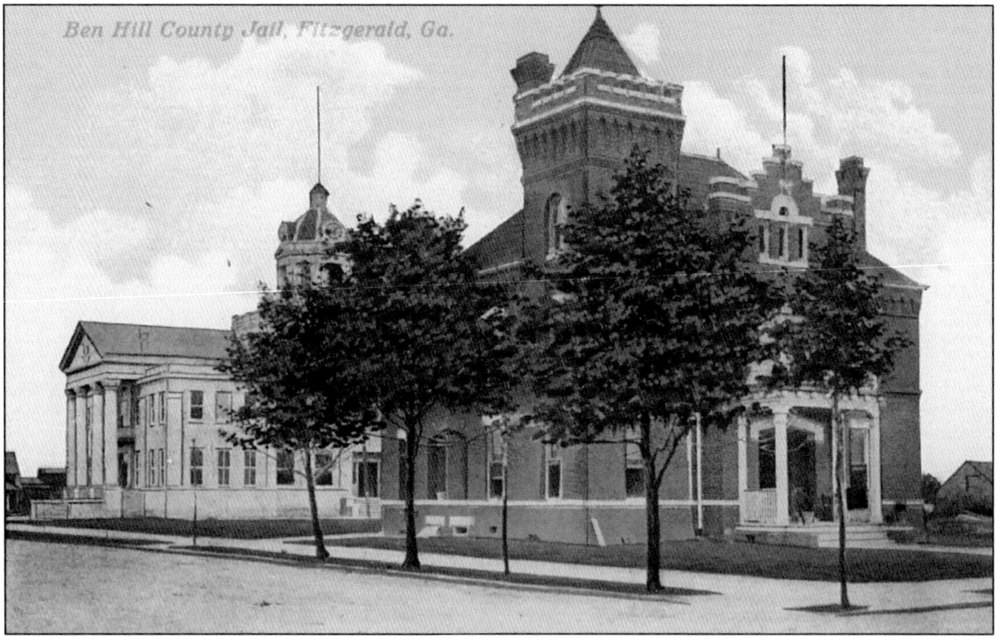

The Ben Hill County Jail at Fitzgerald, c. 1910.

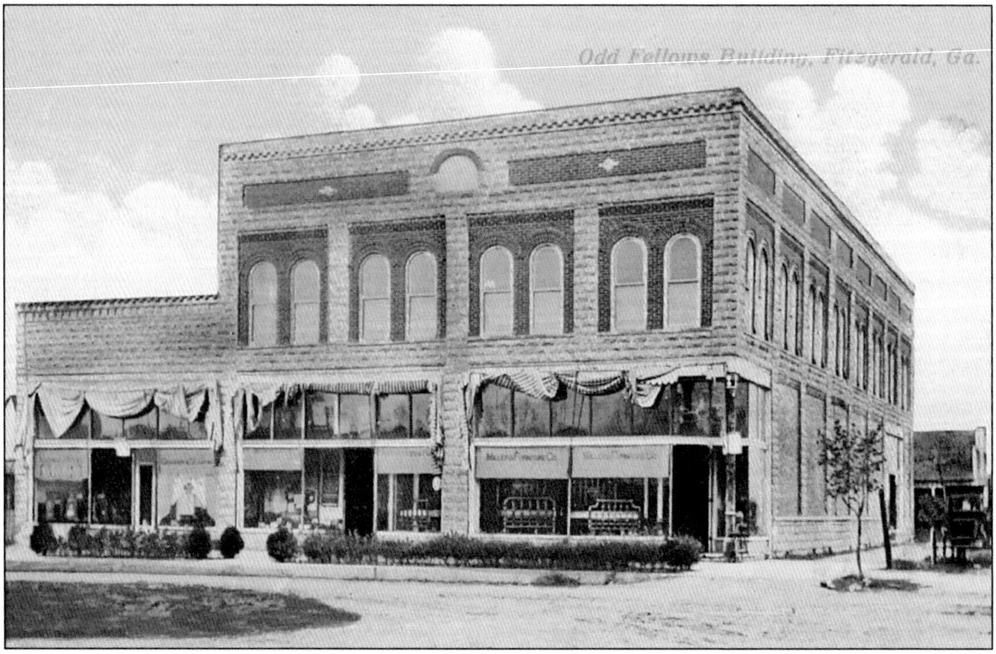

The Odd Fellows Building in Fitzgerald, c. 1910. The corner store was occupied by the C.A. Miller Furniture Company, located at 201 South Main Street.

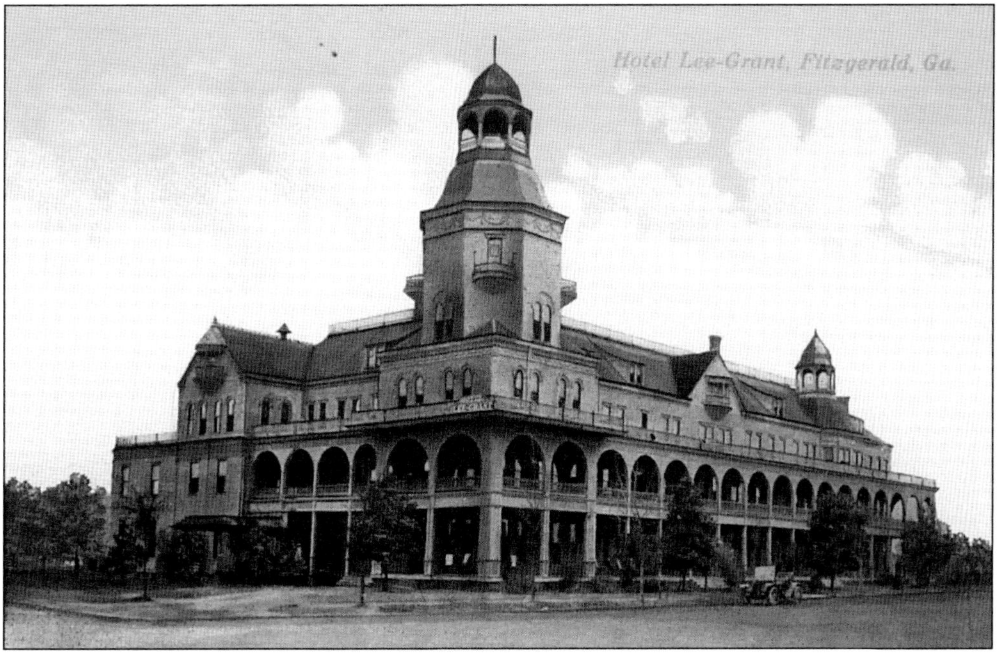

THE MAJESTIC HOTEL LEE-GRANT IN FITZGERALD. The hotel had 100 rooms. In 1910 Mr. Lon Dickey was the proprietor and room rates ranged from $2.50 per night and up.

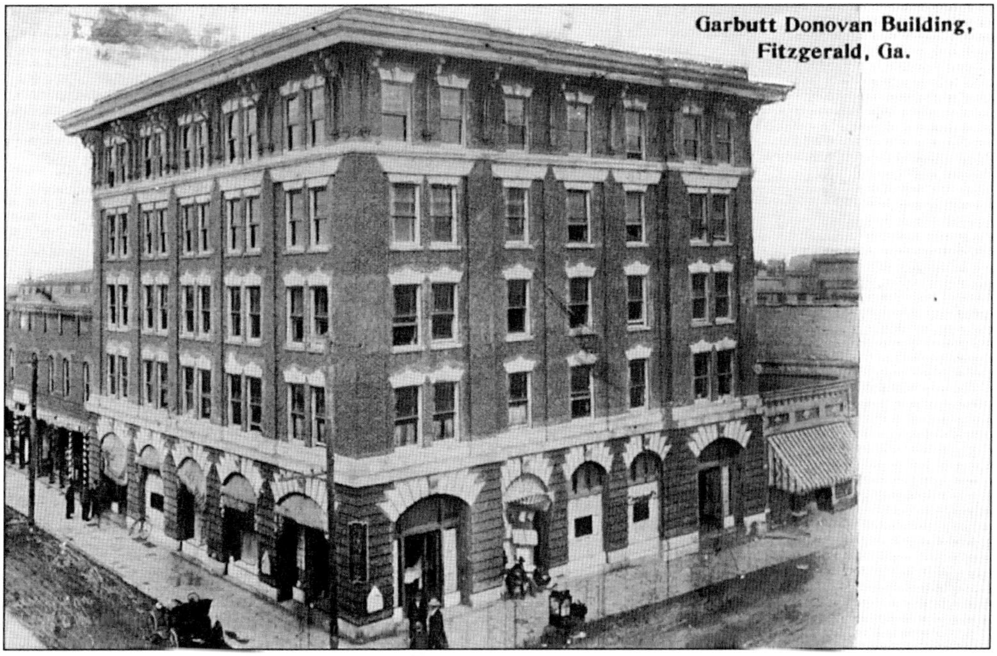

THE GARBUTT DONOVAN BUILDING IN FITZGERALD, C. 1912.

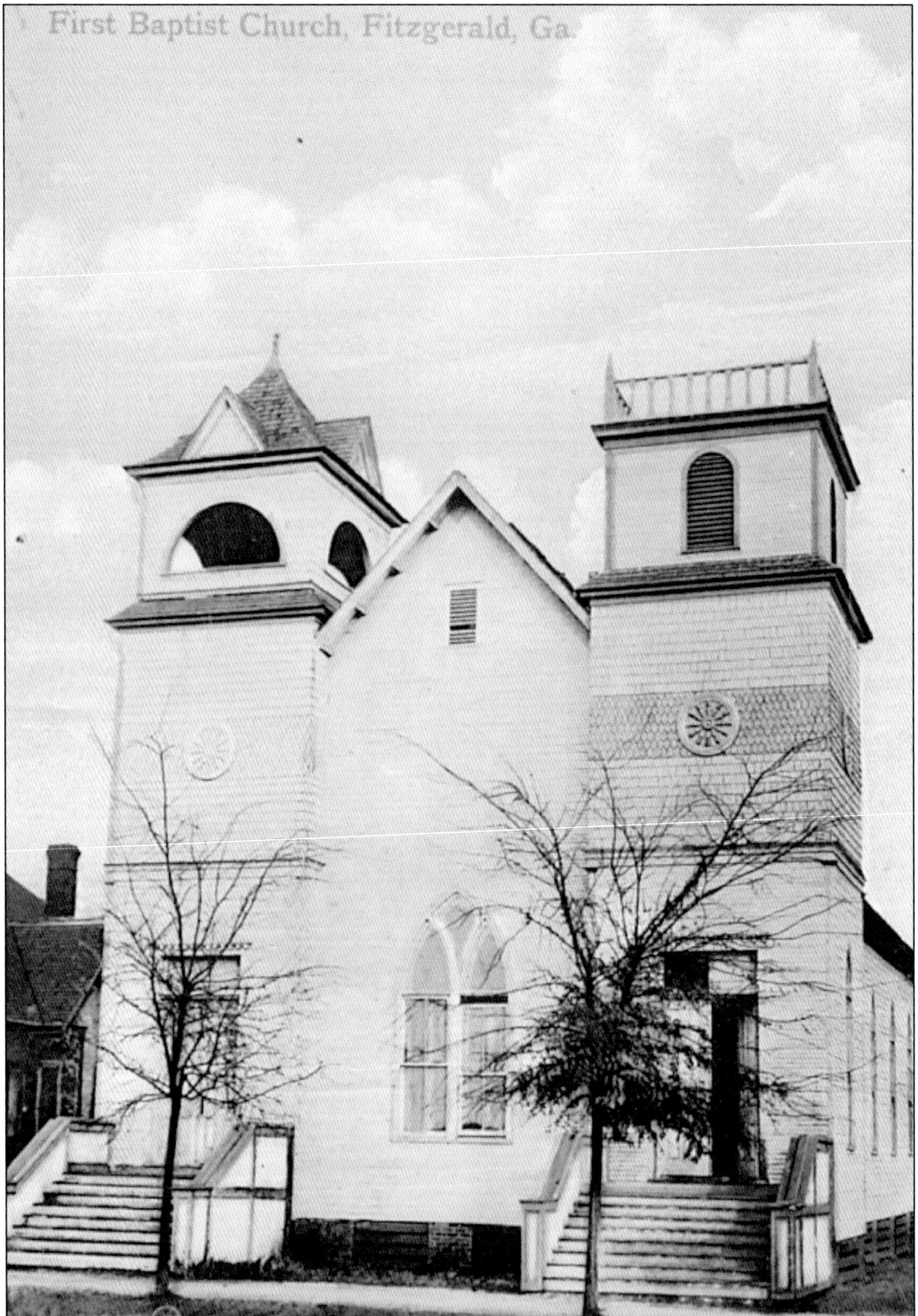

THE FIRST BAPTIST CHURCH IN FITZGERALD, C. 1908. The church was a large wooden structure with a belfry on one side and a tower to broadcast music from the church organ on the other side.

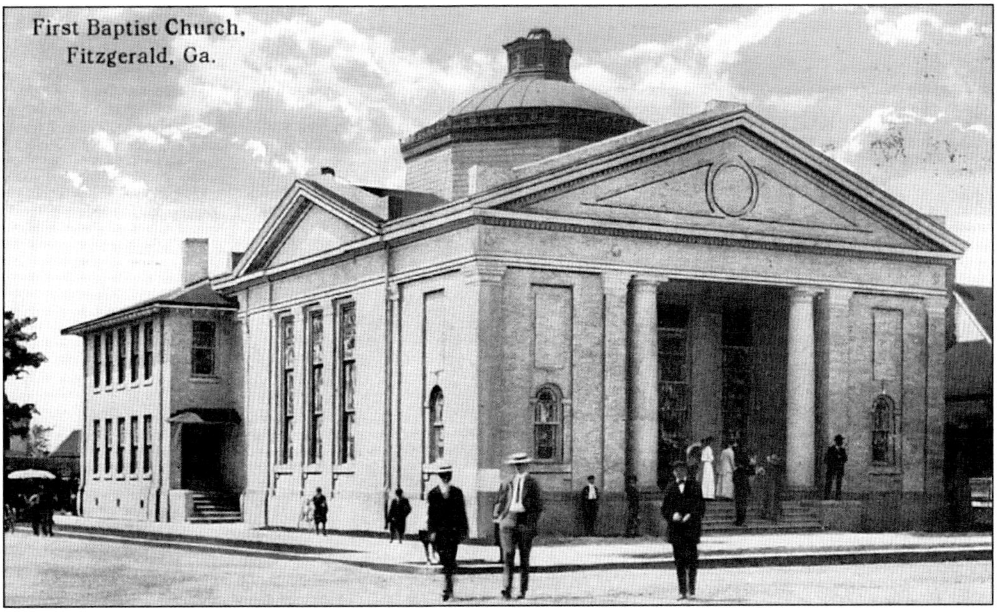

THE FIRST BAPTIST CHURCH IN FITZGERALD, C. 1912.

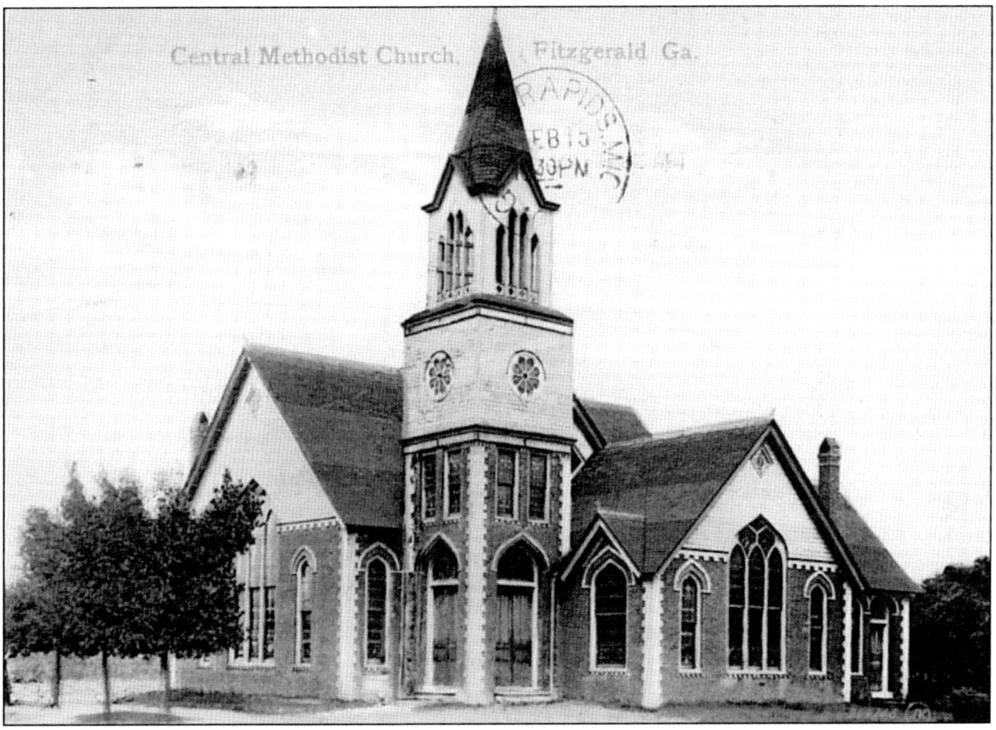

THE CENTRAL METHODIST CHURCH IN FITZGERALD, C. 1907. The church was an elaborate brick structure with a fancy belfry. This card was mailed to Grand Rapids, Michigan, and the message reads in part: "Dear Friend Emma, Well here I am in the Sunny South. It is beautiful weather here. Wish you were with me. I am a going to skip down on to Florida for a day or two, for I want to see the Atlantic Ocean now that I have seen the Pacific. I am a going to stay off at Chattanooga for 2 or 3 days when I go back & see the places of note there. With love, V.P.N."

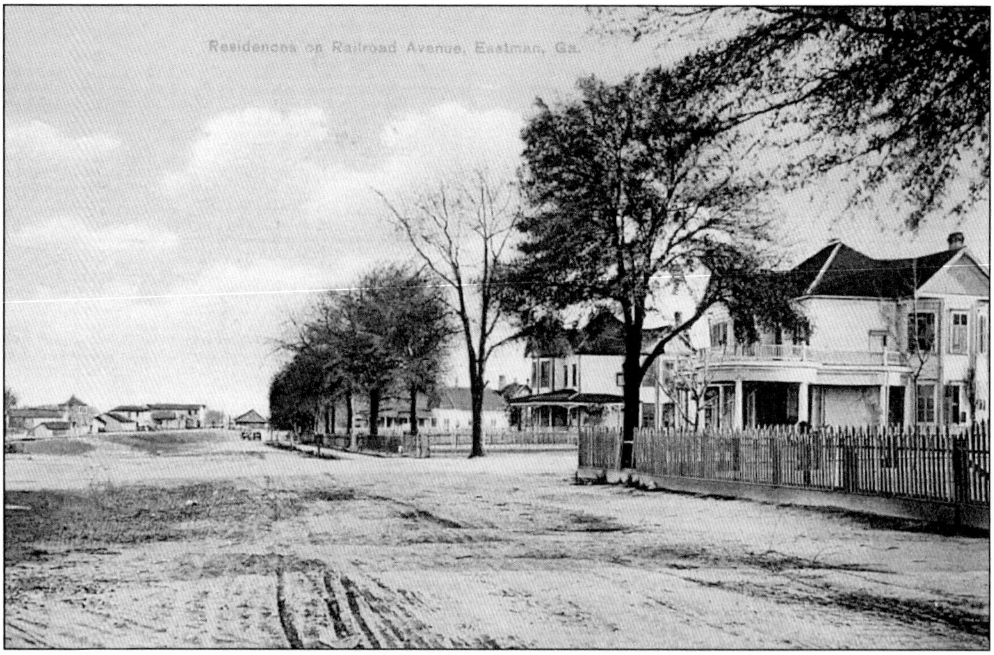

Some Fine Private Homes along Railroad Avenue in Eastman in 1907.

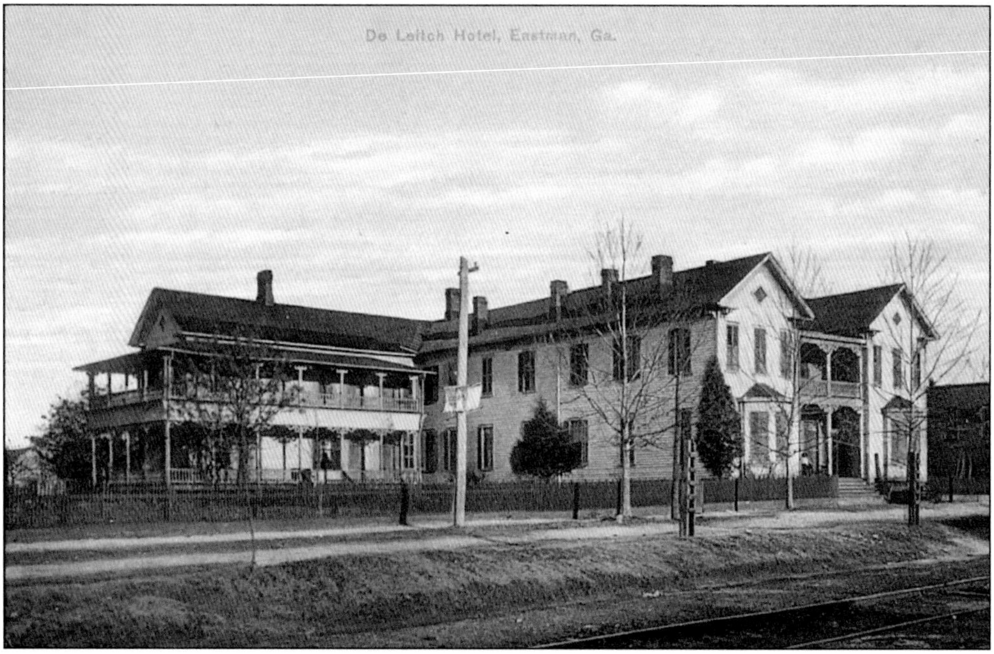

The De Leitch Hotel in Eastman. The hotel was located on Railroad Avenue in Eastman and was operated by Mrs. J.A. Brown.

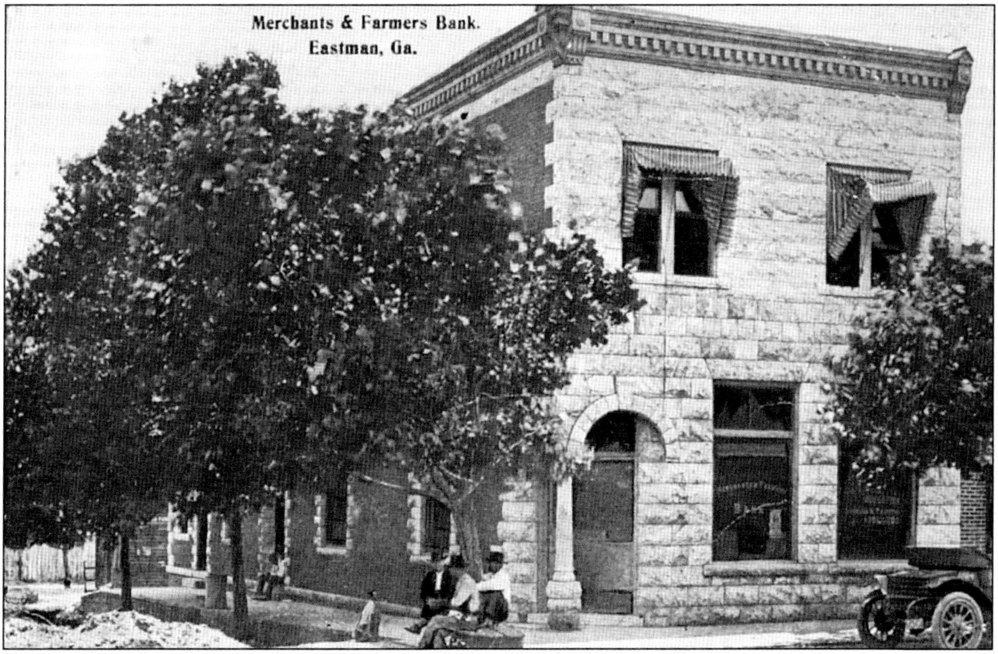

THE MERCHANTS & FARMERS BANK IN EASTMAN. The bank was also located on Railroad Avenue. In 1910 the bank president was D.M. Roberts, J.D. Herman was vice-president, and W.P. Cobb was cashier.

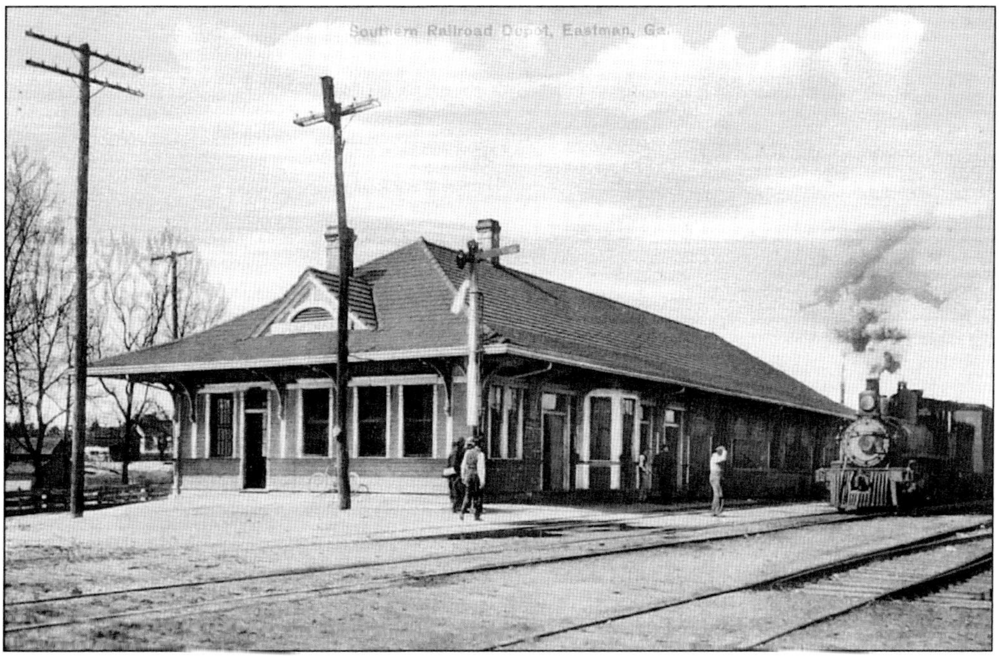

THE SOUTHERN RAILROAD DEPOT AT EASTMAN, C. 1912.

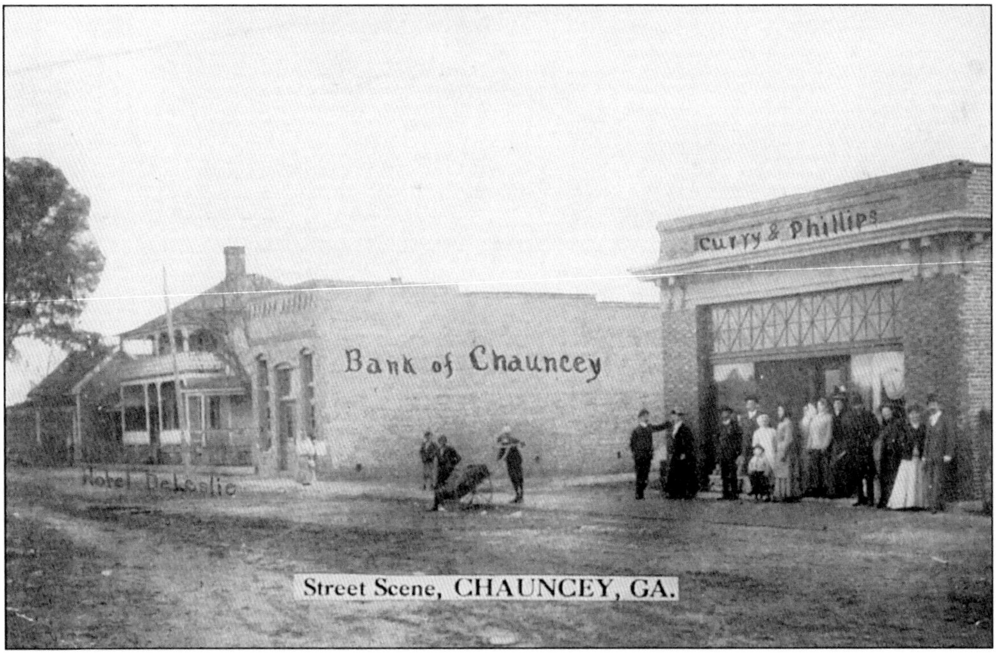

AN EARLY STREET SCENE POST CARD OF CHAUNCEY. The card has the names of three businesses added in ink: Hotel DeLeslie; Bank of Chauncey; and Curry & Phillips.

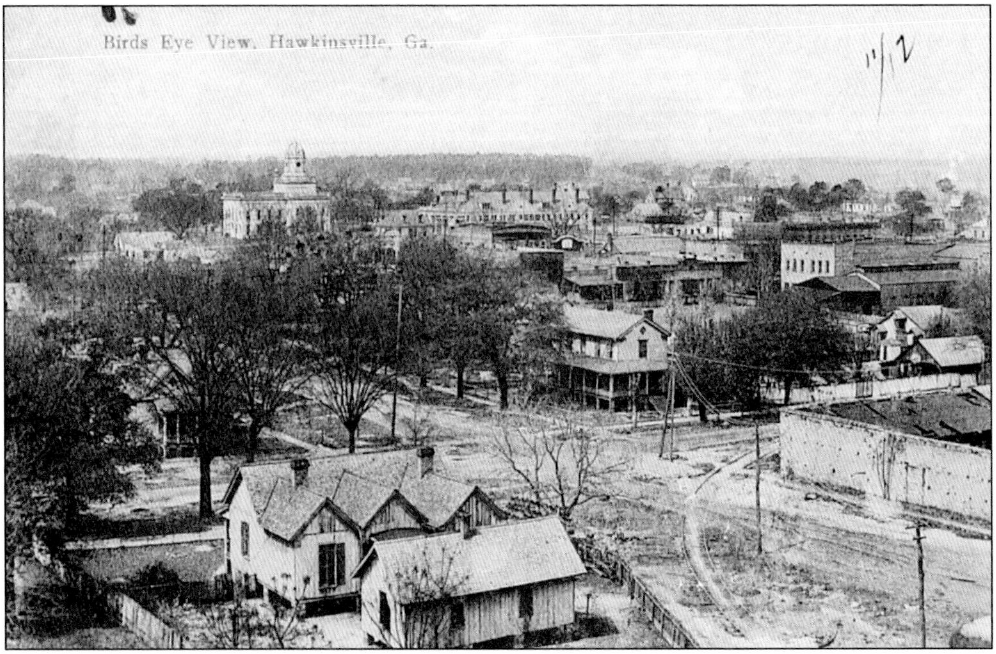

A BIRD'S-EYE VIEW OF HAWKINSVILLE, C. 1908.

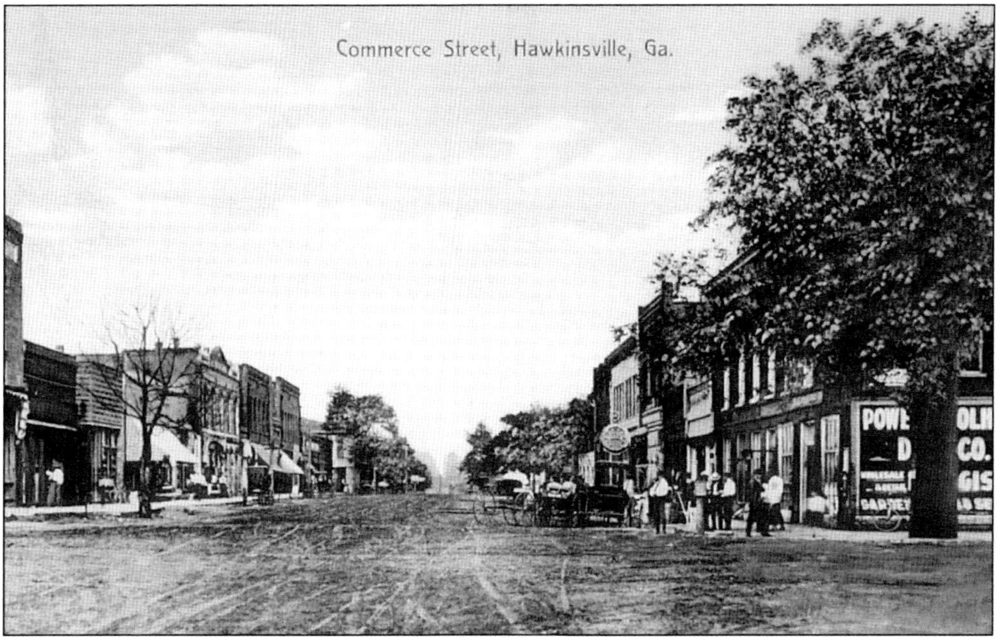

COMMERCE STREET IN HAWKINSVILLE, C. 1908. The Powell-Polhill Drug Store was located in the corner building on the right.

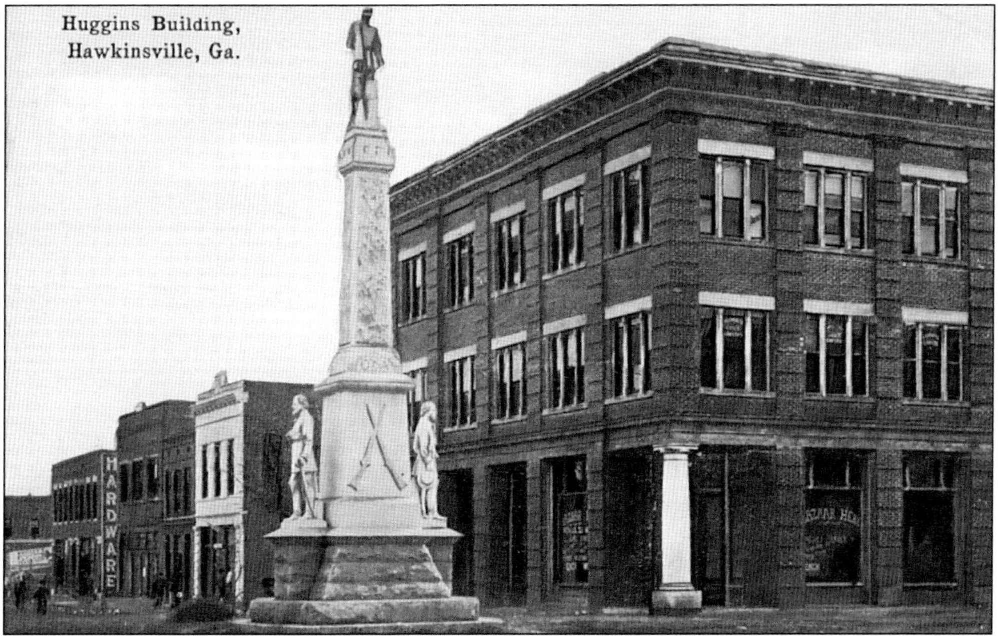

THE CONFEDERATE MONUMENT, HAWKINSVILLE. When the monument was erected in Hawkinsville in 1907 it was placed in the middle of town in front of the Huggings Building. The 30-foot shaft includes the statue of a soldier on top, with likenesses of Generals Lee and Jackson on either side of the base. Increased traffic caused the monument to be moved to the intersection of Lumpkin and Commerce Street. After the monument was struck by an automobile at that location in the 1930s, it was moved to its present location on the courthouse lawn.

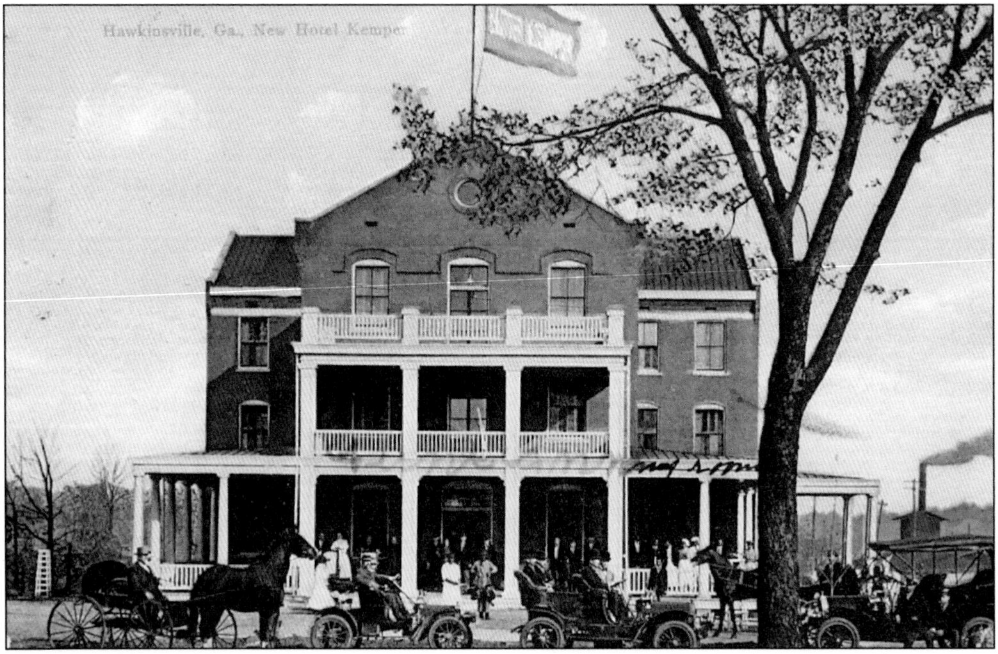

The New Hotel Kemper in Hawkinsville. The hotel appeared to be doing a good business in this 1910 view. Mrs. S.E. Brannon operated the hotel at this time.

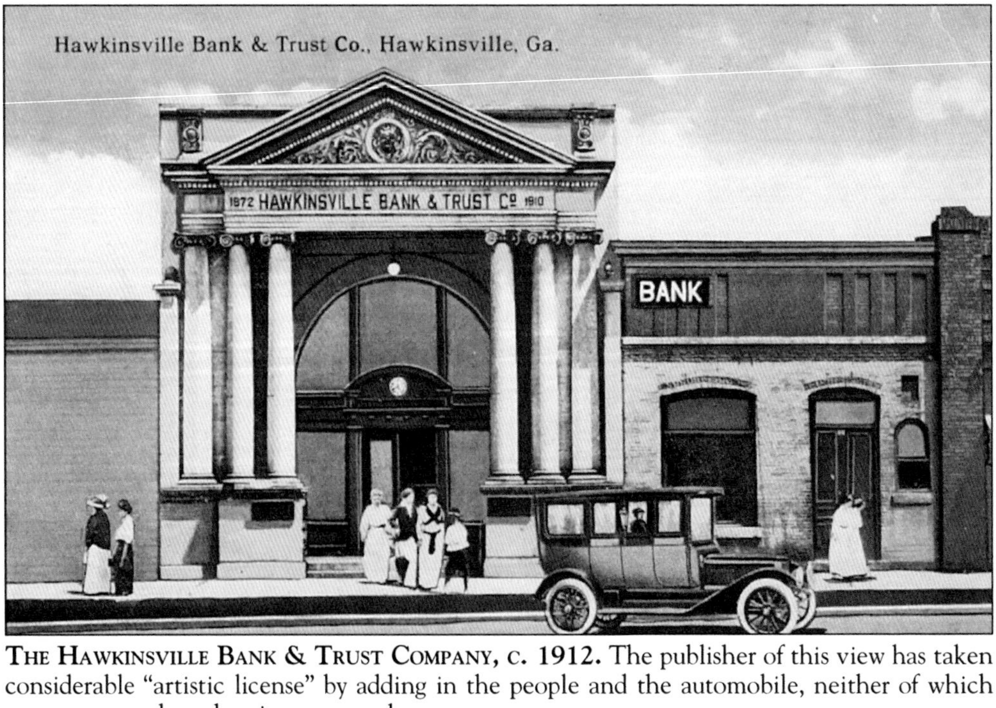

The Hawkinsville Bank & Trust Company, c. 1912. The publisher of this view has taken considerable "artistic license" by adding in the people and the automobile, neither of which were present when the picture was taken.

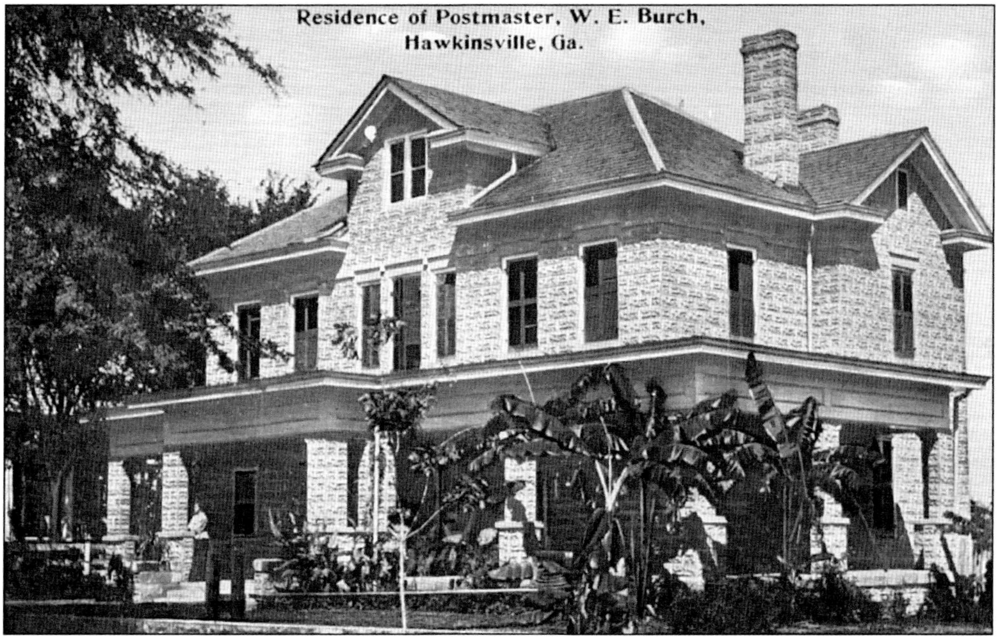

THE STATELY RESIDENCE OF W.E. BURCH, POSTMASTER OF HAWKINSVILLE, C. 1912.

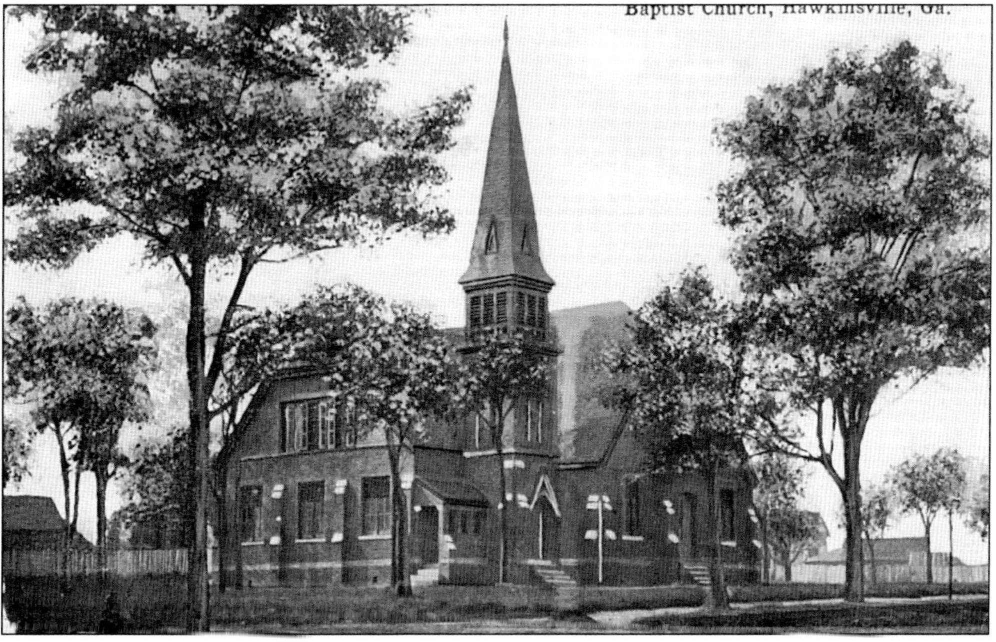

THE BAPTIST CHURCH IN HAWKINSVILLE.

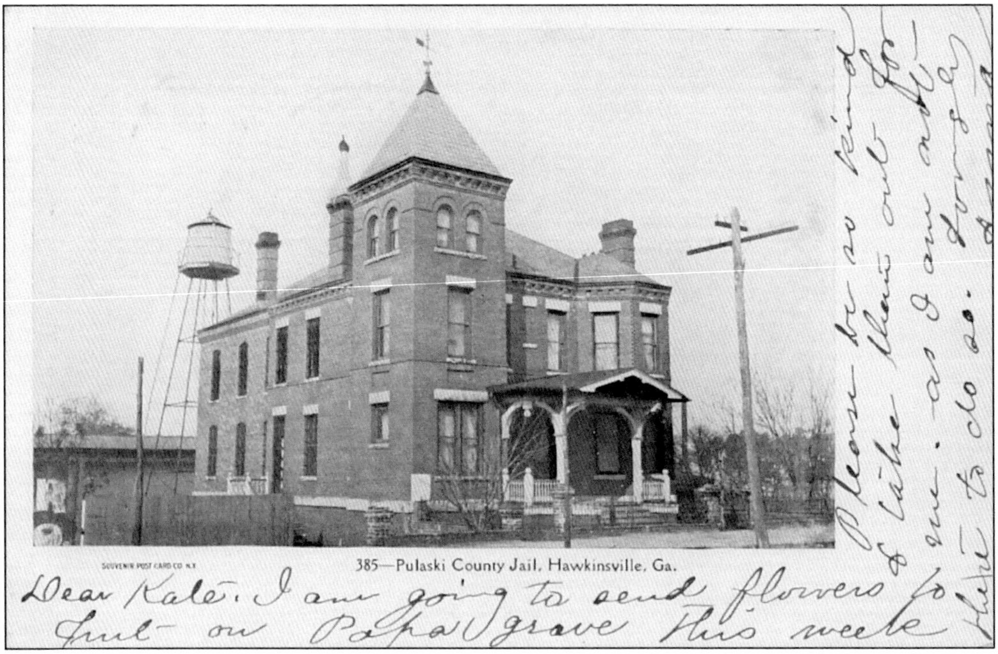

THE PULASKI COUNTY JAIL IN HAWKINSVILLE ABOUT 1907. The card was mailed to Baltimore, Maryland, and the message reads: "Dear Kate, I am going to send flowers to put on Papa's grave this week. Please be so kind & take them out for me as I am not there to do so. Lovingly Anna."

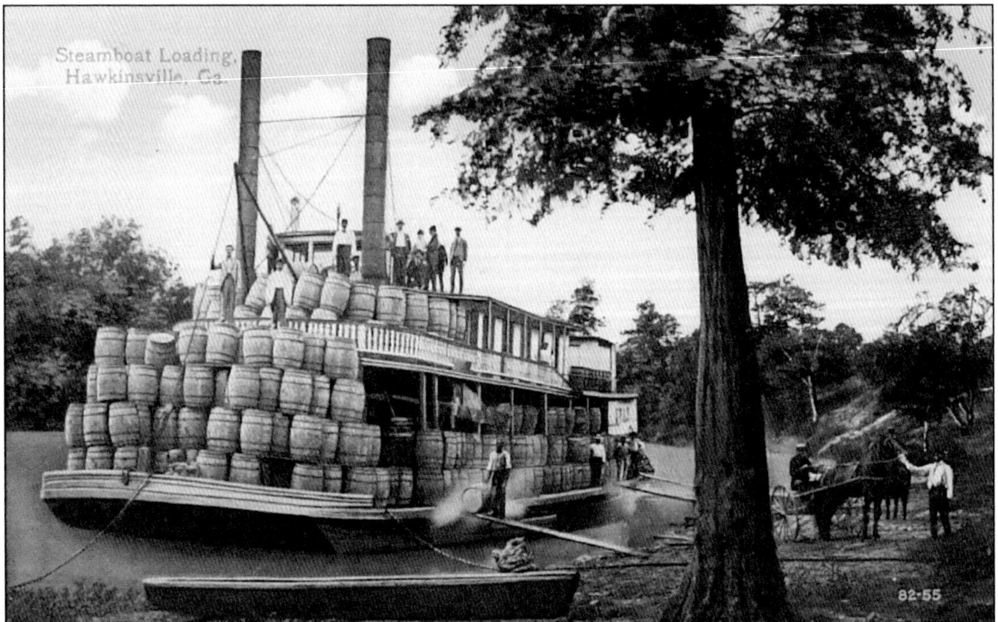

A MAGNIFICENT STERN-WHEELER STEAMBOAT IN THE OCMULGEE RIVER AT HAWKINSVILLE. Here the vessel is at the dock and taking on barrels of naval stores.

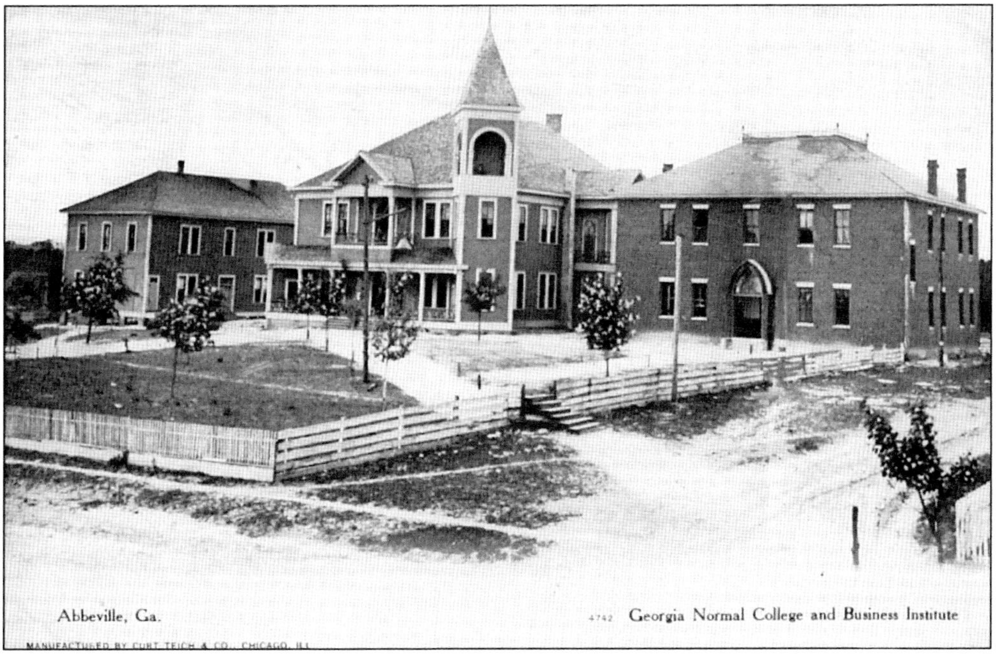

The Georgia Normal College and Business Institute at Abbeville. This card was mailed to Douglas, Georgia, on January 2, 1909, and carried this message: "Justin died this morning at 3 A.M. Will bring him home this P.M. & will bury him in the morning. So sad, Amanda."

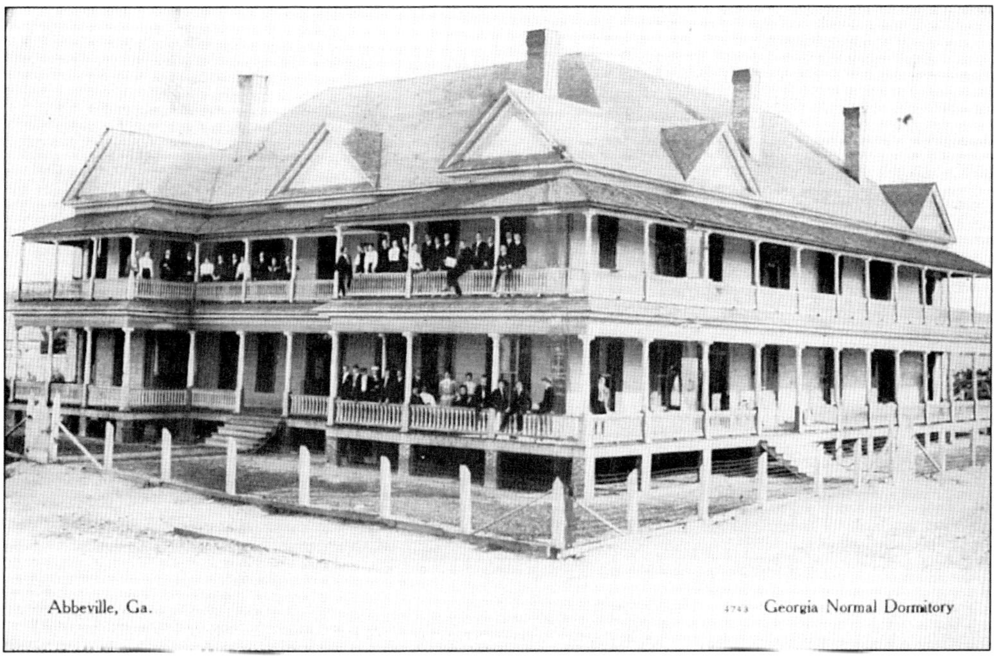

The Dormitory at the Georgia Normal College and Business Institute at Abbeville.

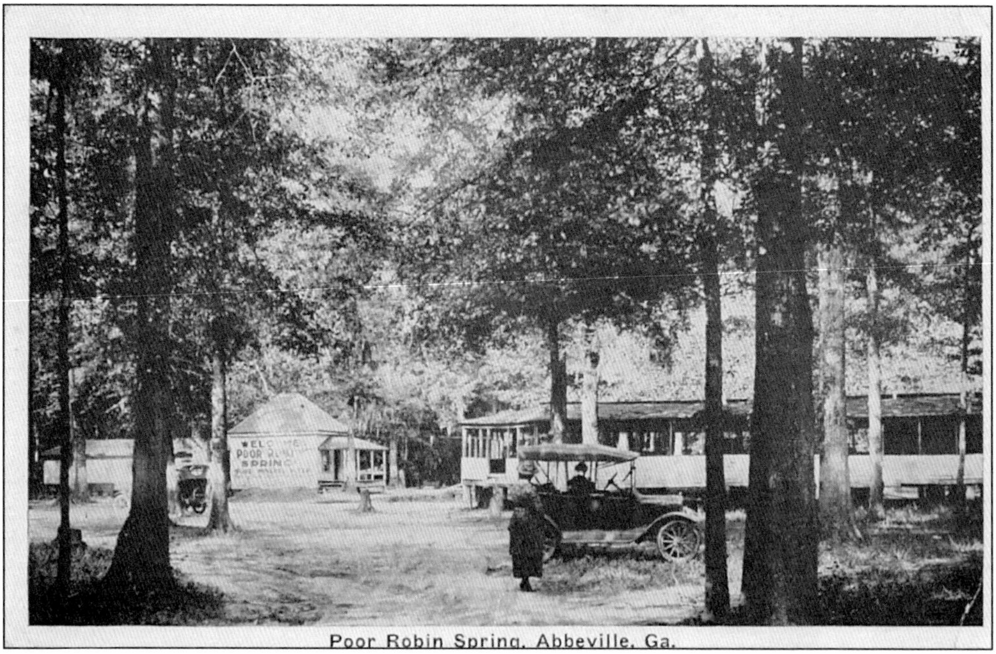

Poor Robin Spring. Tourists patronized Poor Robin Spring at Abbeville to partake of the mineral water.

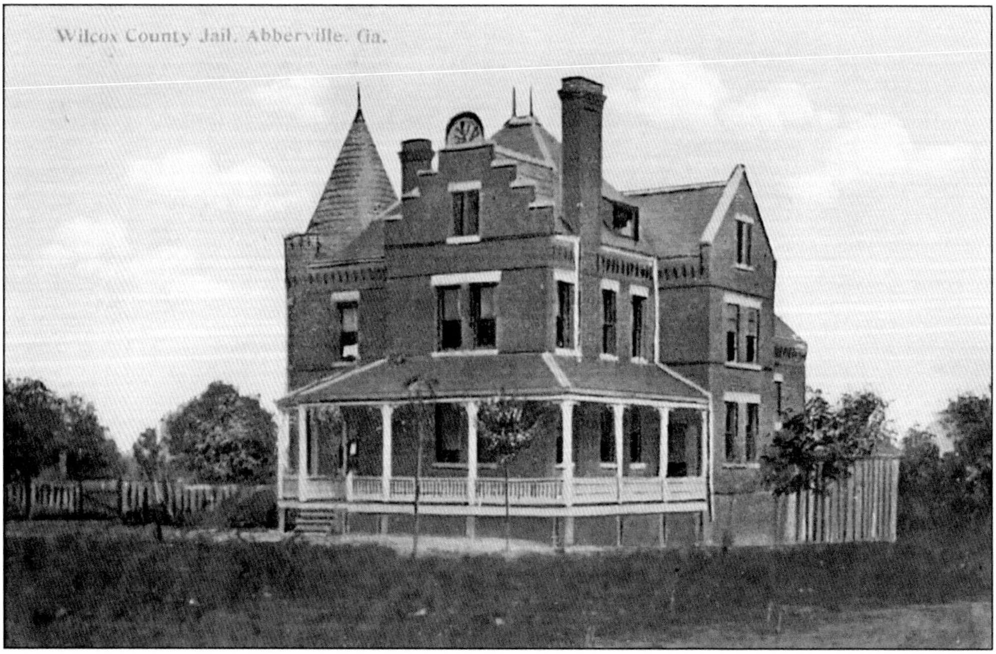

The Wilcox County Jail at Abbeville, c. 1912. The jail was an attractive building that looked more like a fine Victorian-style home.

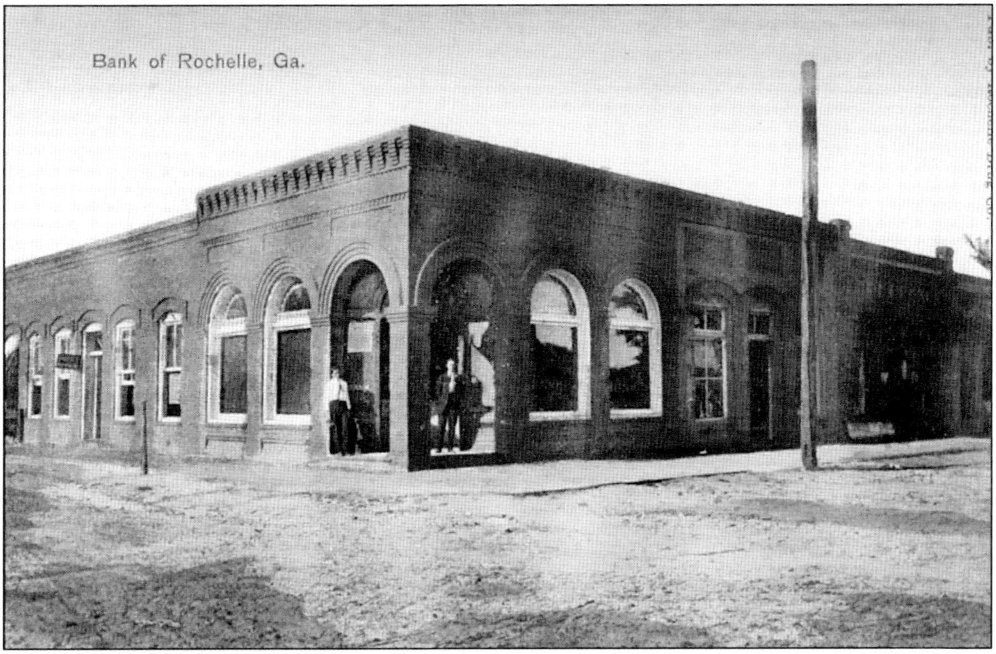

THE BANK OF ROCHELLE. In 1910, the president of the Bank of Rochelle was J.N. King. H. Mashburn was vice-president, and S.V. Hicks was cashier.

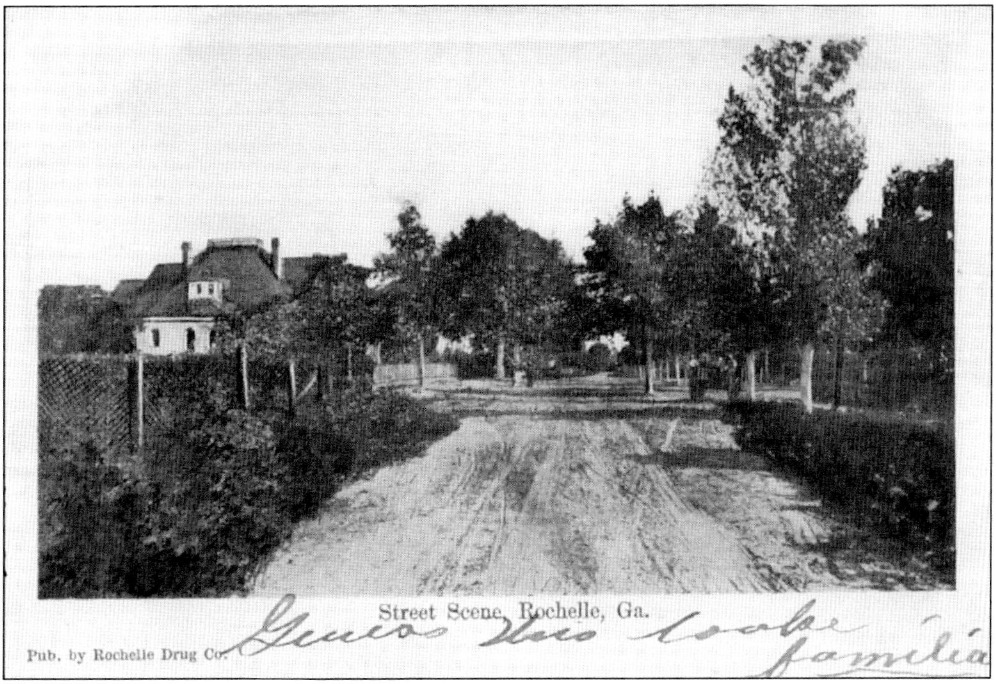

A STREET SCENE IN ROCHELLE, C. 1910. The bored writer who mailed this card to Mount Vernon, Georgia, wrote: "Well you just aught to be hear. There's not a thing doing. Guess things are on a boom there. from J.C.F."

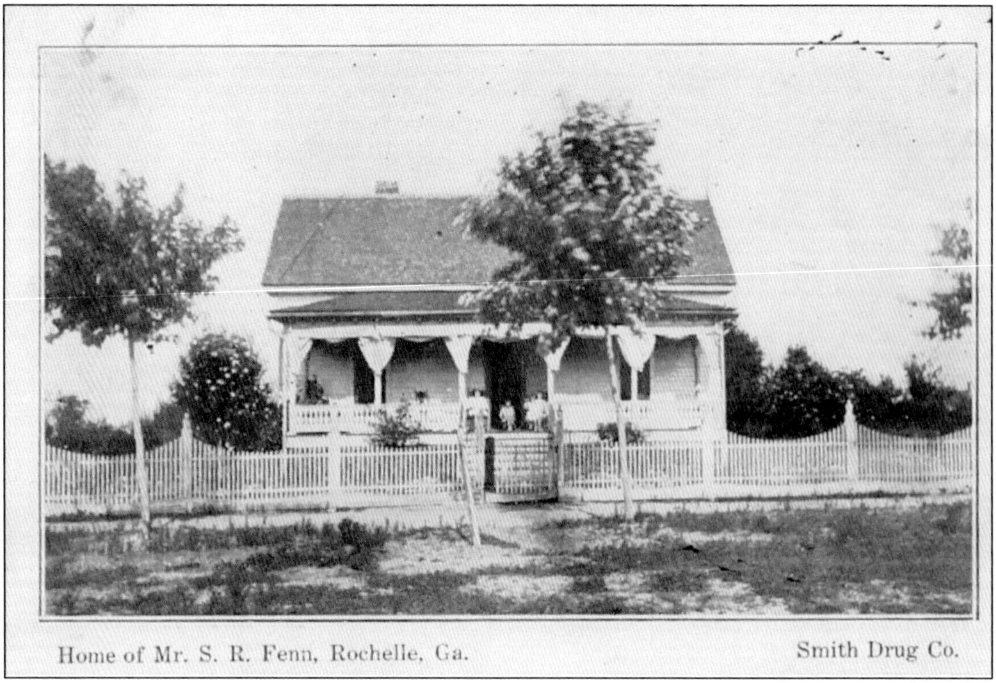

THE HOME OF MR. S.R. FENN IN ROCHELLE. Mr. Fenn operated a general merchandise store.

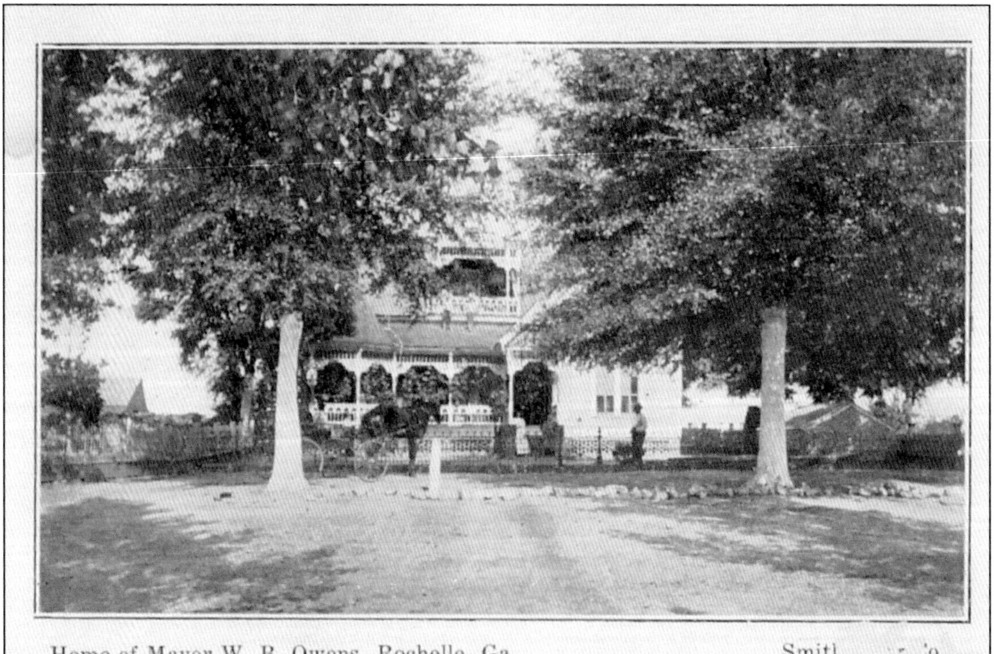

THE HOME OF MR. W.B. OWENS. Owens was mayor of Rochelle, and also operated a general merchandise store. This card was mailed to Corona, California, on November 19, 1909, with the following message: "If you were in Norfolk tonight what would you order?" The receiver of the card wrote "Ham" beneath.

Four

CAMDEN, CHARLTON, PIERCE, AND WARE COUNTIES

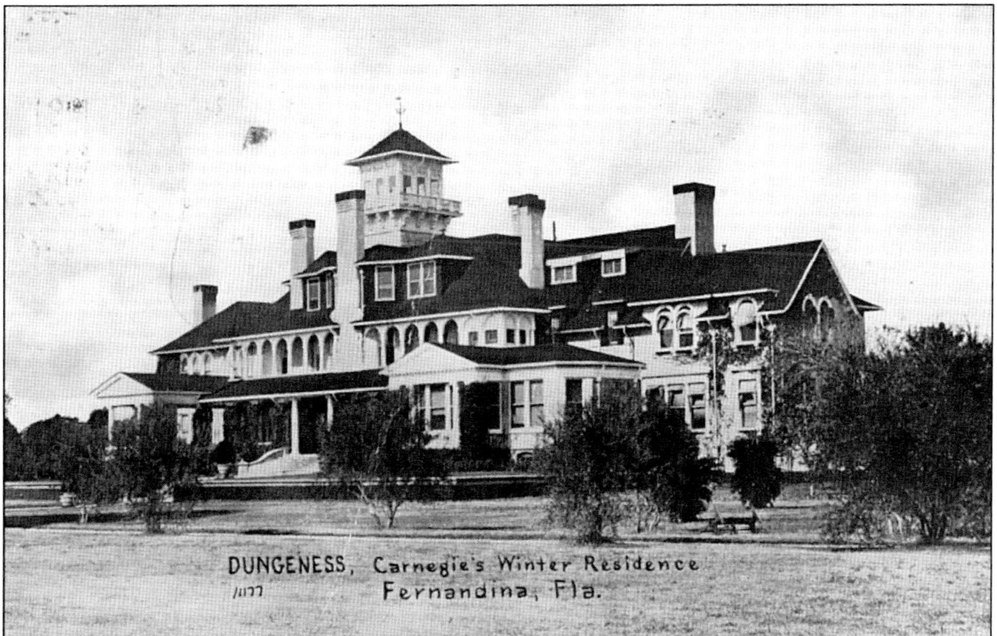

DUNGENESS, THE HOME OF ANDREW CARNEGIE ON CUMBERLAND ISLAND. The home was built in the 1880s by Andrew's father, Thomas Carnegie. The home had been empty for many years when it was burned by arsonists in the 1960s.

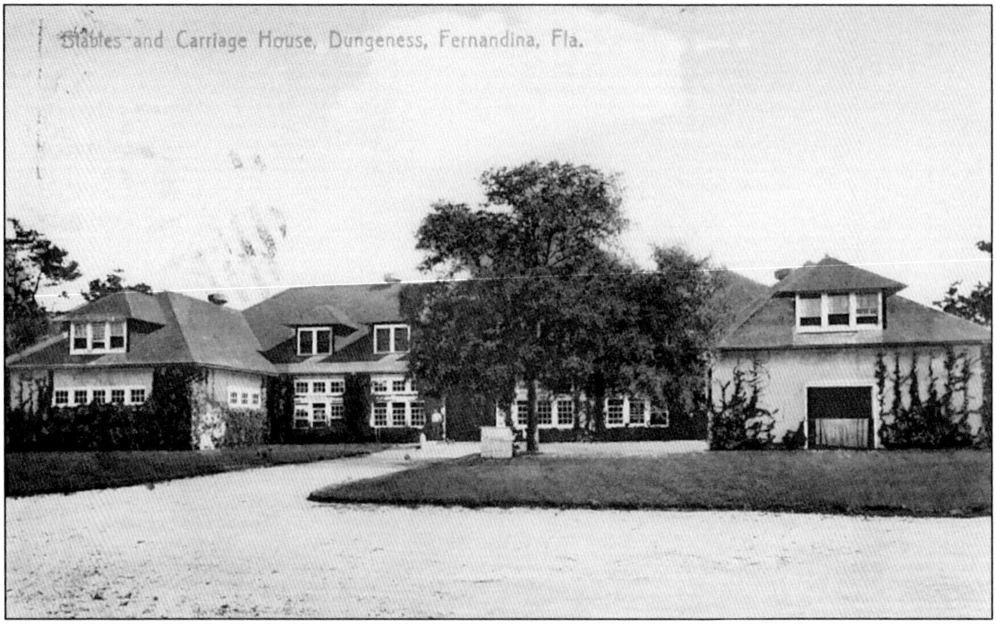

THE STABLES AND CARRIAGE HOUSE ON THE GROUNDS OF DUNGENESS, ON CUMBERLAND ISLAND.

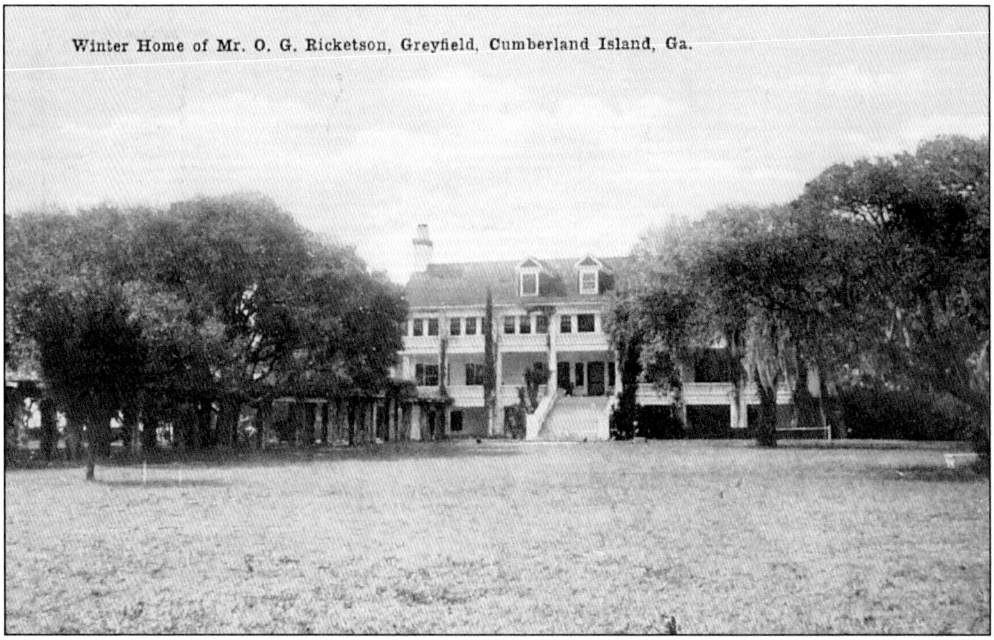

GREYFIELD, THE WINTER HOME OF MR. O.G. RICKETSON WHEN THIS POST CARD WAS MADE. The building still stands and is operated as an inn for visitors to Cumberland Island.

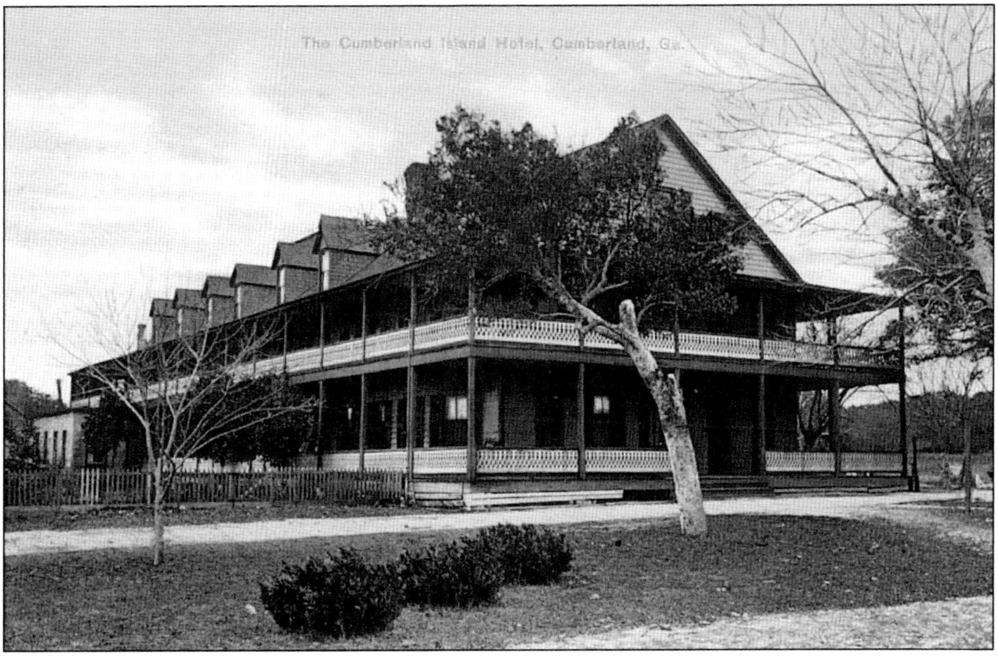

THE CUMBERLAND ISLAND HOTEL, SHOWN HERE IN 1910. The house was built by W.P. Bunkley and was operated by his nephew, L.A. Miller.

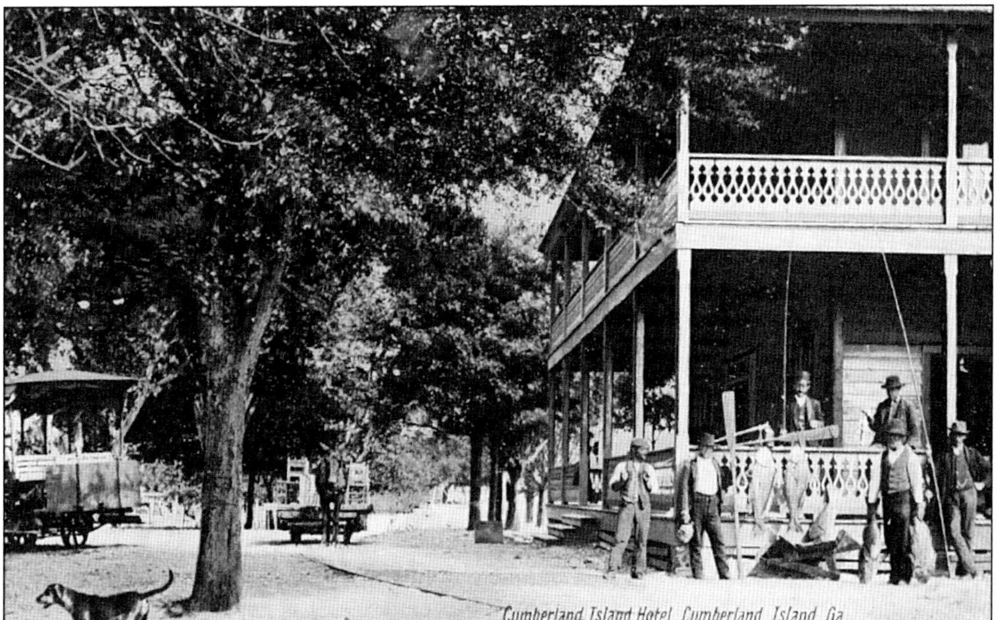

GUESTS OF THE CUMBERLAND ISLAND HOTEL SHOW OFF THEIR CATCH OF FISH. On the left can be seen the mule-drawn trolley cars that hauled guests and their luggage from the boat dock to the hotel.

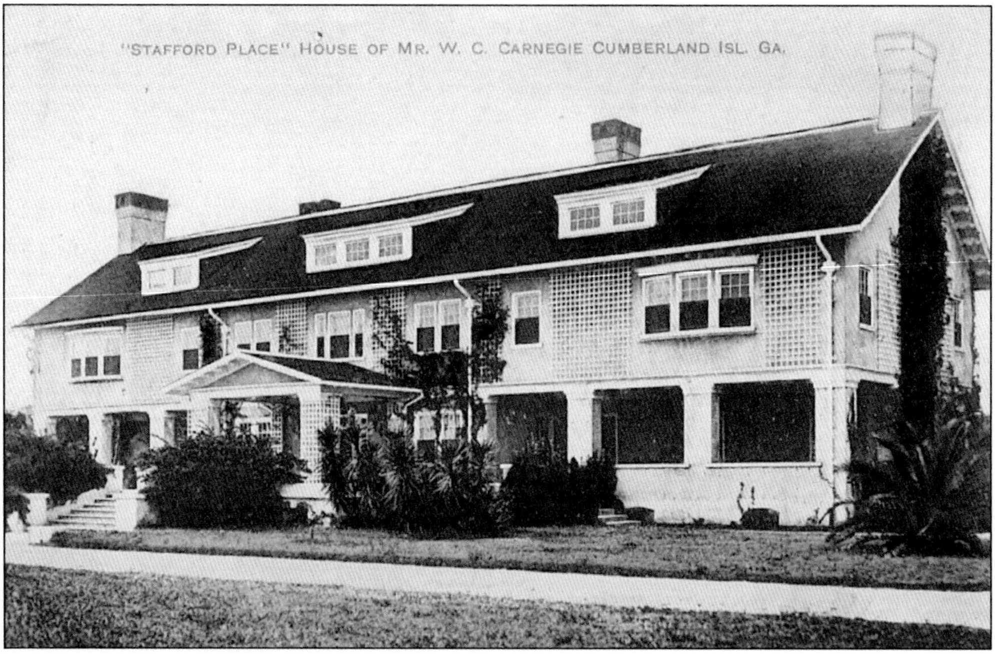

Mr. W.C. Carnegie's Stafford Place on Cumberland Island.

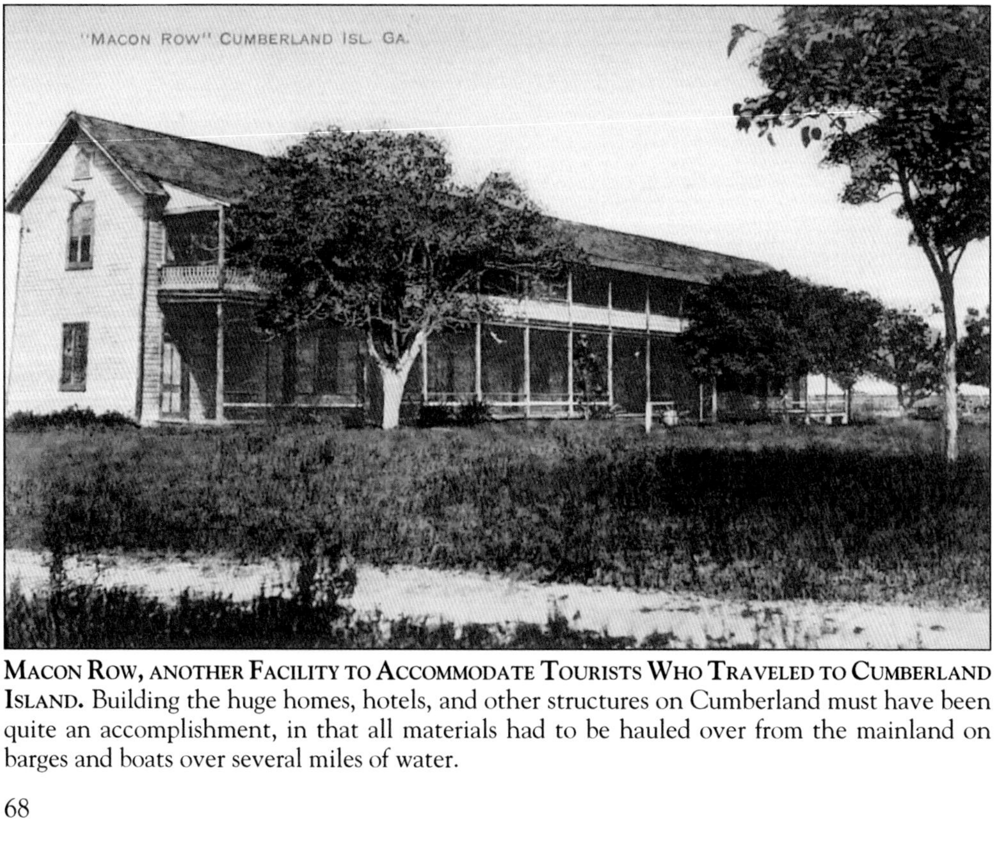

Macon Row, another Facility to Accommodate Tourists Who Traveled to Cumberland Island. Building the huge homes, hotels, and other structures on Cumberland must have been quite an accomplishment, in that all materials had to be hauled over from the mainland on barges and boats over several miles of water.

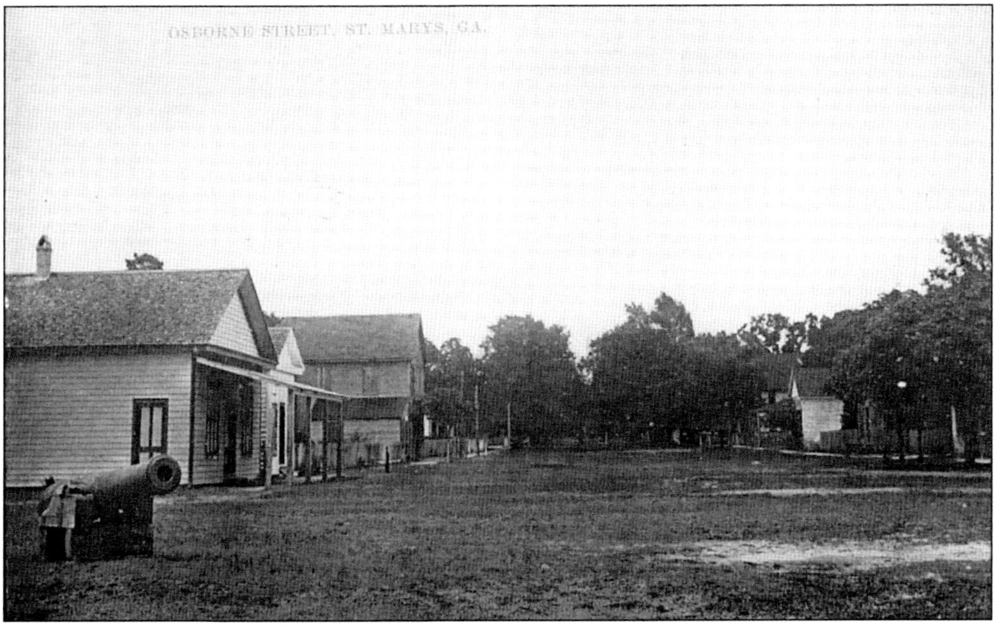

OSBORNE STREET IN SAINT MARYS. The street looks well fortified in this 1908 view.

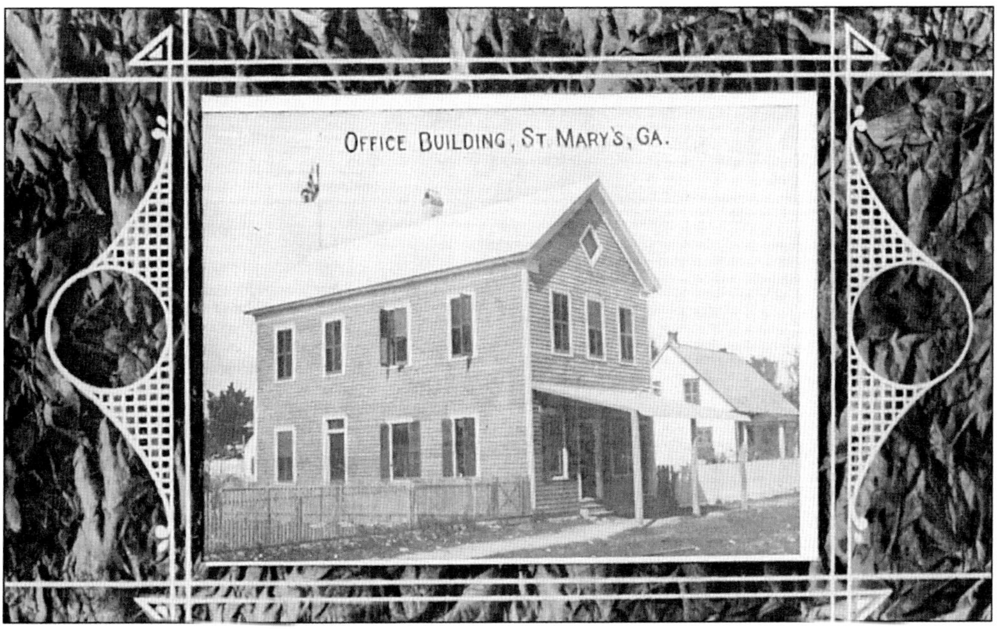

THE "OFFICE BUILDING" IN SAINT MARYS, C. 1912.

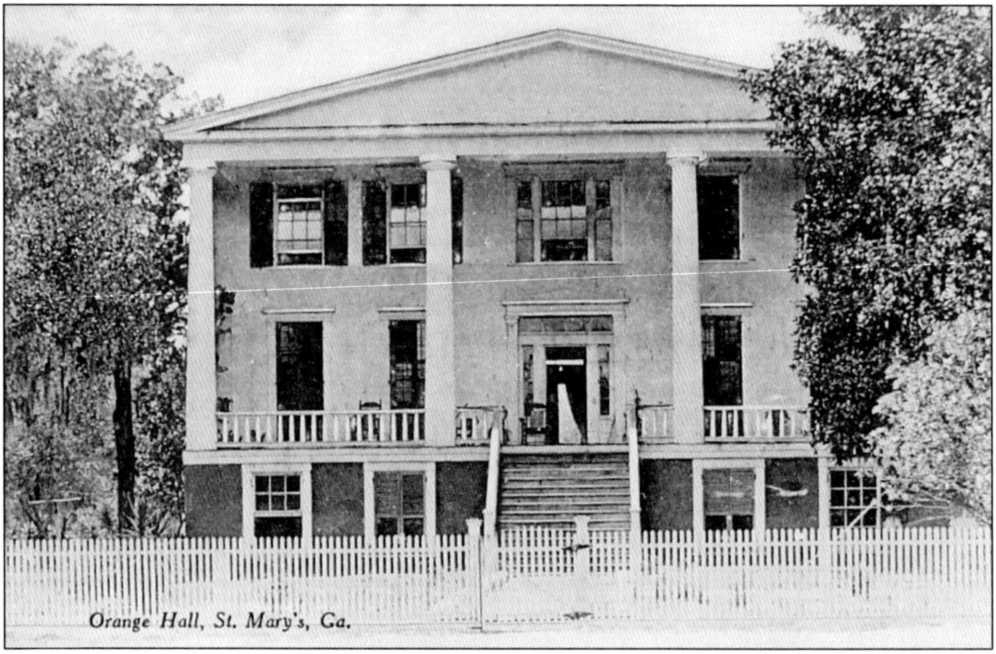

ORANGE HALL IN SAINT MARYS. The building was built about 1832 as the parsonage for the Presbyterian church. It got its name from the grove of orange trees around it.

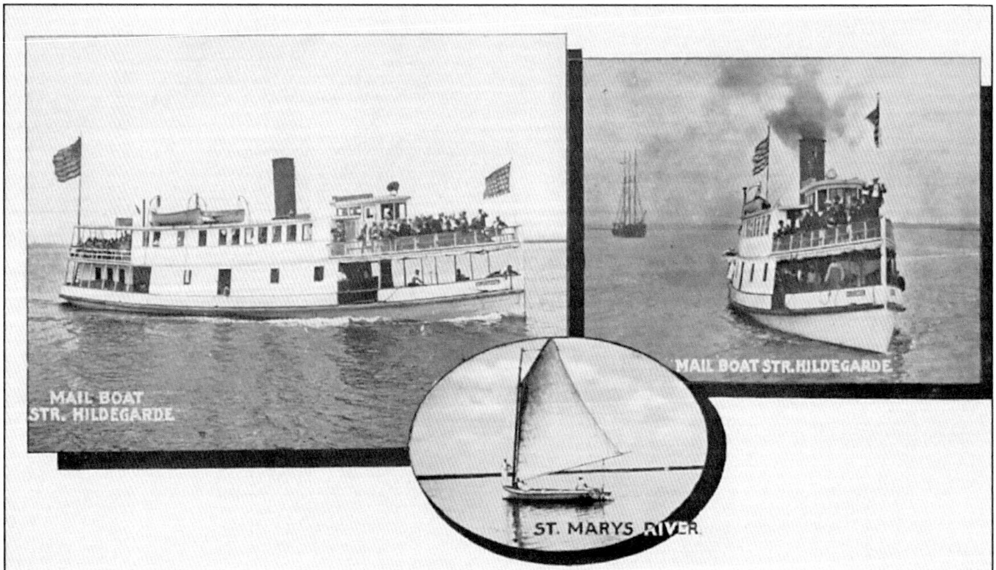

THE STEAMER *HILDEGARDE*, THE MAIL BOAT THAT SERVED SOME OF GEORGIA'S OFFSHORE ISLANDS AROUND THE TURN OF THE CENTURY.

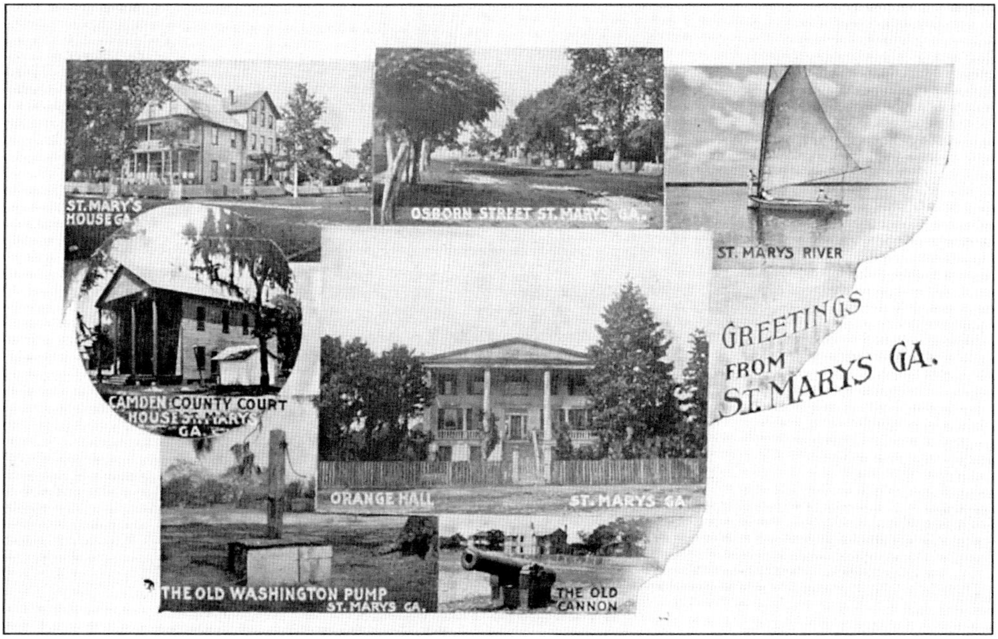

A COMPOSITE VIEW CARD OF SAINT MARYS. The card shows several old landmarks as they appeared about 1907.

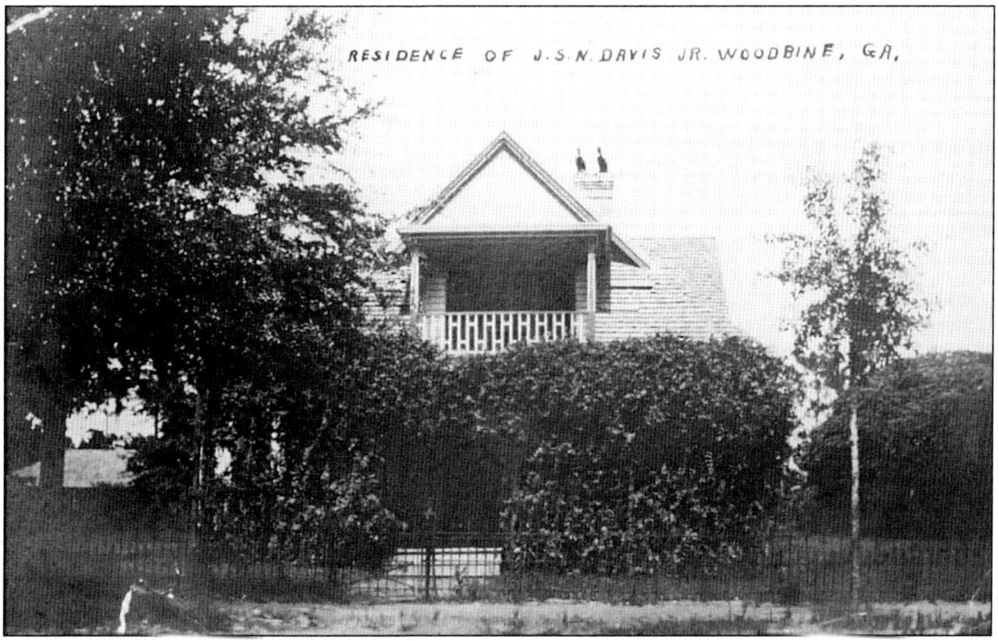

THE RESIDENCE OF J.S.N. DAVIS AT WOODBINE, C. 1912.

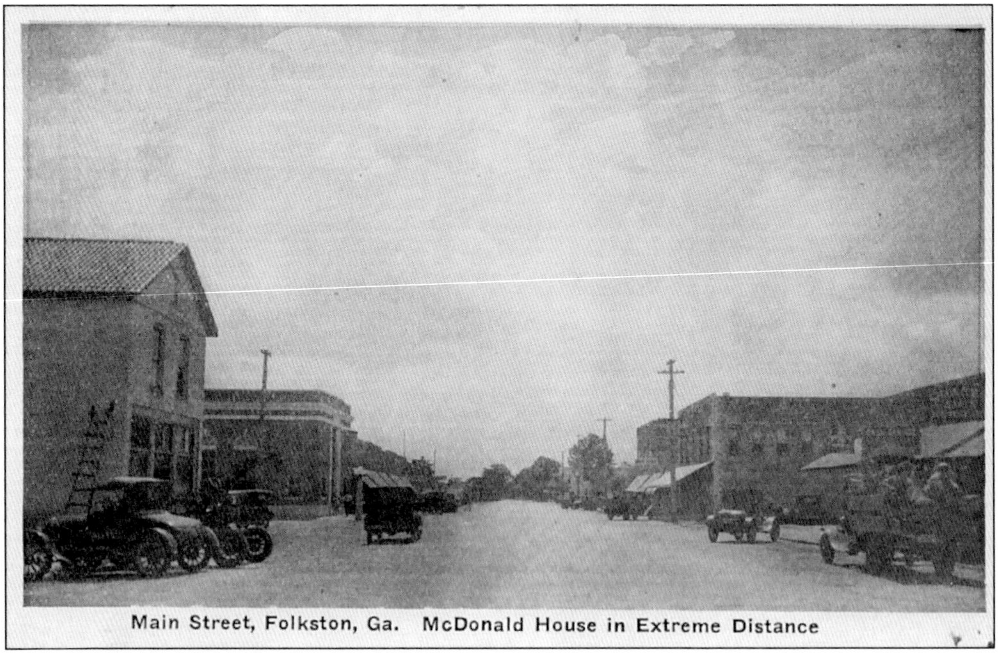

MAIN STREET IN FOLKSTON IN THE EARLY 1920S.

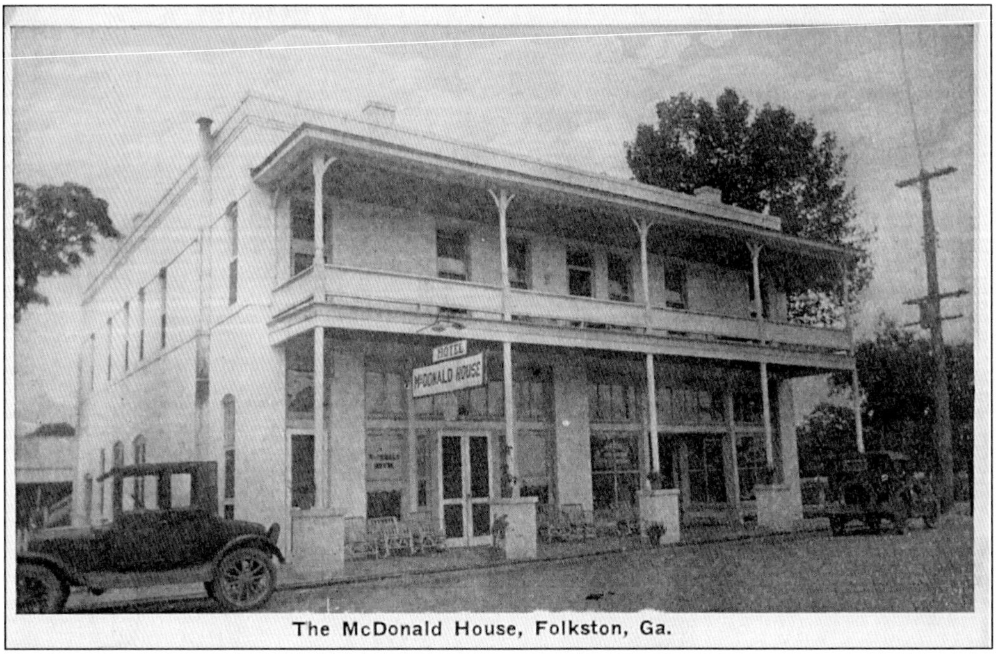

THE MCDONALD HOUSE HOTEL IN FOLKSTON IN THE EARLY 1920S.

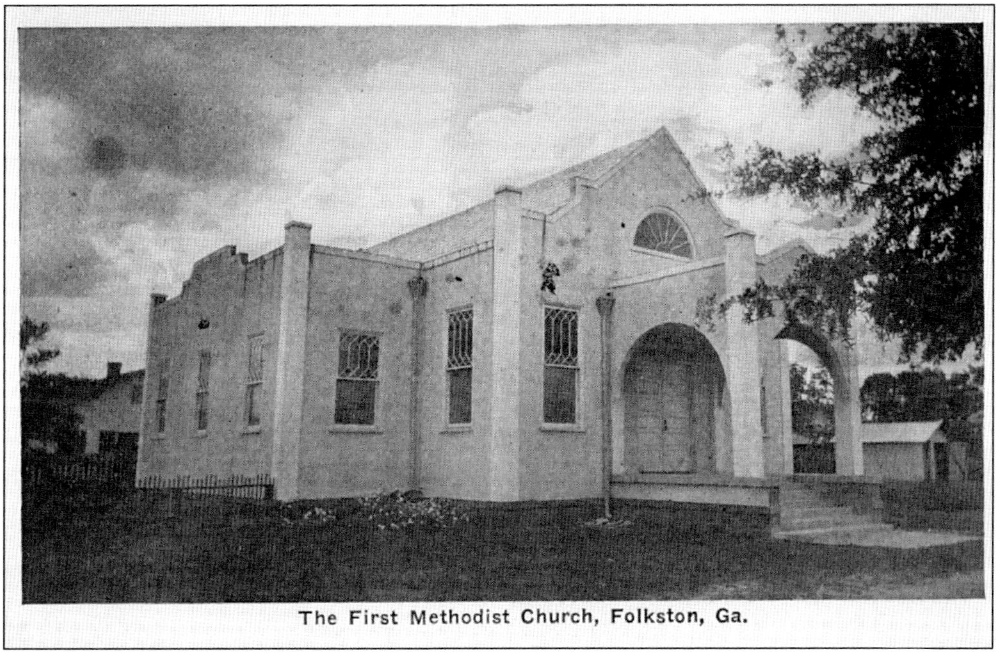

THE FIRST METHODIST CHURCH IN FOLKSTON.

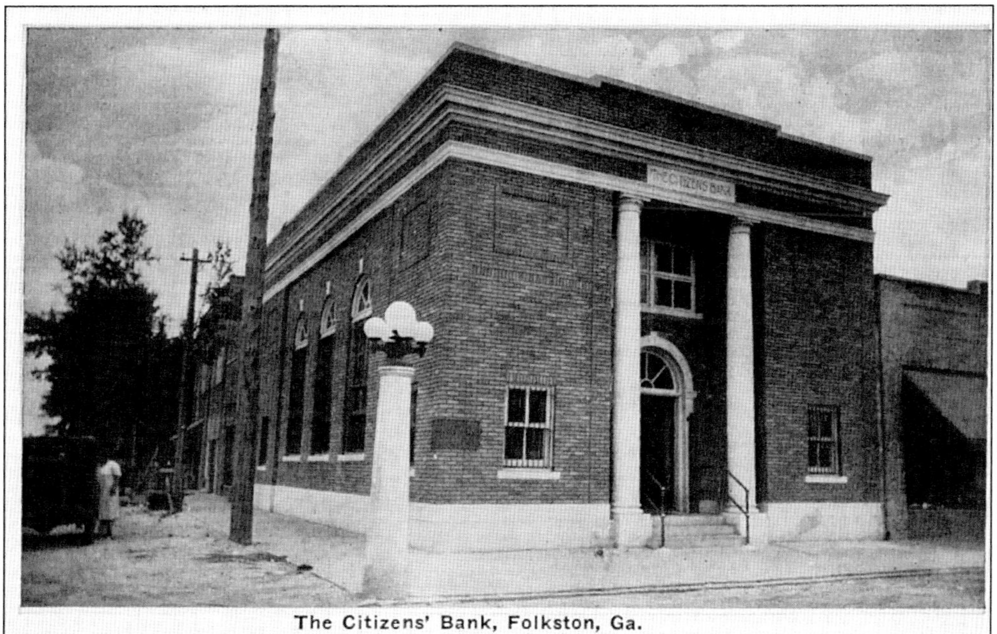

THE CITIZEN'S BANK IN FOLKSTON IN THE EARLY 1920S. The bank was a substantial-looking concern.

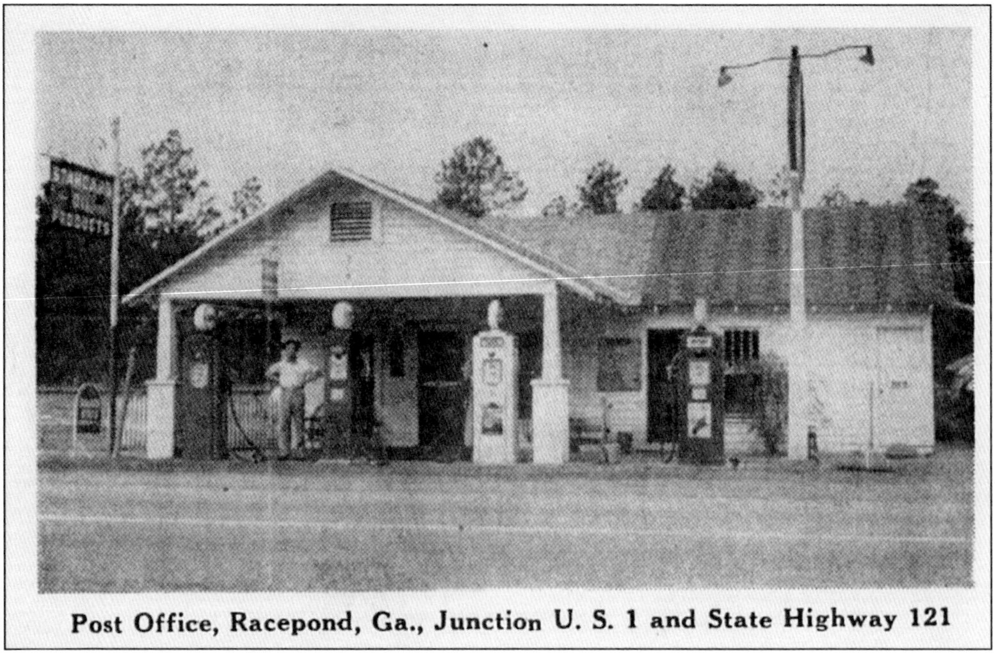

The Post Office, Racepond. The post office was located in this Standard Oil service station at Racepond, at the junction of U.S. Highway #1 and State Highway #121 in the 1930s.

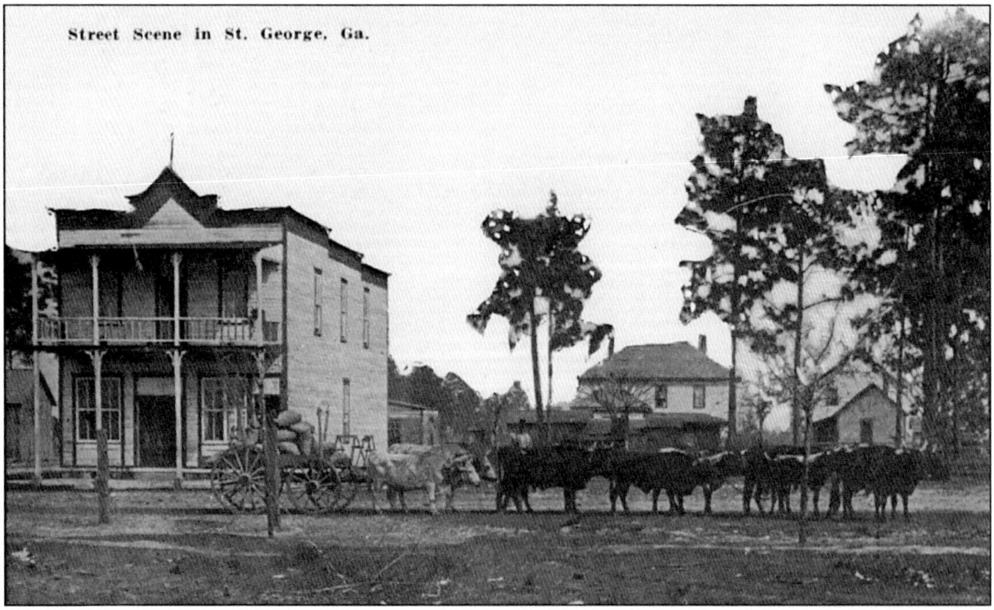

An early Street Scene Post Card of St. George. This view shows a team of 10 oxen pulling a wagon through town. This card was mailed to Hudson, Michigan, on March 20, 1912, and states: "Wished you wer down here now, it would nock your rheumatism. 80 and 85 in the shade—June weather in Michigan. Peaches are large as walnuts and evrything growing to beat the band. I have potatoes over a foot high and no bugs to bother. Plenty of strawberries now and all kinds of green stuff. We can eat 3 meals per day and feel good. Hope you are the same. E.G.H."

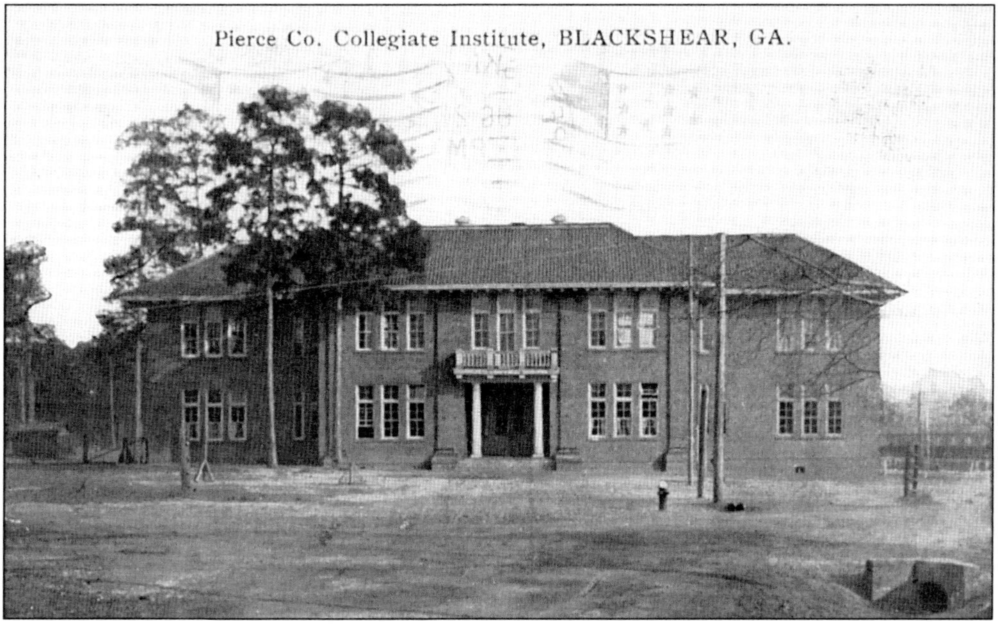

THE PIERCE COUNTY COLLEGIATE INSTITUTE IN BLACKSHEAR IN THE 1910s.

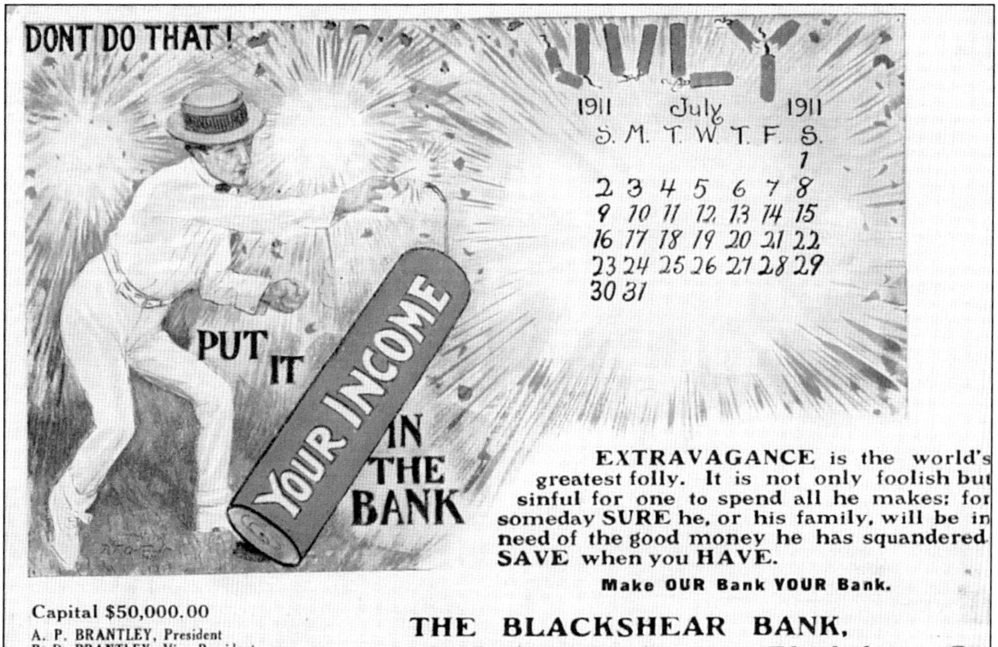

A 1911 ADVERTISING CARD FOR THE BLACKSHEAR BANK. The card admonishes that "Extravagance is the world's greatest folly."

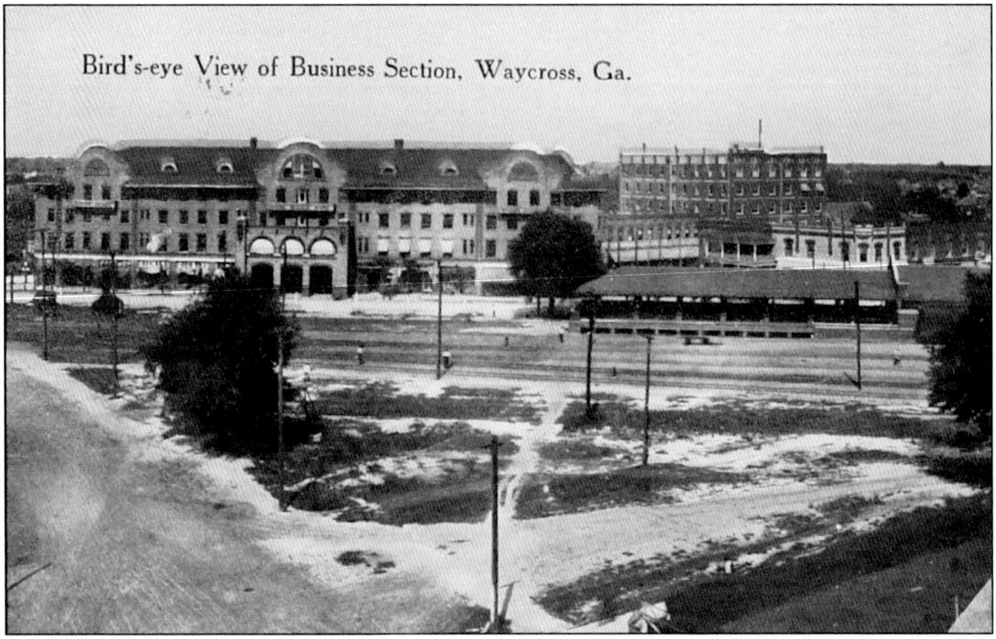

A BIRD'S-EYE VIEW OF THE BUSINESS SECTION OF WAYCROSS IN THE EARLY 1910S.

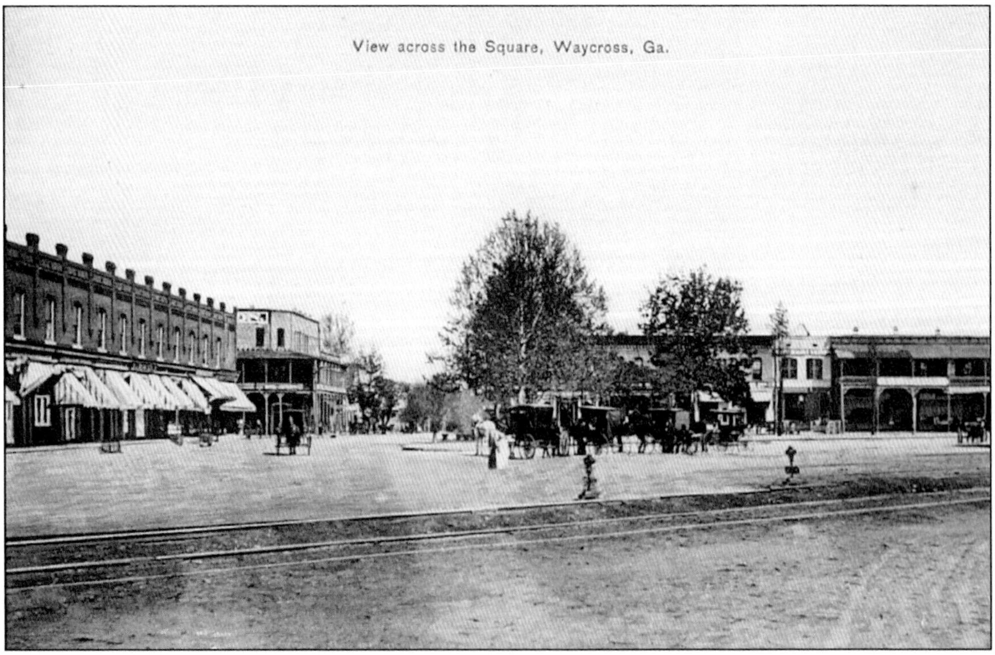

A VIEW ACROSS THE SQUARE IN WAYCROSS. The railroad tracks are shown running through the middle of town.

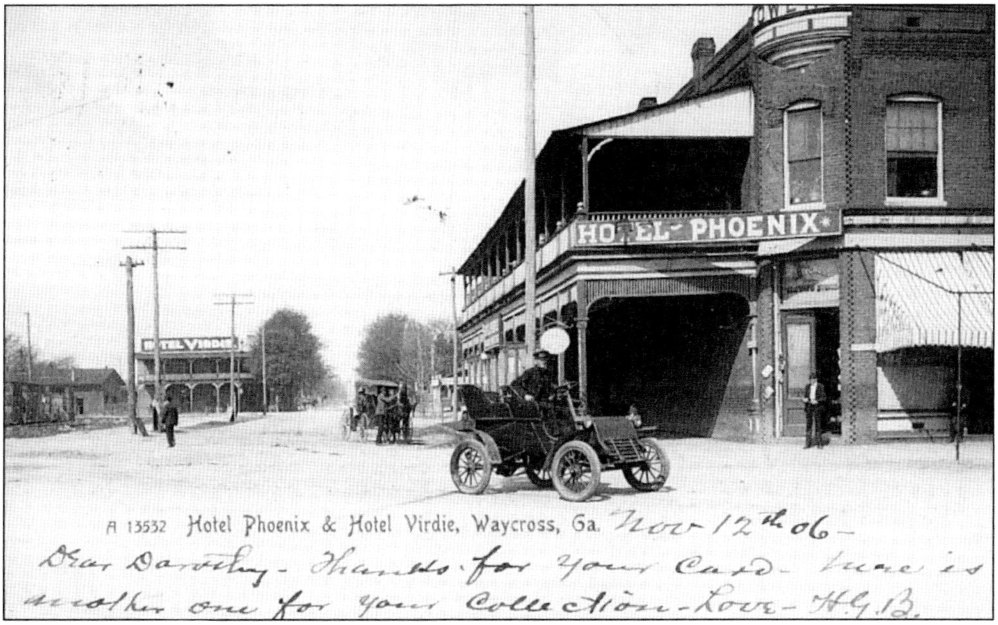

A c. 1905 View of the Hotel Phoenix in Waycross. This view also shows the Hotel Virdie in the distance.

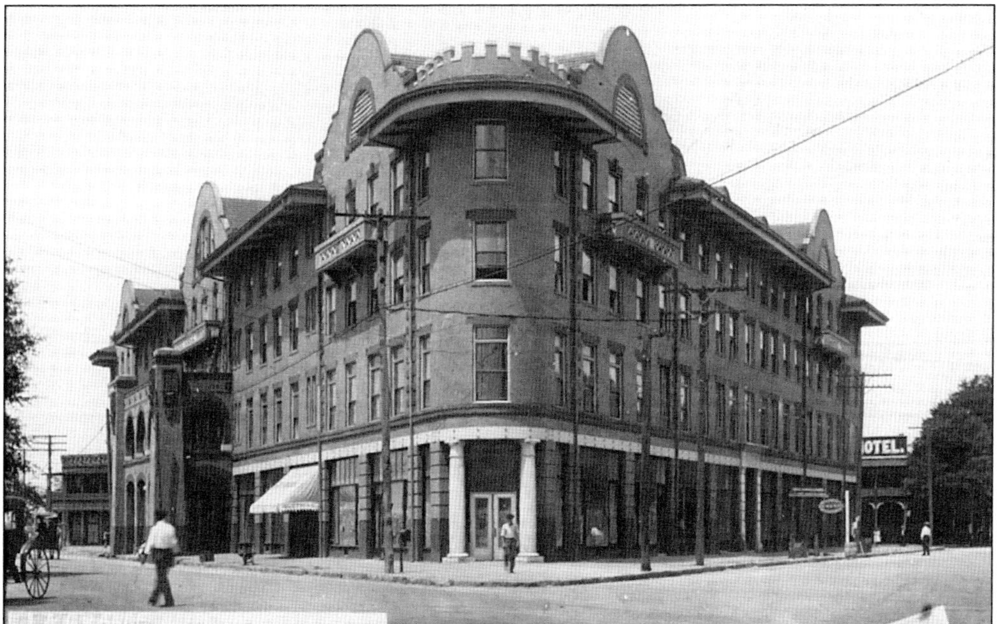

A Real-Photo View of the LaGrande Hotel in Waycross, c. 1908. This card was mailed to Manchester, Virginia, and has a most interesting message apparently written from a young lady to her former teacher who had moved away. Part of the message reads: "Dear Miss Hancock, when I read your card and saw you were coming back I just hollered and ran across to tell V.S. the news and it just a pouring rain and I stepped in a hole of water and got wet all over, so you know I am proud you are coming back. I knew you would. It is about 10:30 and scary for we had a lynching in town this afternoon. Everybody better get in bed. by by Vera."

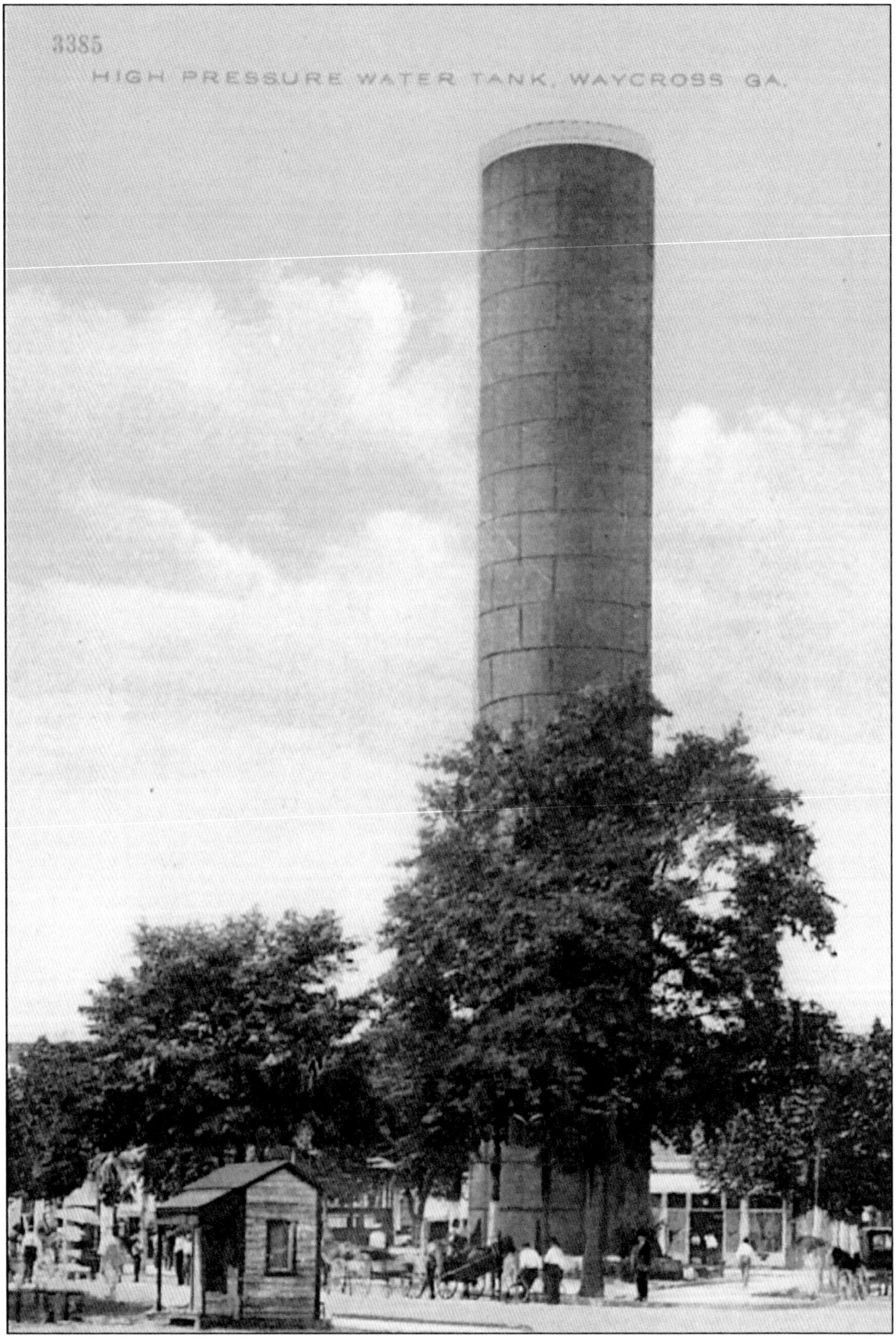

THE WAYCROSS WATER TANK. This large, high-pressure water tank in Waycross provided water for the town.

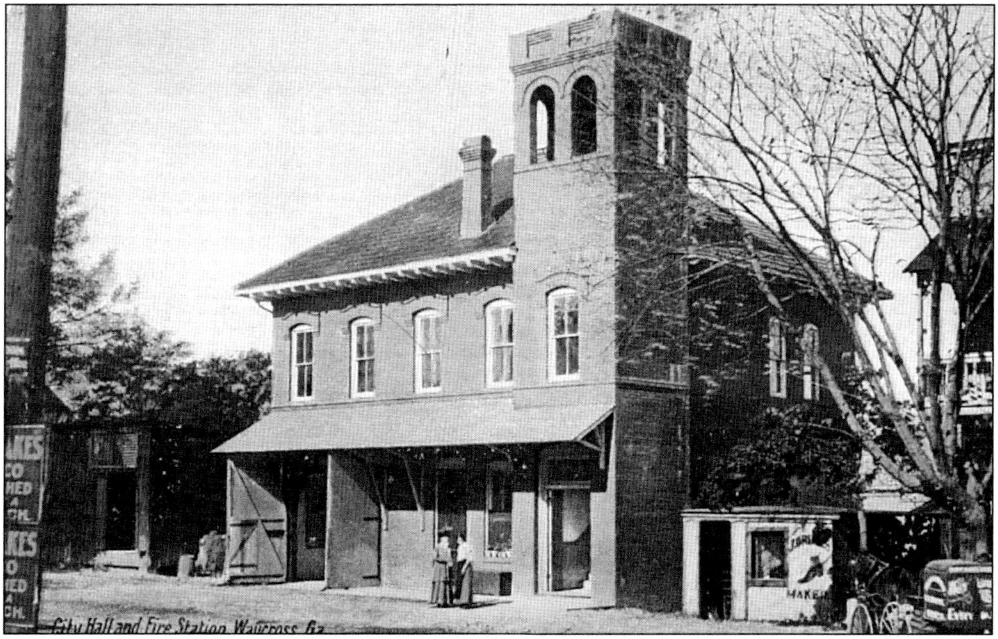

THE CITY HALL AND FIRE STATION IN WAYCROSS, C. 1910.

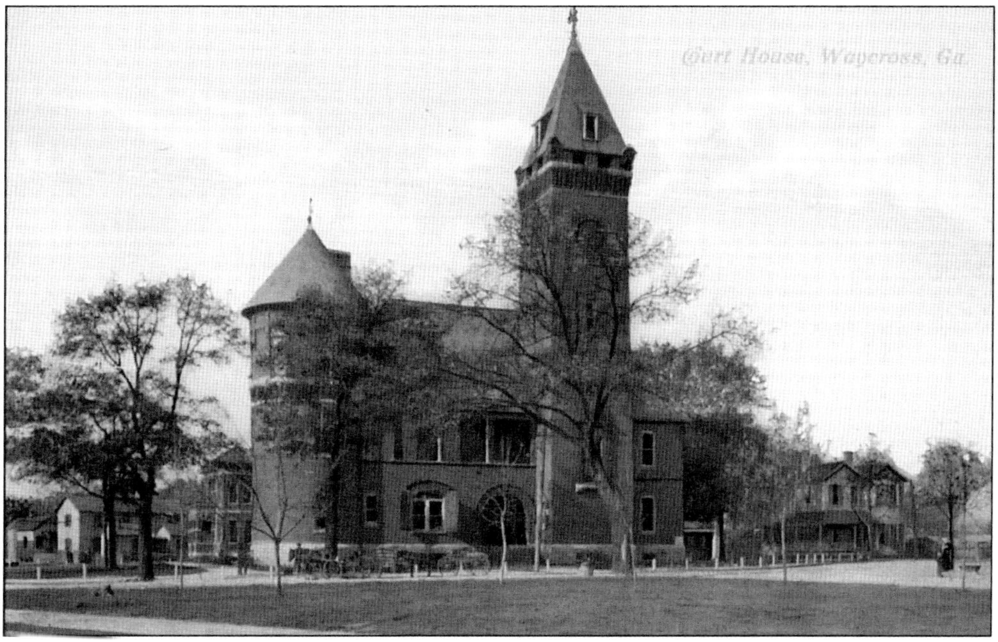

THE WARE COUNTY COURTHOUSE BUILDING IN WAYCROSS. The building was built in 1891 and saw service until 1957.

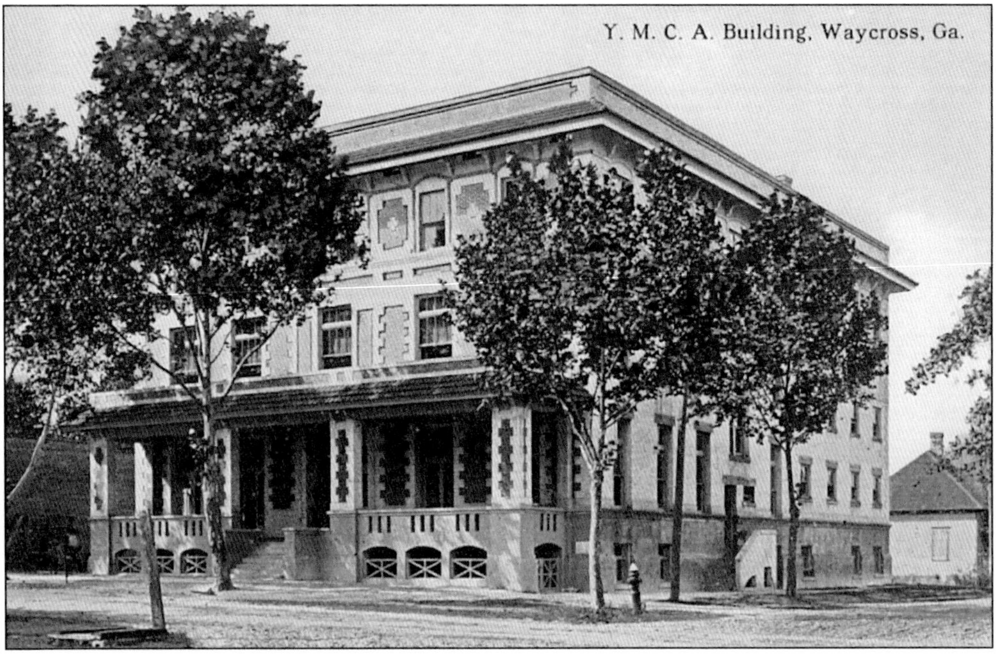

THE YMCA BUILDING IN WAYCROSS.

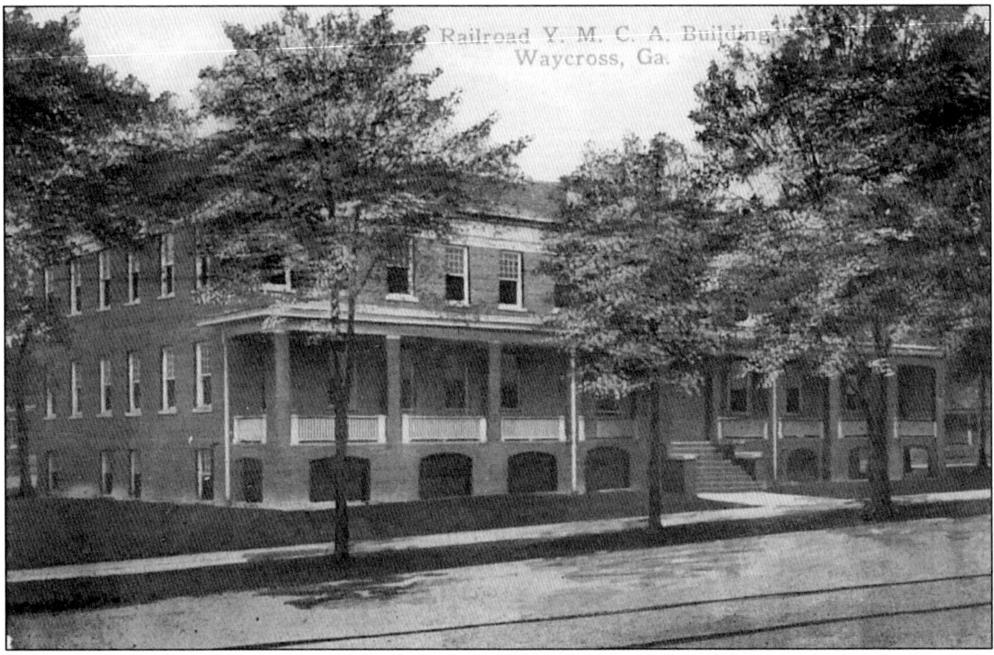

THE RAILROAD YMCA BUILDING IN WAYCROSS.

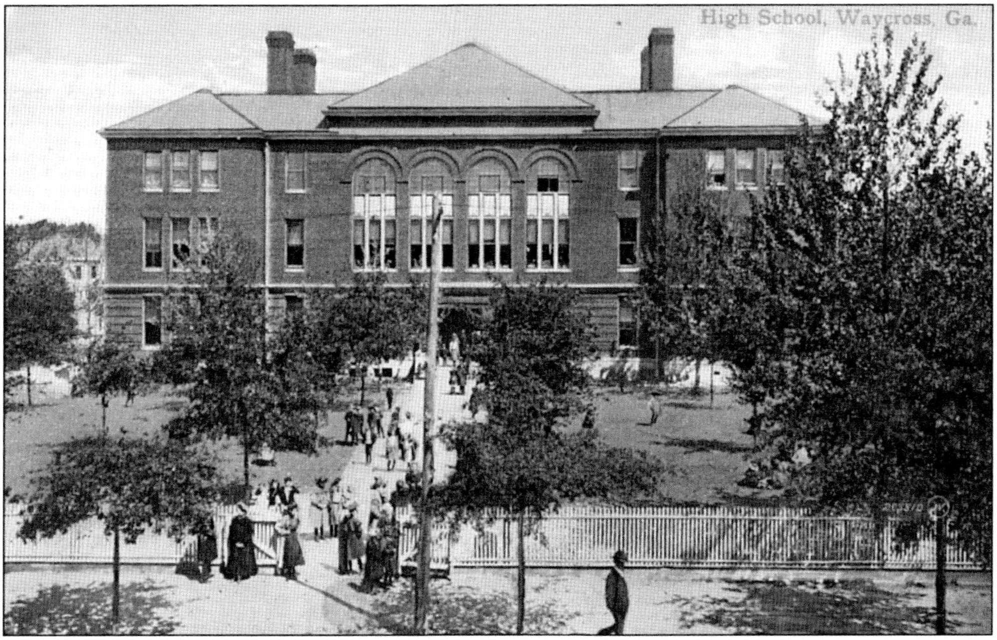

THE HIGH SCHOOL IN WAYCROSS, C. 1910.

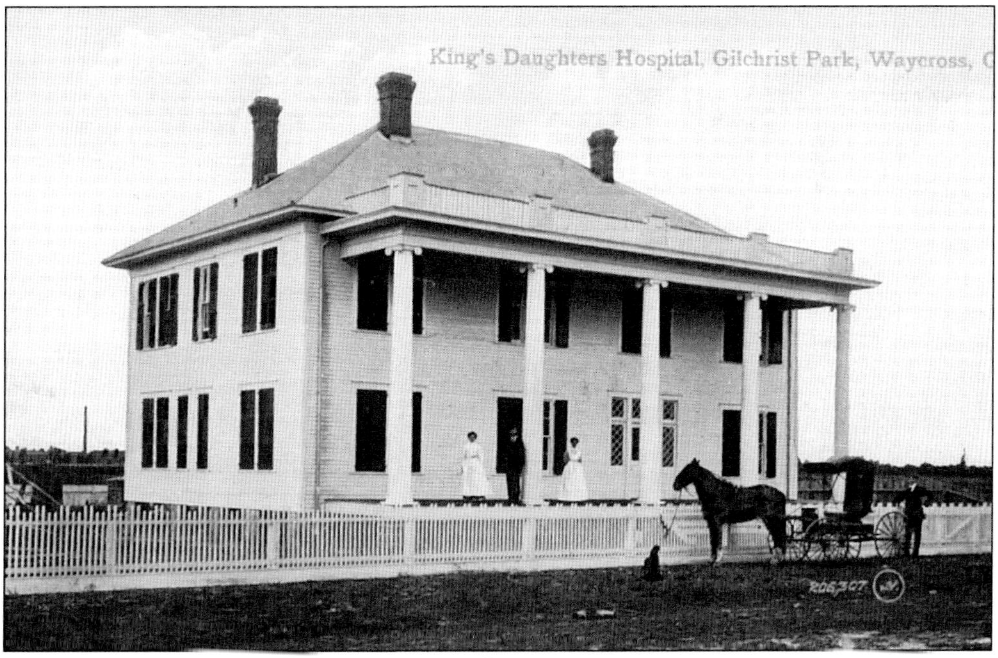

KING'S DAUGHTERS HOSPITAL AT GILCHRIST PARK IN WAYCROSS.

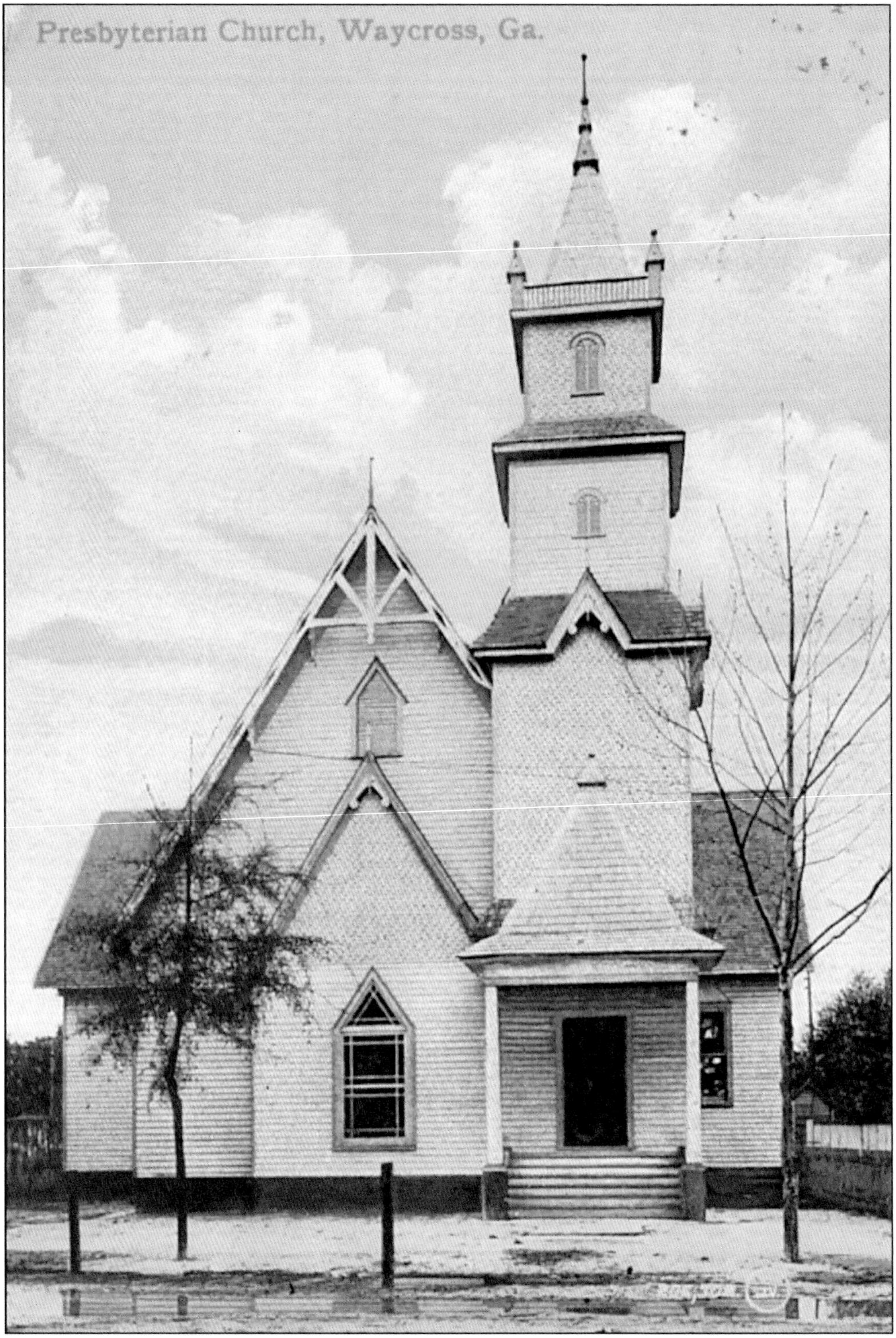

The Presbyterian Church in Waycross in the 1910s. The church was a beautiful wooden building with a multi-level steeple and belfry.

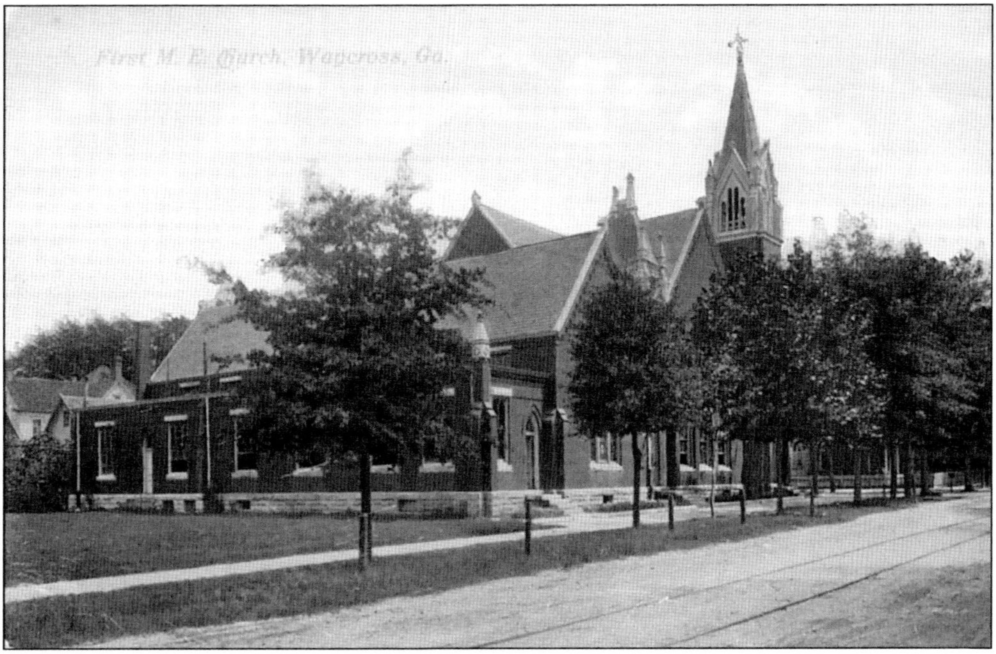

THE FIRST METHODIST EPISCOPAL CHURCH IN WAYCROSS, c. 1912.

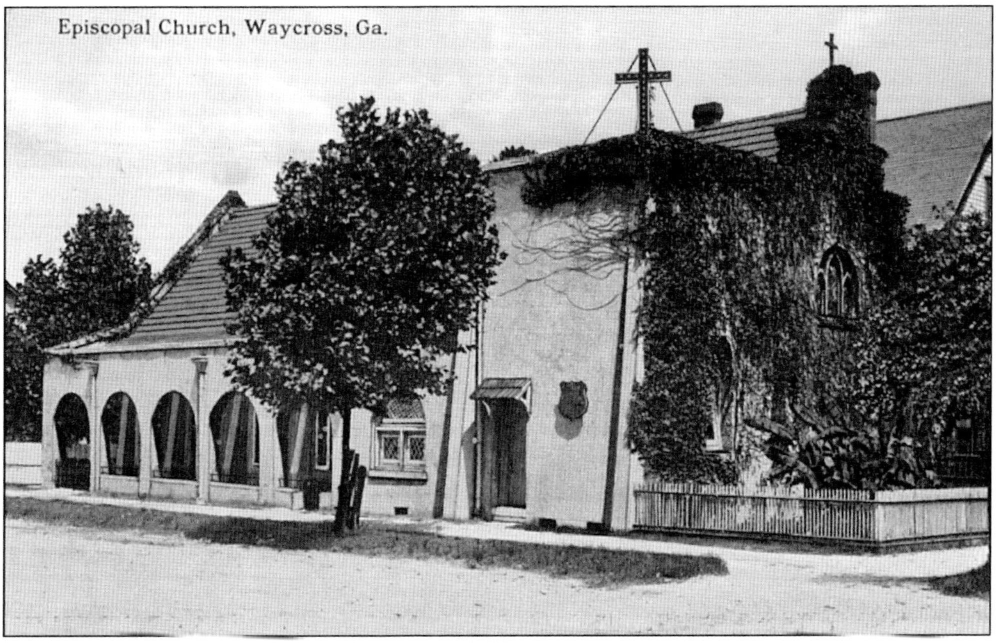

THE EPISCOPAL CHURCH IN WAYCROSS, c. 1912.

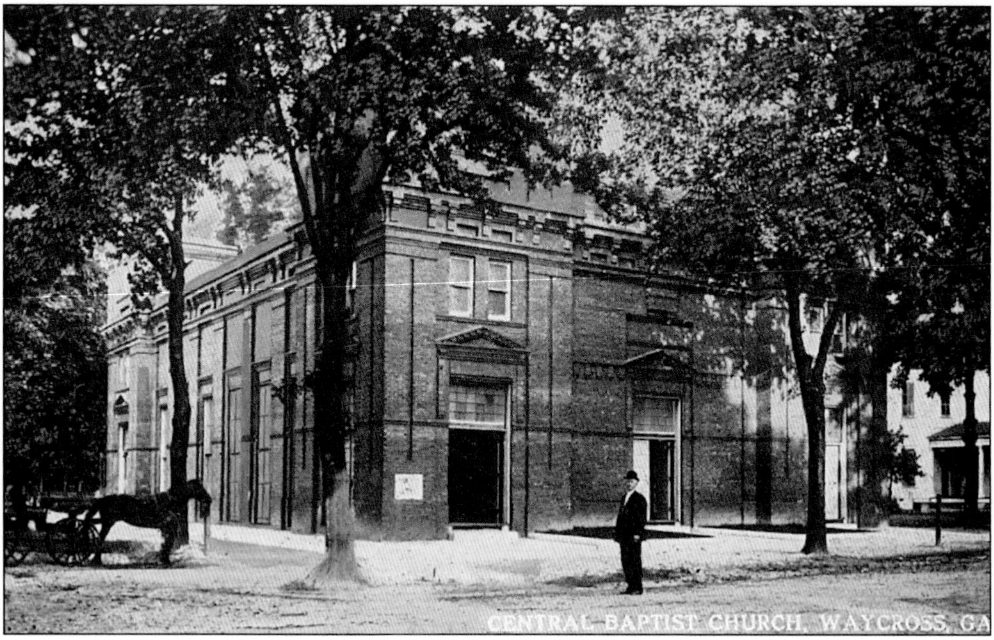

The Central Baptist Church in Waycross, c. 1912.

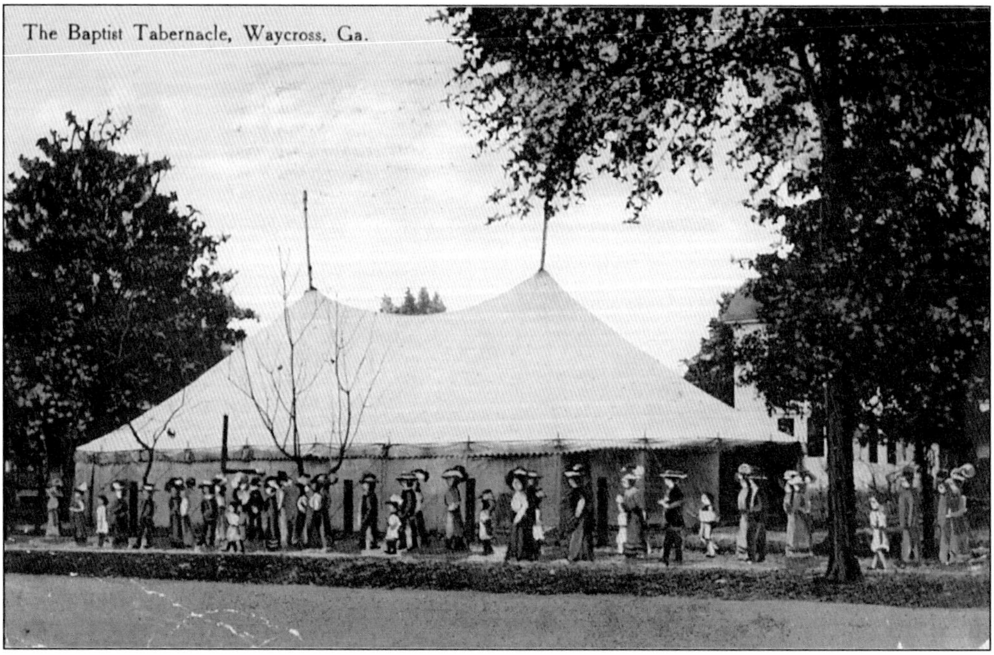

The Baptist Tabernacle in Waycross. The members met in a large tent.

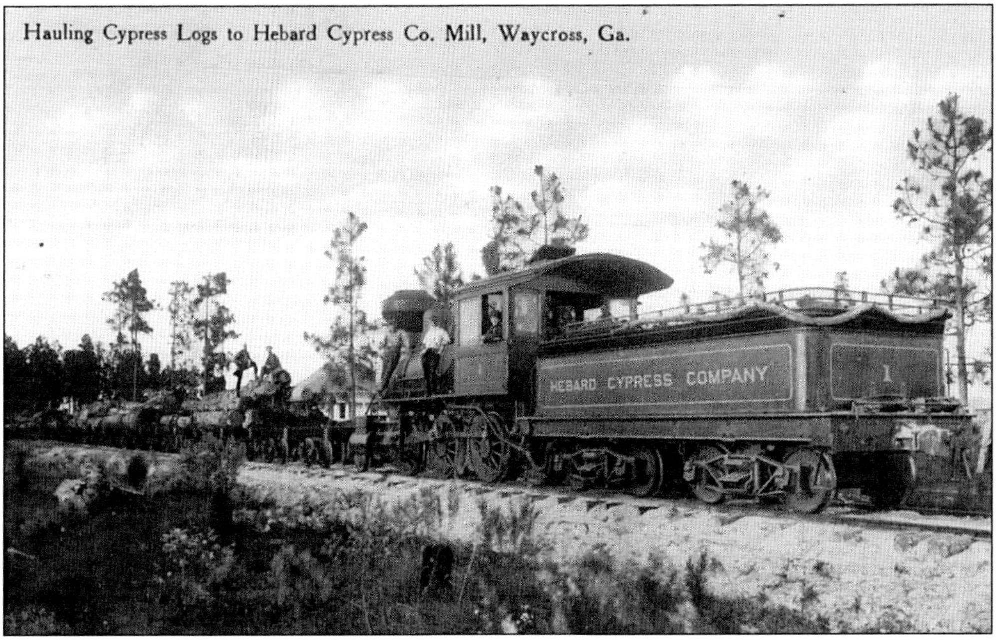

THE HEBARD CYPRESS COMPANY MILL IN WAYCROSS. The mill had its own railroad to haul logs to their huge mill.

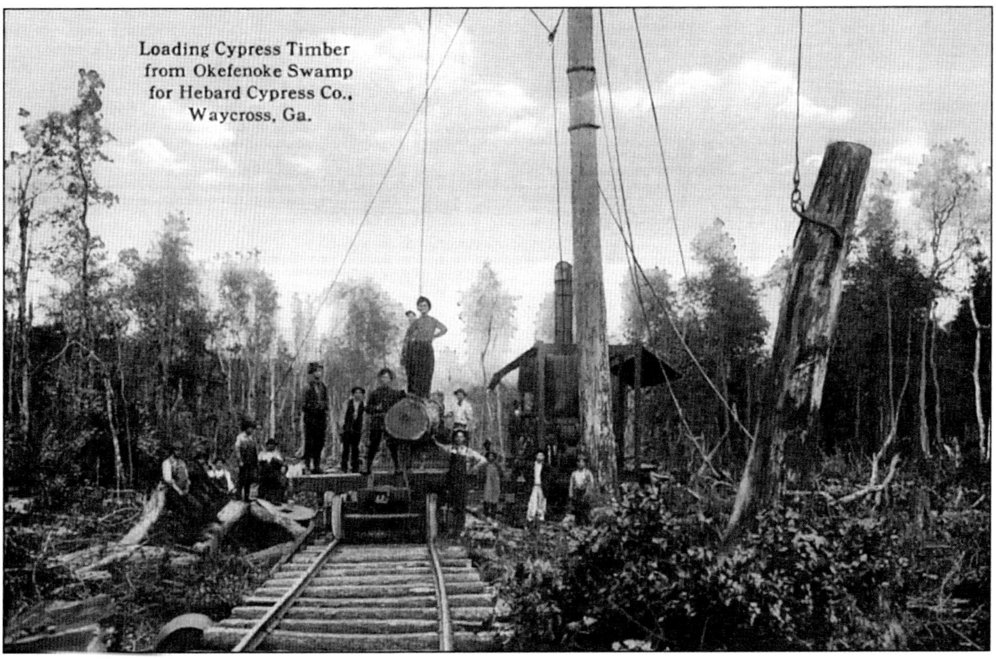

WORKERS WITH THE HEBARD CYPRESS COMPANY MILL IN WAYCROSS. The men are shown here loading cypress logs in the Okefenokee Swamp.

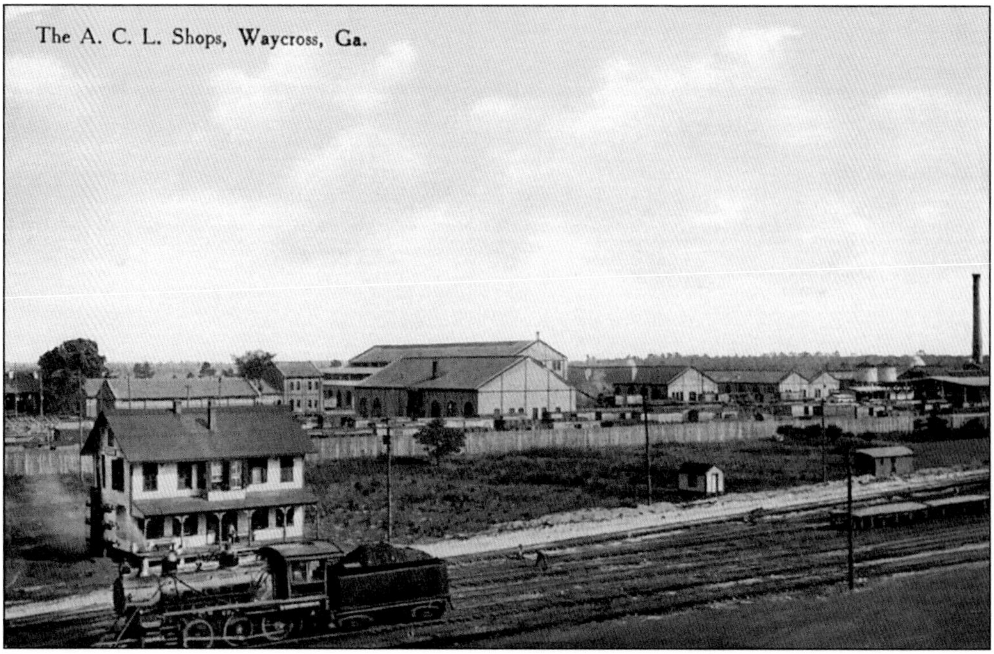

THE ATLANTIC COAST LINE RAILROAD SHOPS IN WAYCROSS, C. 1912. A written note on the message side states: "The pay roll at these shops is $120,000 per month. 88 trains go through here every day. Chas. H."

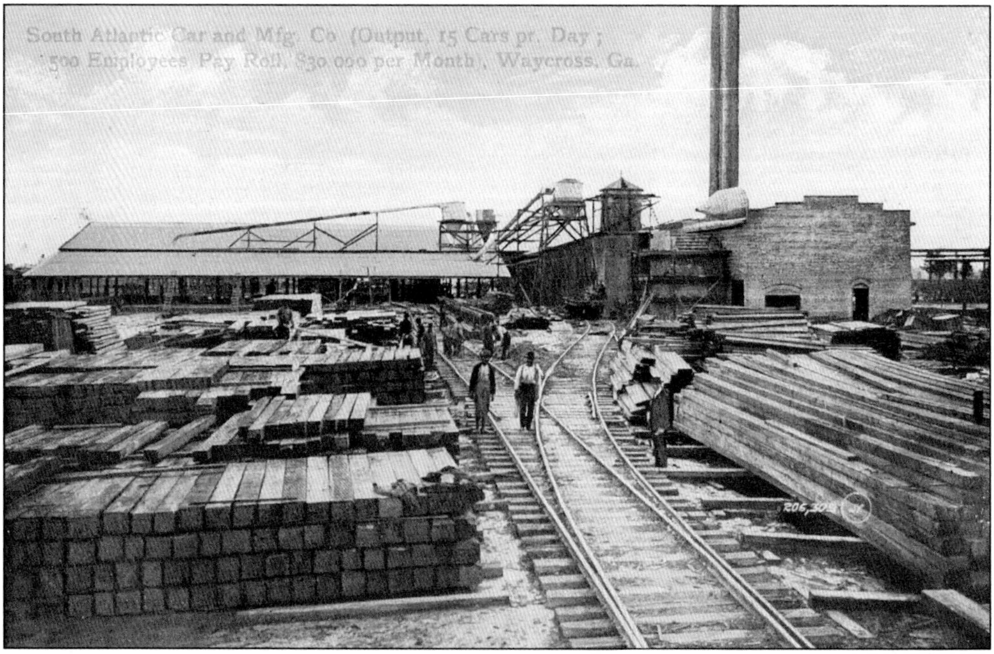

THE SOUTH ATLANTIC CAR AND MANUFACTURING COMPANY IN WAYCROSS. The company manufactured railroad cars. The printed message on this c. 1910 card claimed that their 500 employees built 15 cars a day and that the company had a payroll of $30,000 per month.

Five

Glynn, Liberty, Long, McIntosh, and Wayne Counties

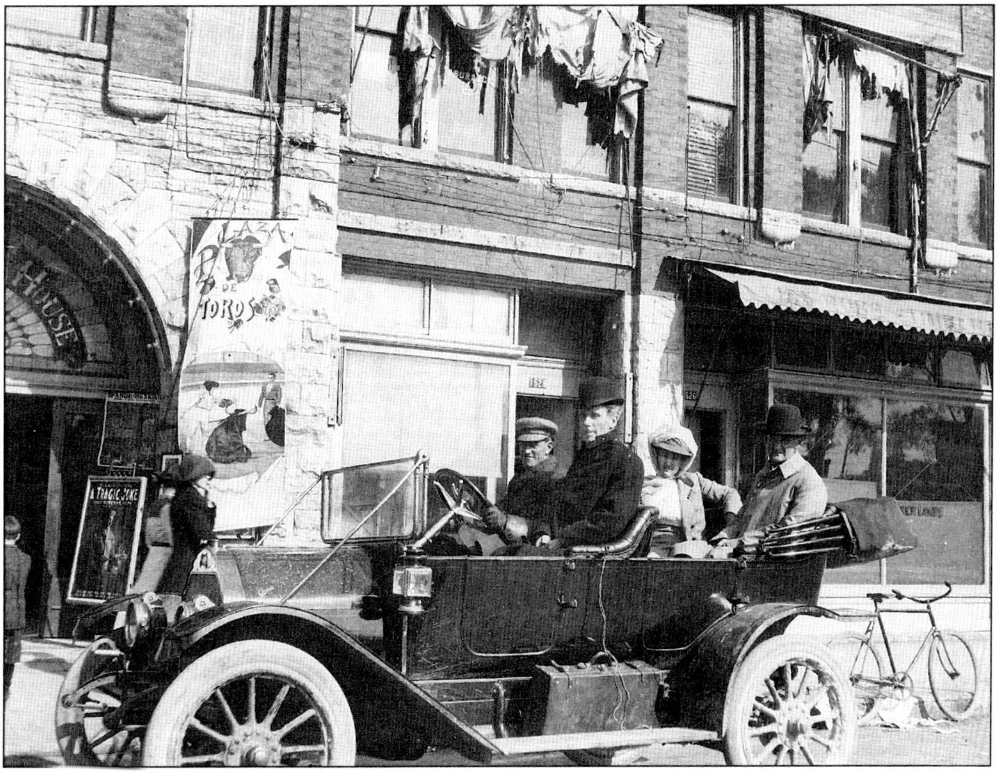

A Real-Photo Post Card of Brunswick in 1912. This view shows some of the businesses in the 1500 block of Newcastle Street.

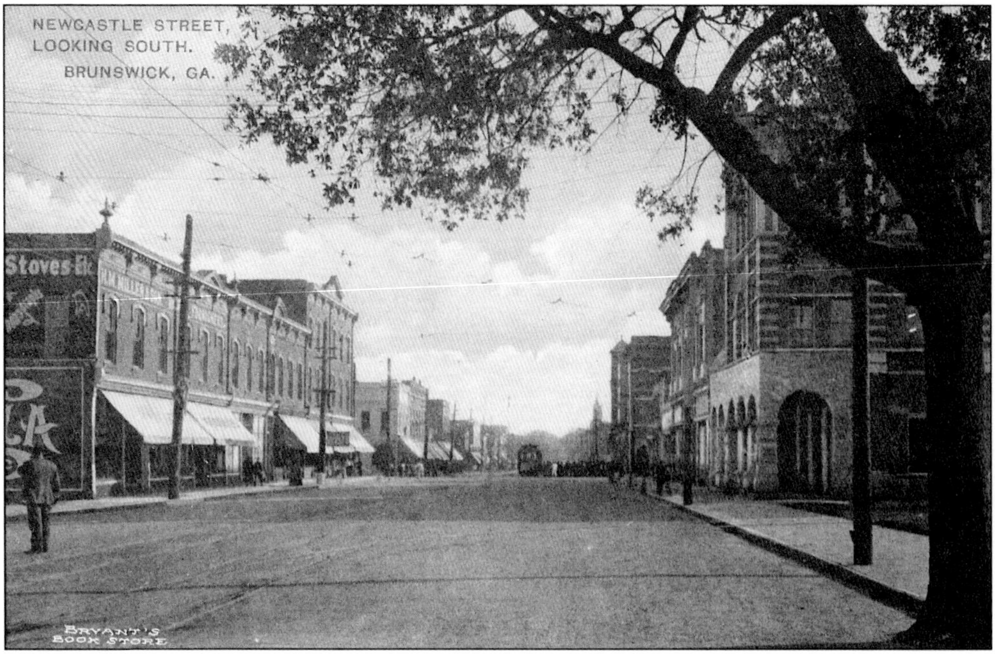

NEWCASTLE STREET LOOKING SOUTH IN BRUNSWICK, C. 1914.

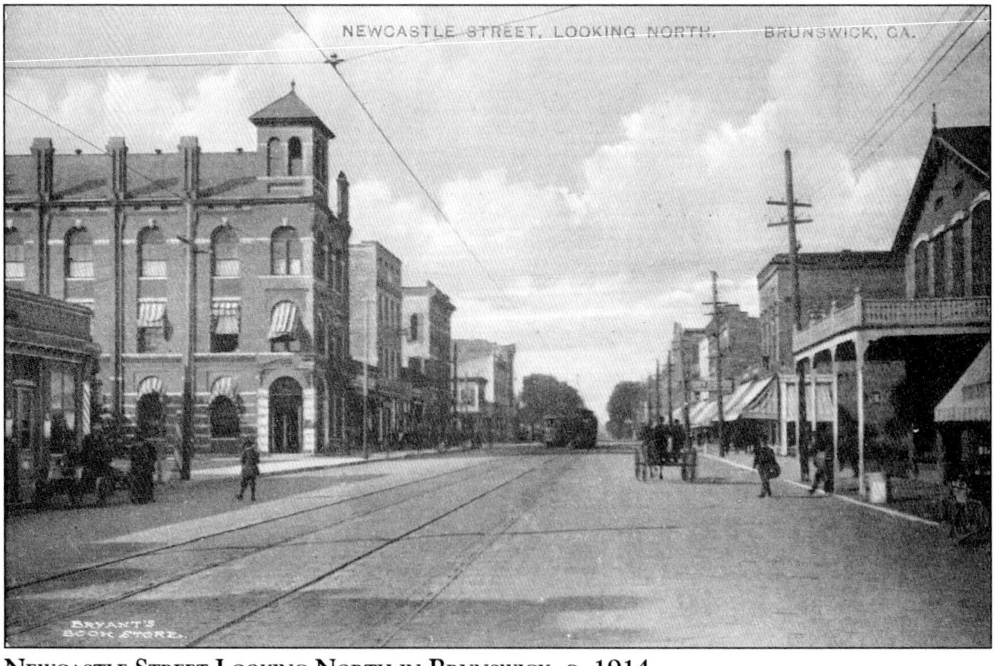

NEWCASTLE STREET LOOKING NORTH IN BRUNSWICK, C. 1914.

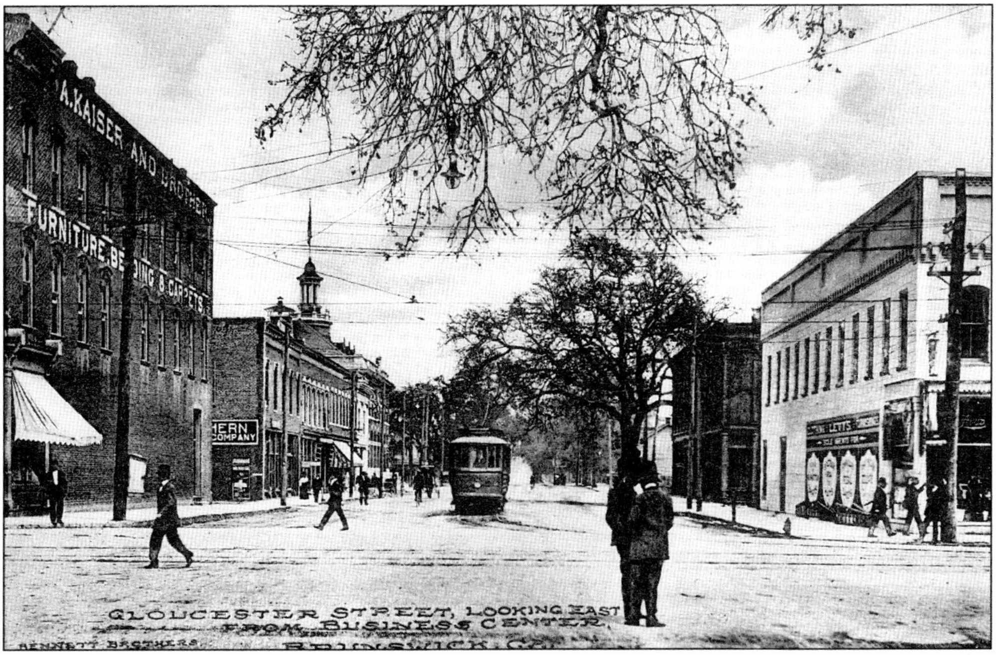

GLOUCESTER STREET LOOKING EAST FROM THE BUSINESS CENTER OF BRUNSWICK, C. 1912. The unsigned card was mailed to a young lady in Mystic, Connecticut, and simply said: "You give me the fidgets."

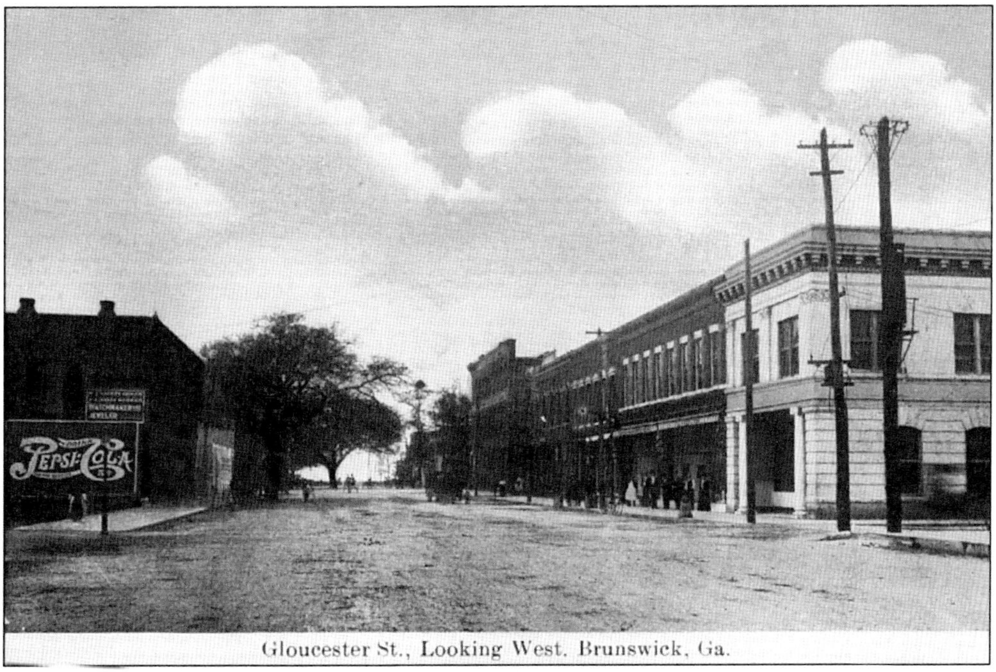

GLOUCESTER STREET LOOKING WEST IN BRUNSWICK IN 1911. This view shows a prominent Pepsi-Cola sign painted on one of the buildings.

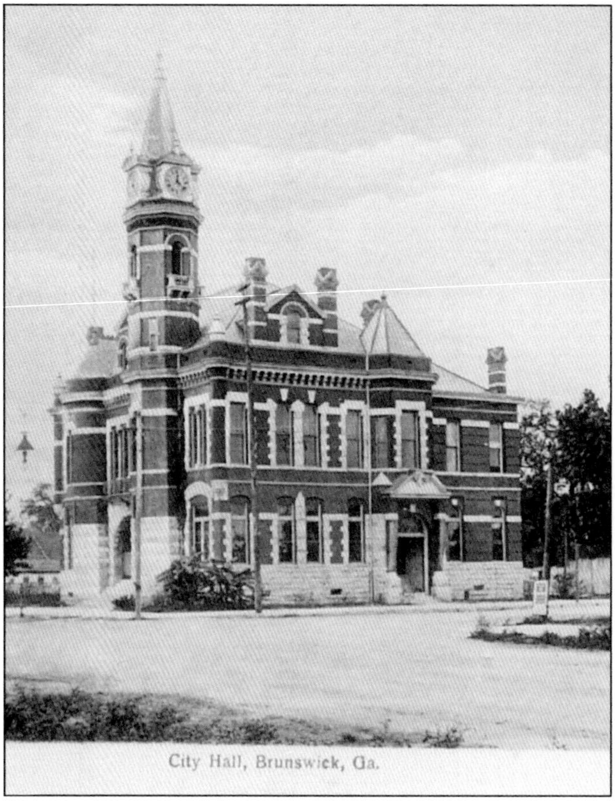

The City Hall Building in Brunswick. A majestic building, it is shown as it appeared c. 1907.

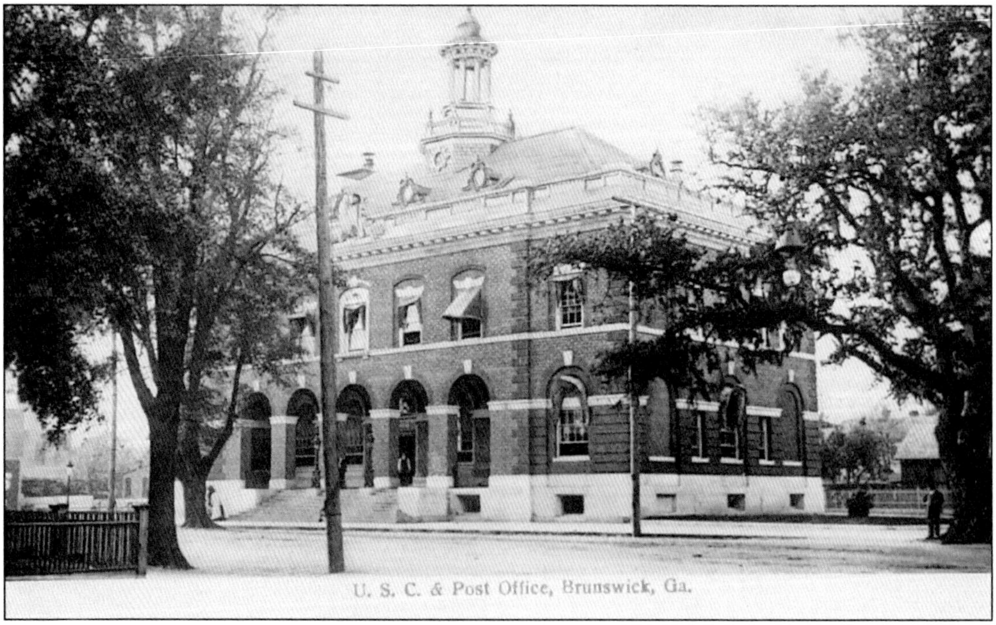

The U.S. Customs and Post Office Building in Brunswick, c. 1907. This was also an impressive structure.

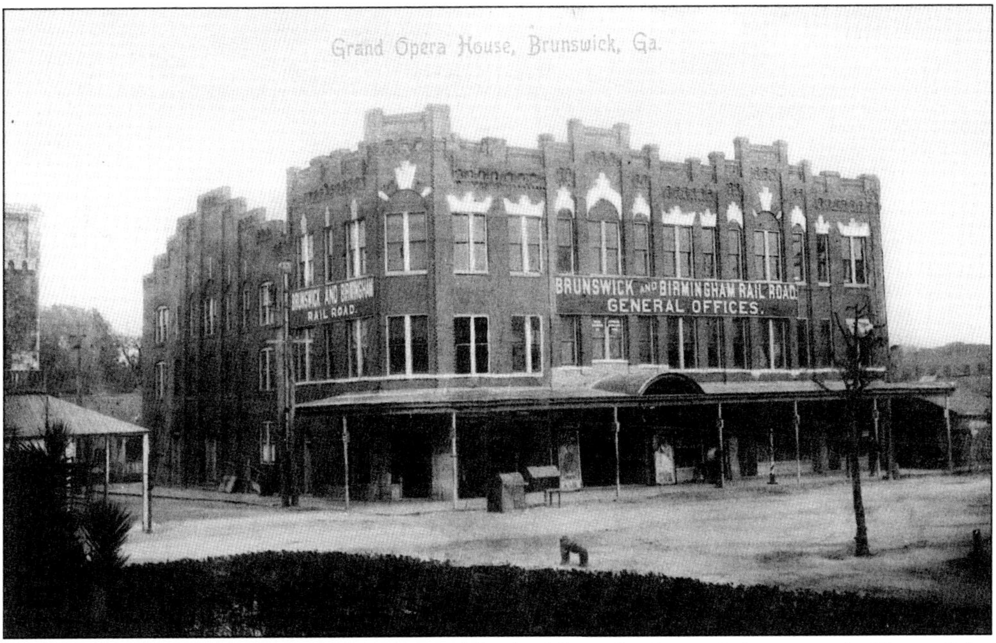

The Grand Opera House in Brunswick. The building also housed the general offices of the Brunswick and Birmingham Rail Road.

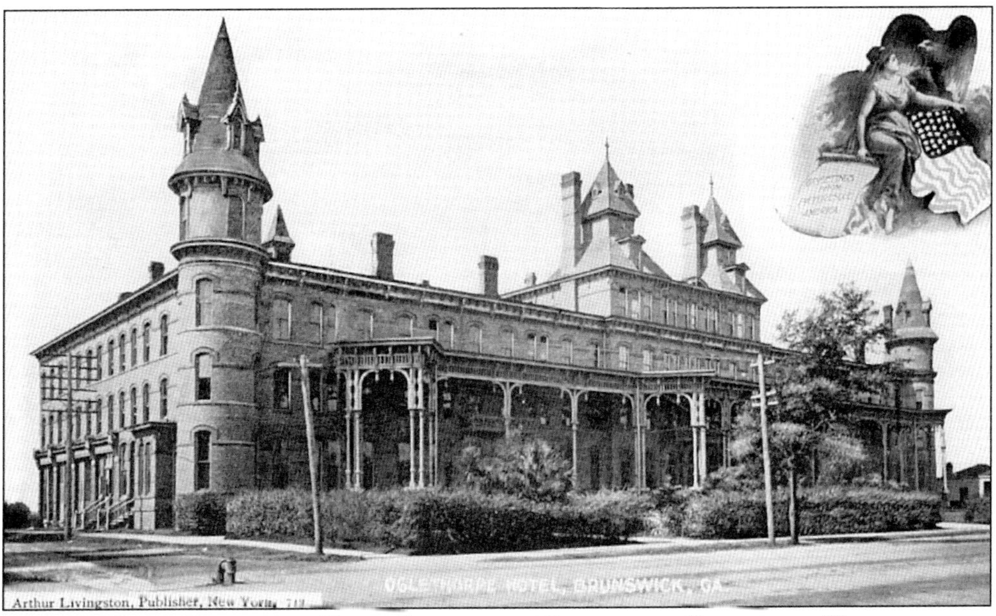

Another Regal Building in Early Brunswick, Home of the Oglethorpe Hotel.

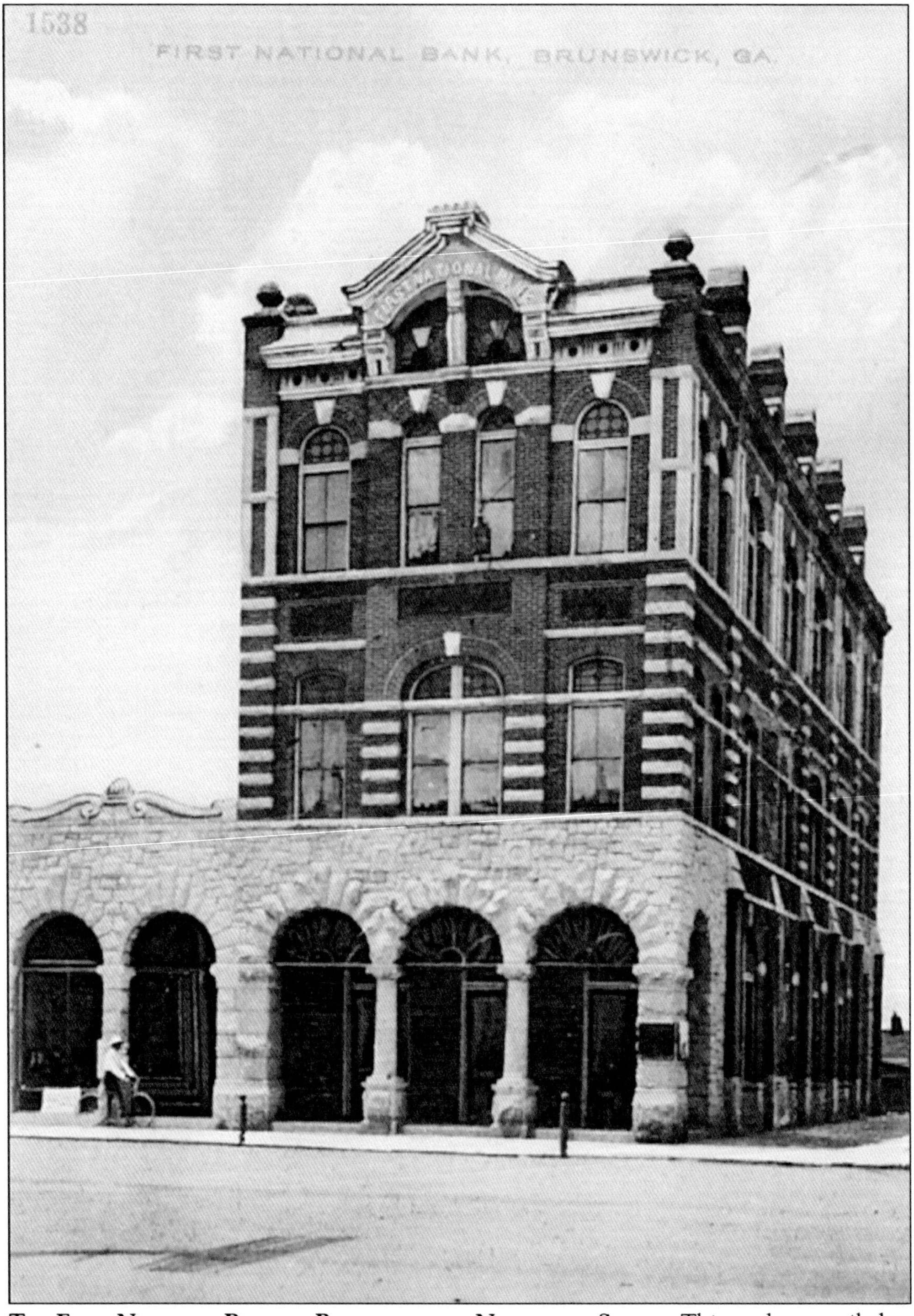

The First National Bank of Brunswick, on Newcastle Street. This card was mailed to Oxford, New York, on May 27, 1911, with the message: "It is so pleasant here that one can feel reconciled to the trouble and discomforts of southern traveling to get here. While it is 6 miles to the ocean, the breeze is most refreshing. C.S.D."

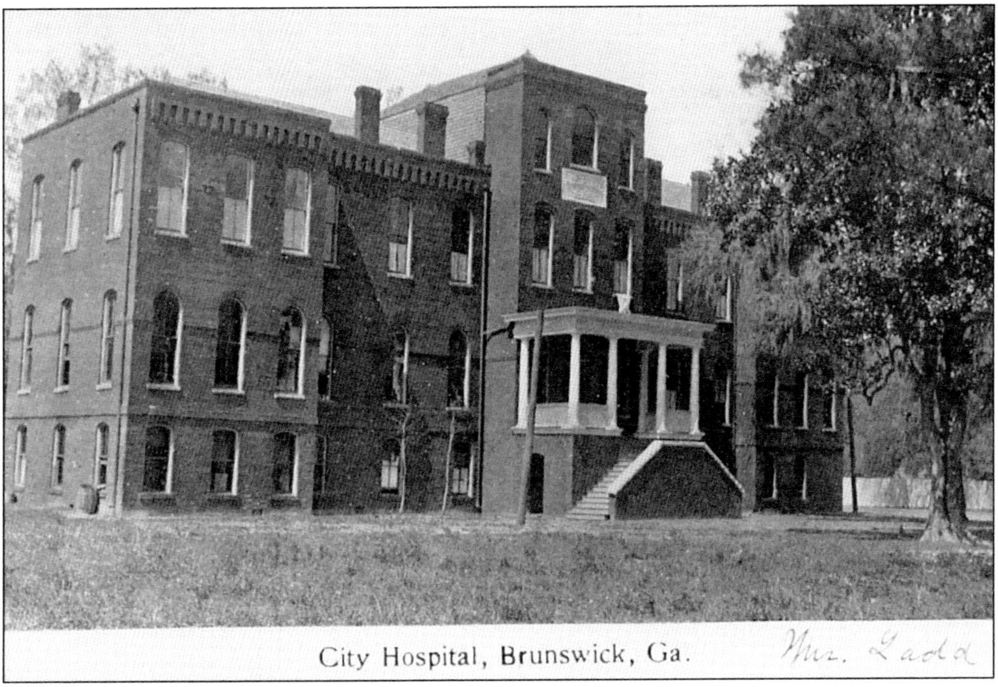

A PRE-1907 CARD SHOWING THE CITY HOSPITAL AT BRUNSWICK.

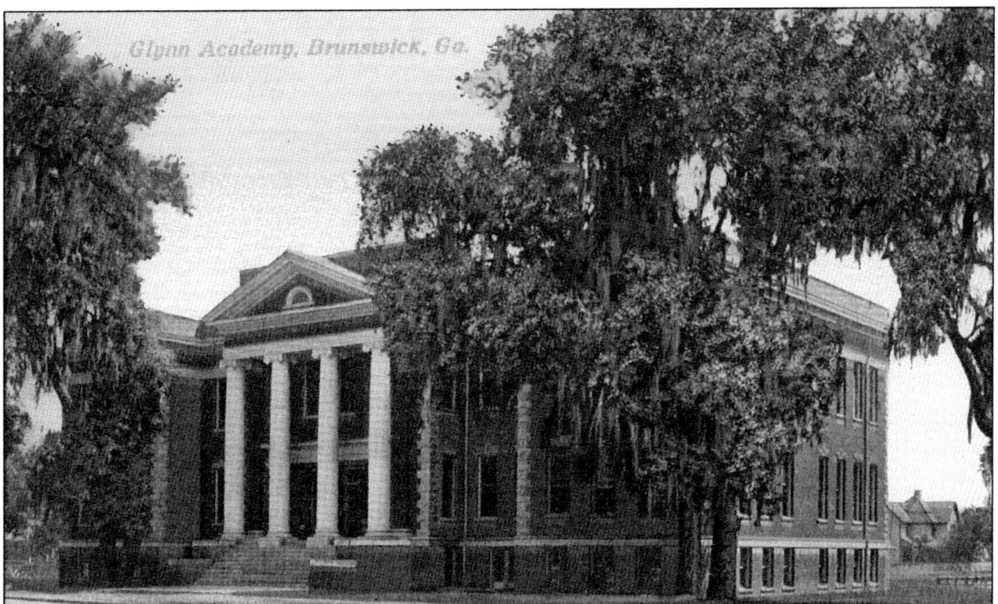

GLYNN ACADEMY IN BRUNSWICK. The school was situated in a grove of live oak trees draped with Spanish moss.

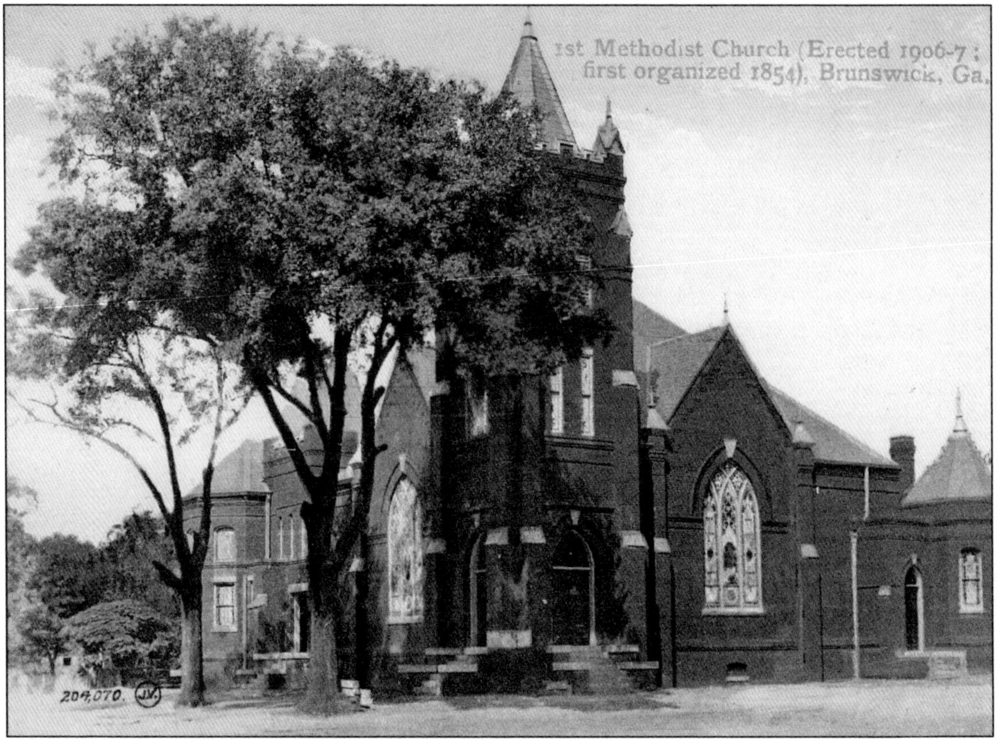

THE FIRST METHODIST CHURCH IN BRUNSWICK, C. 1908. The printed message on this card states that the church was organized in 1854 and this building was erected 1906–1907.

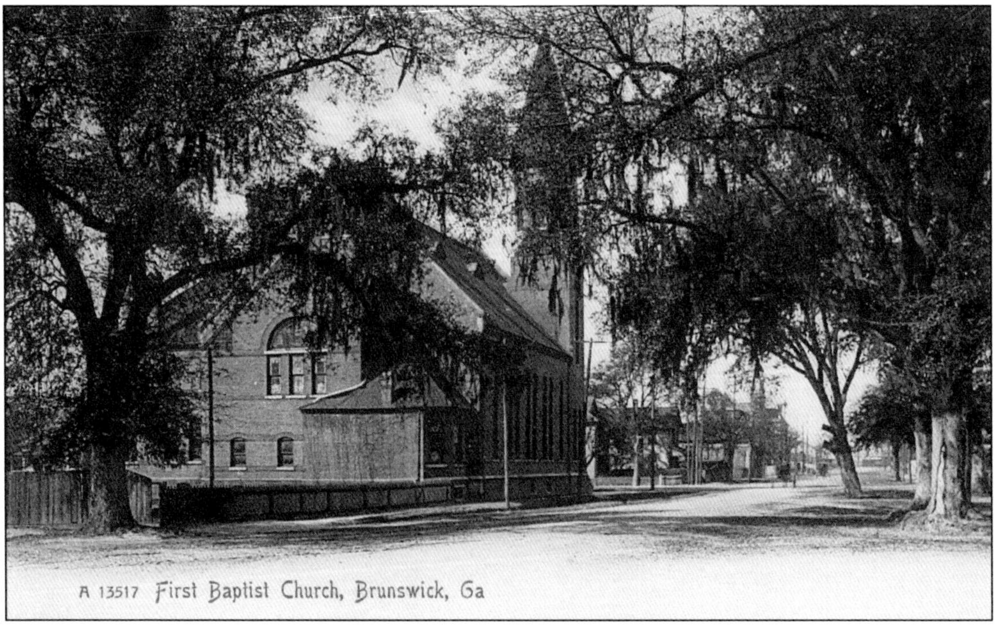

A PRE-1907 VIEW OF THE FIRST BAPTIST CHURCH IN BRUNSWICK.

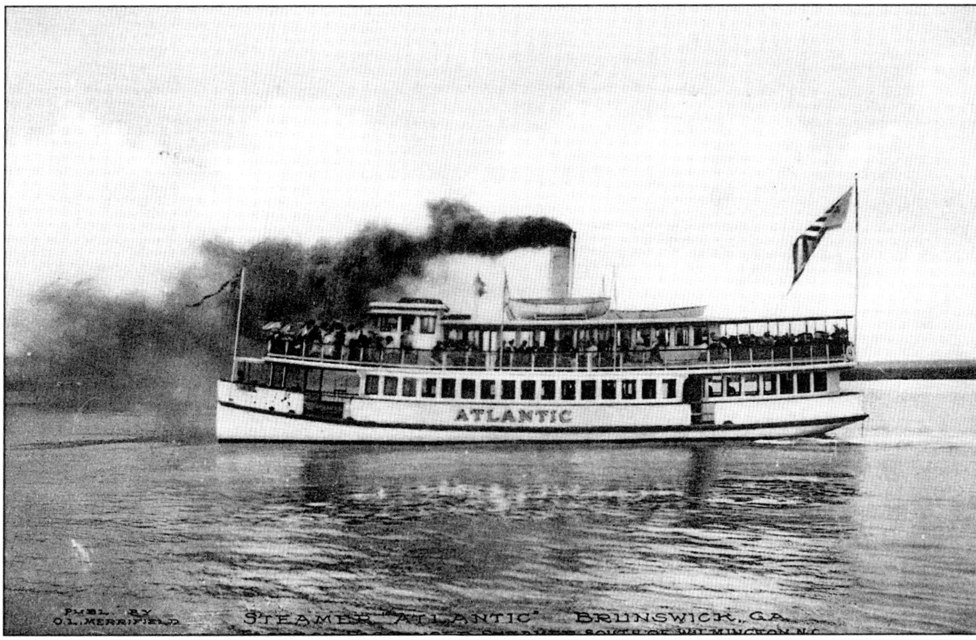

The Steamer *Atlantic* at Sea off the Coast of Brunswick. A printed note on this card claimed it to be the "fastest passenger steamer south of Wilmington, N.C."

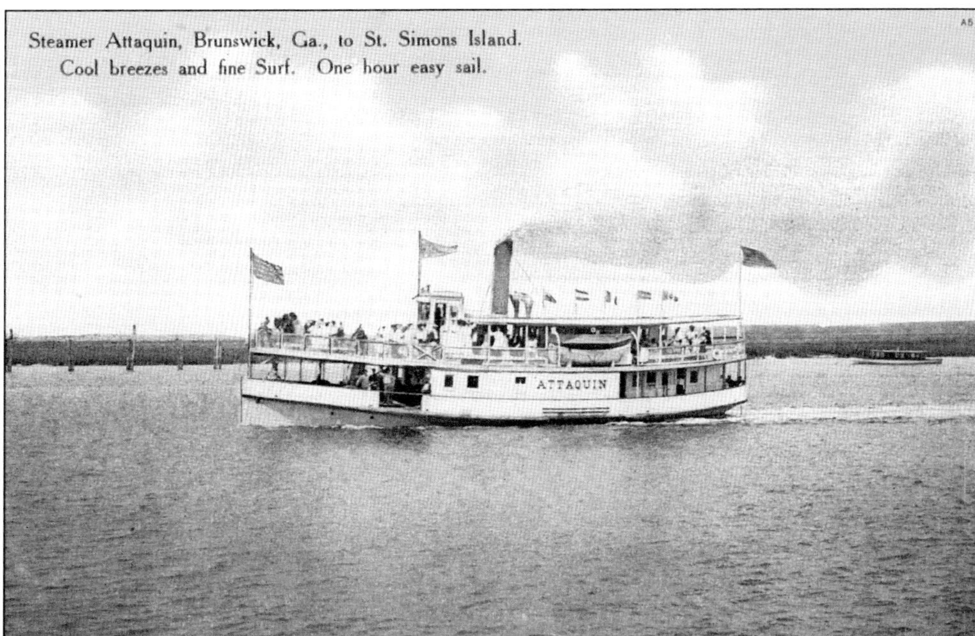

The Steamer *Attaquin*. The ship ran from Brunswick to St. Simons Island in "One hour easy sail." It would be many years before the causeway was built to St. Simons Island and tourists could drive their automobiles there.

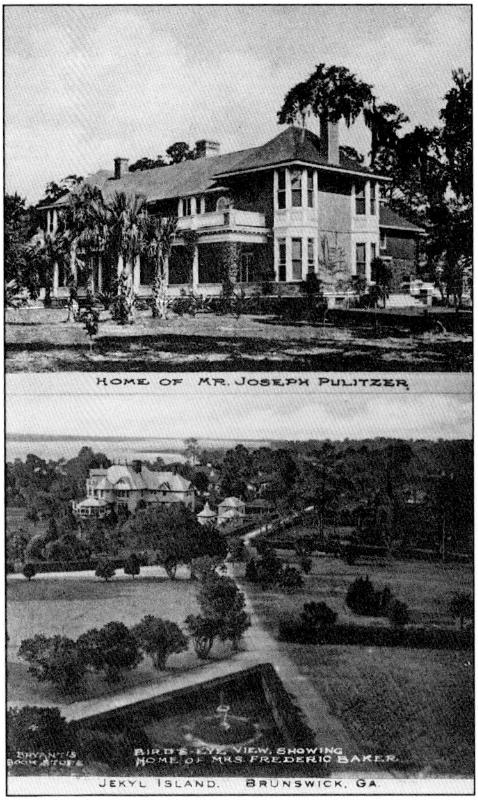

A Combination View Card Showing Two of the so-called "Cottages" Built on Jekyll Island by Wealthy Northerners around the Turn of the Century. The top one is the home of Joseph Pulitzer and the bottom one shows a bird's-eye view of the home of Mrs. Frederic Baker.

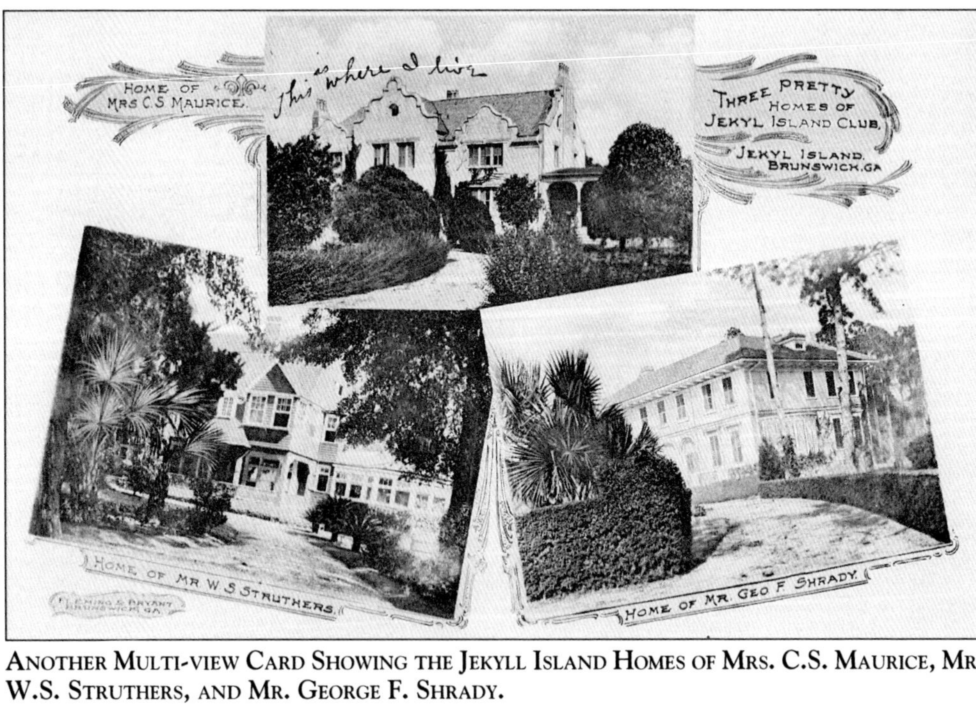

Another Multi-view Card Showing the Jekyll Island Homes of Mrs. C.S. Maurice, Mr. W.S. Struthers, and Mr. George F. Shrady.

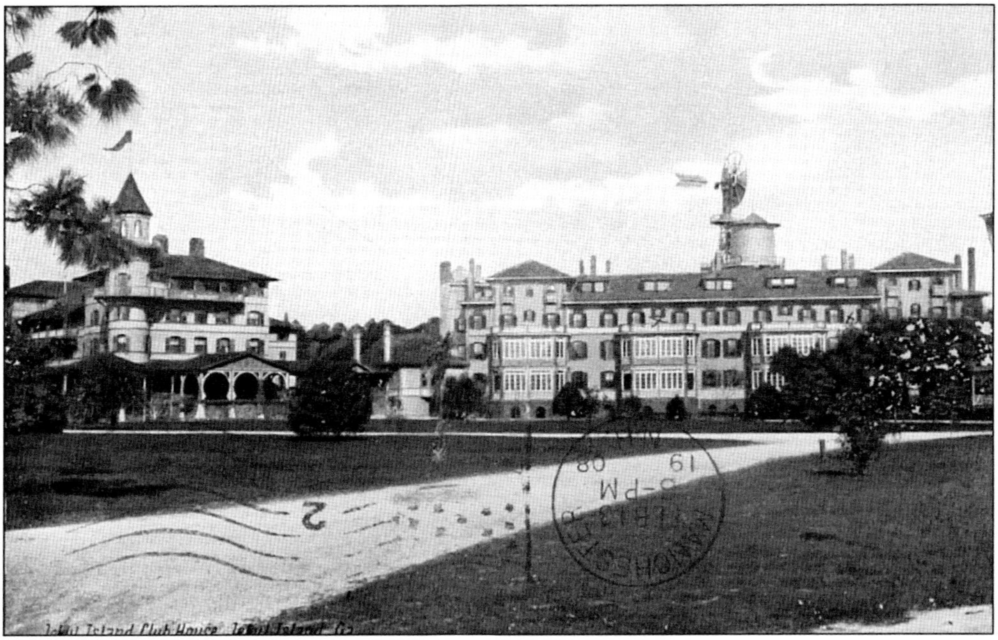

A View of the Jekyll Island Club House. This was where the winter residents stayed who did not have private houses on Jekyll.

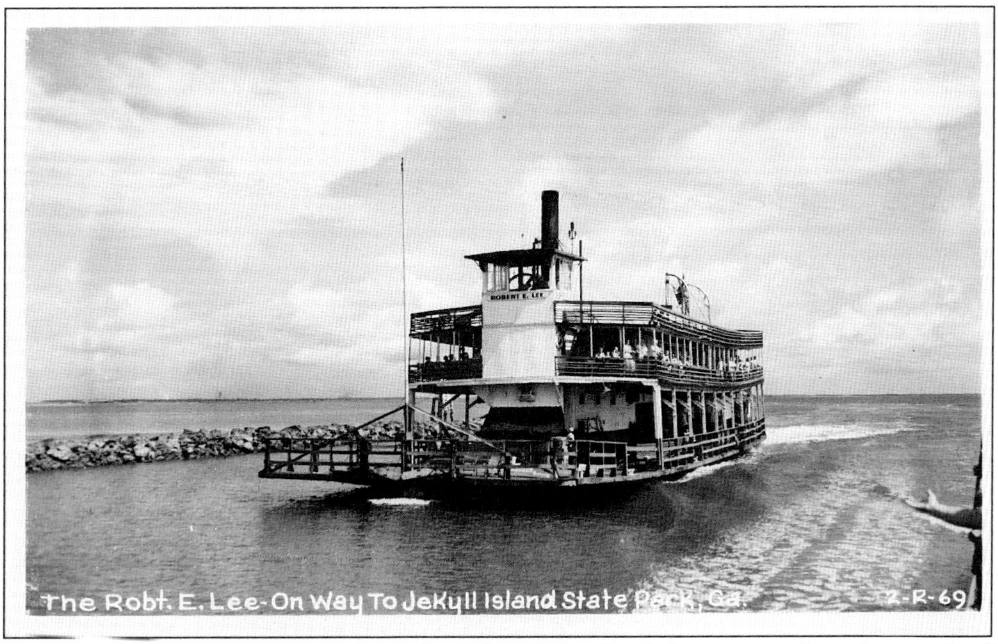

The Robert E. Lee. A modern boat, the *Robert E. Lee* hauled passengers from the mainland to offshore destinations.

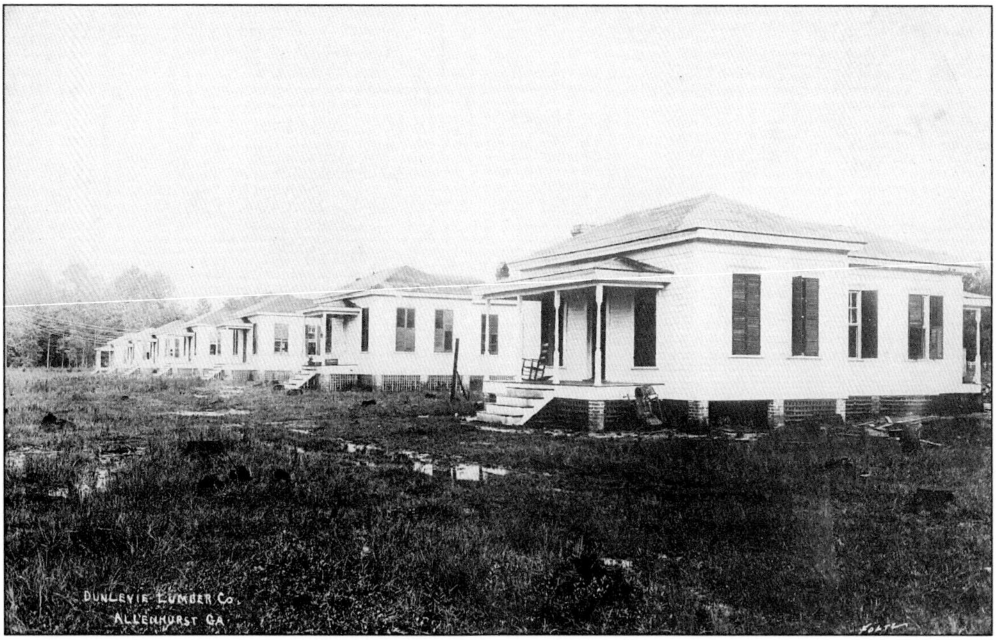

HOUSES FOR WORKERS AT THE DUNLEVIE LUMBER COMPANY IN ALLENHURST IN 1912.

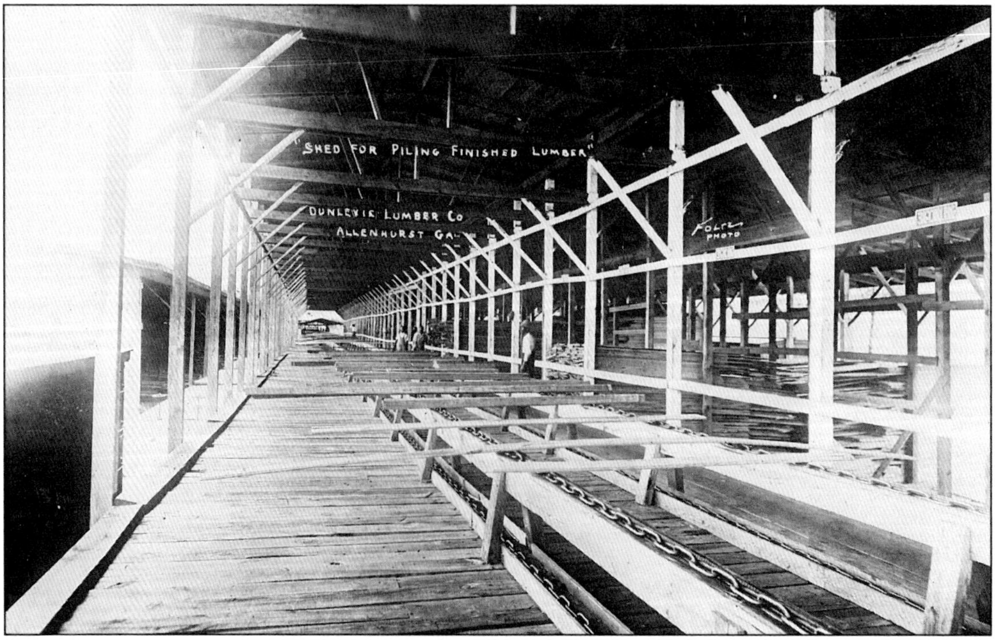

A SHED FOR STORING FINISHED LUMBER AT THE DUNLEVIE LUMBER COMPANY IN ALLENHURST IN 1912.

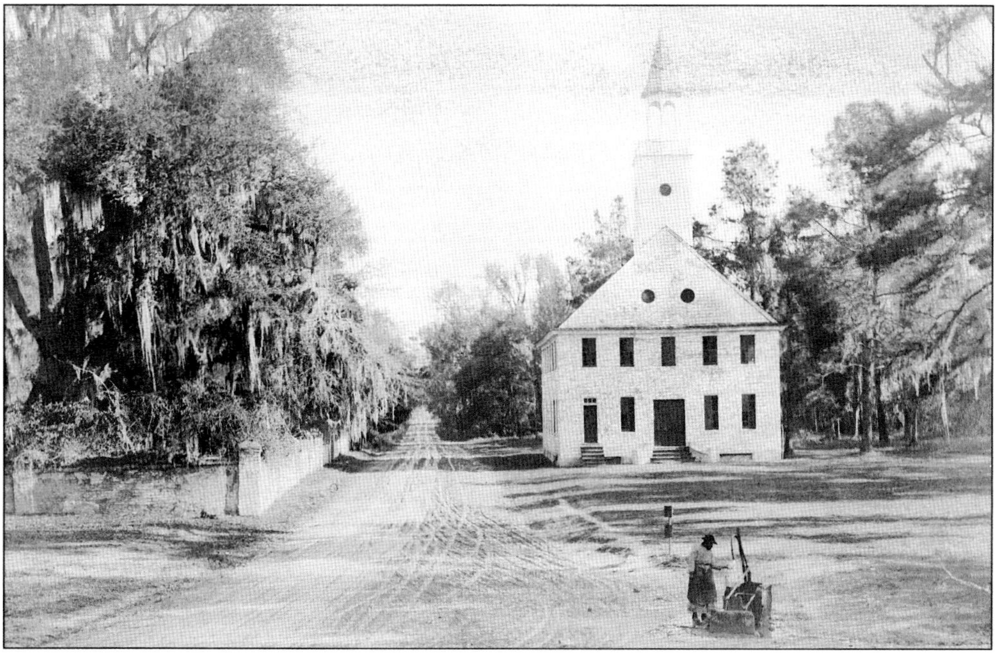

The Congregationalist Church at Midway. The card has a typed statement which says in part: "My father took this picture about 1916. Church is 135 years old, slaves worshiped on 2nd floor, Nabobs on 1st floor. Large old cemetery with heavy brick wall on left, best camp ground between here and Fla. to the left. Gen. Sherman on his march to the sea crossed the road here. All the timber except in cemetery has grown since the war."

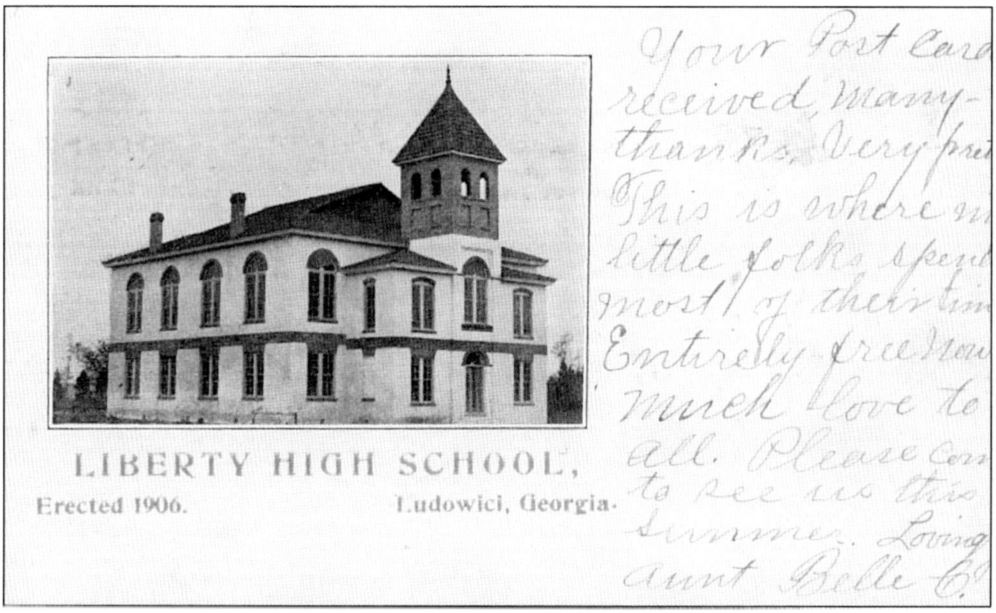

Liberty High School in Ludowici, Erected in 1906.

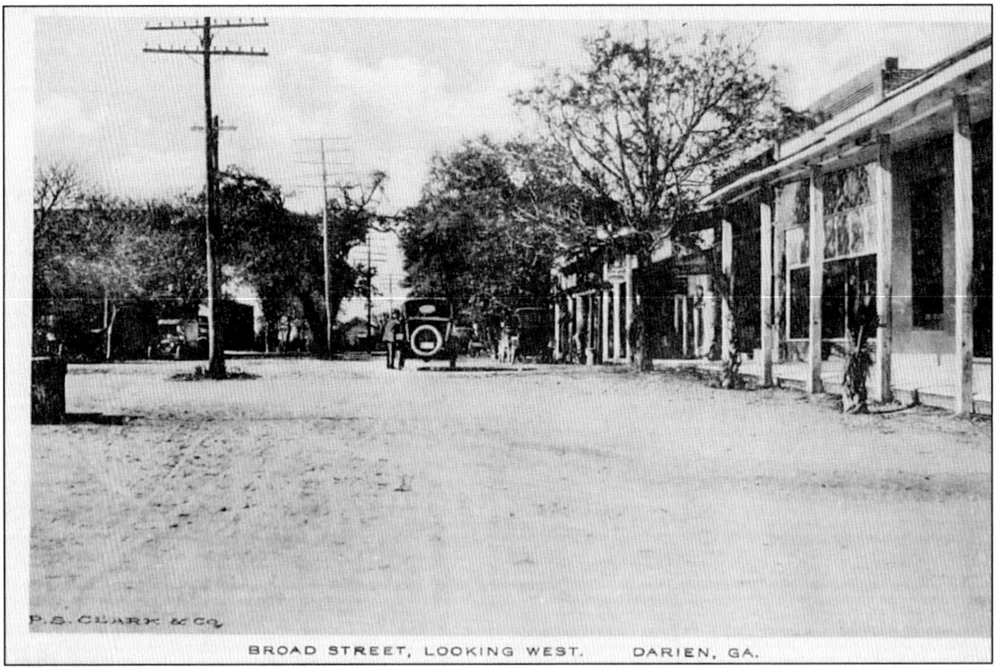

Broad Street Looking West in Darien, c. 1912.

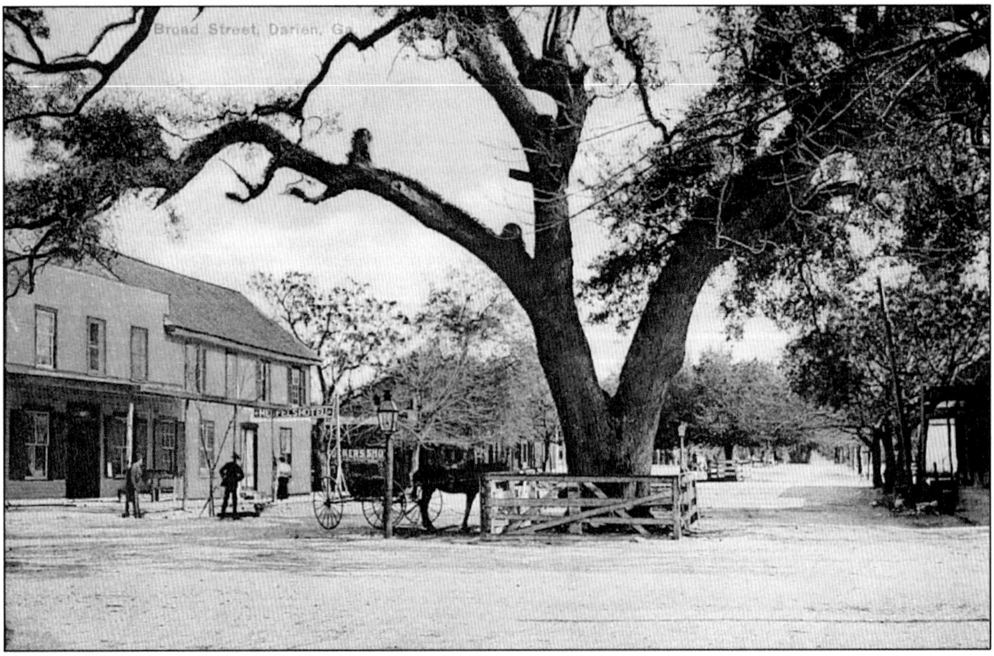

Broad Street in Darien, c. 1908. The huge live oak tree is protected from horses and mules, which would gnaw the bark if they could.

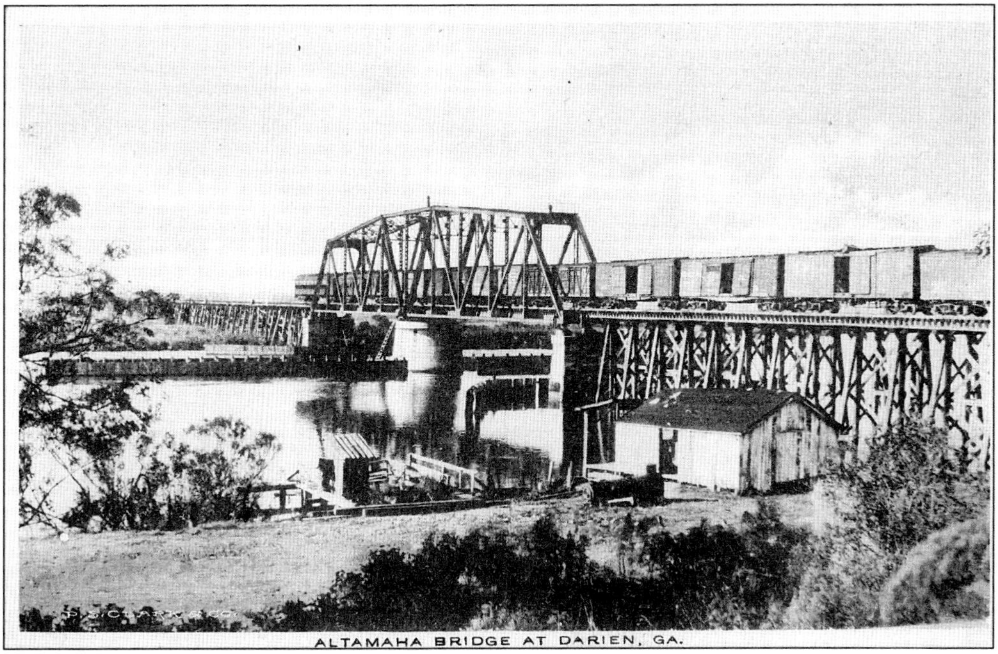

A RAILROAD TRESTLE. There was no bridge for automobile traffic across the Altamaha River at Darien in the early days, but the railroad did have a trestle there.

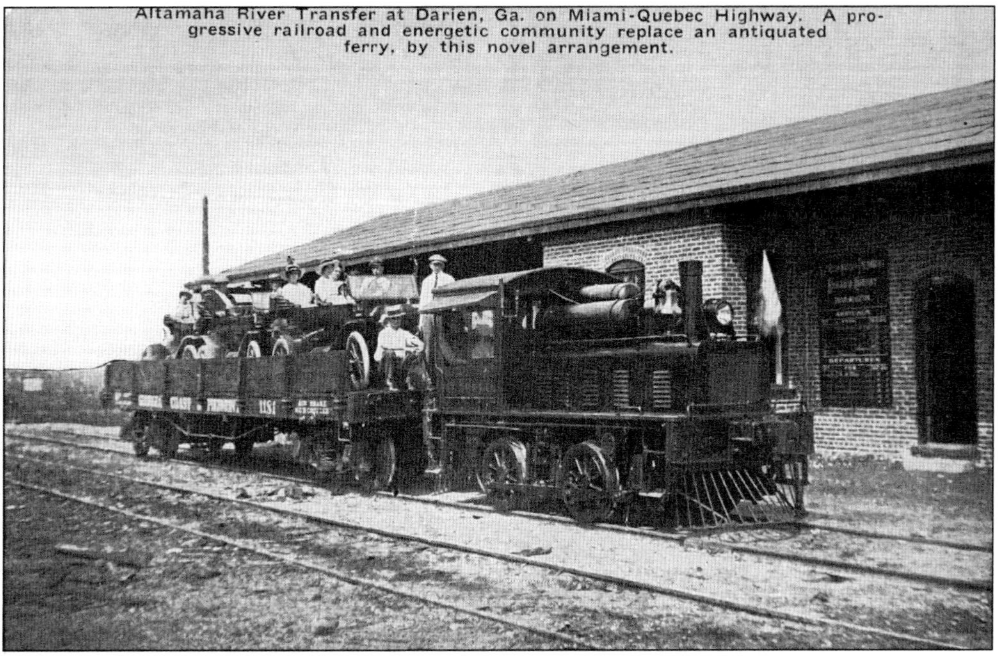

TRANSPORTING AUTOMOBILES. Automobiles were driven onto railroad flat cars on either side of the Altamaha River and ferried across by train.

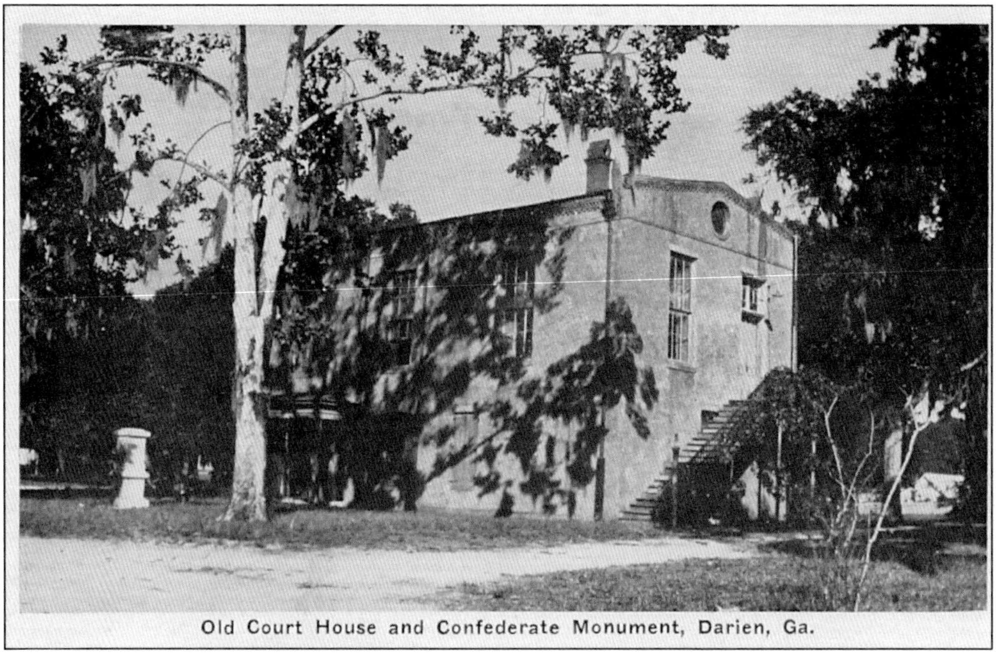

THE MCINTOSH COUNTY COURTHOUSE IN DARIEN, BUILT IN 1872. The building was remodeled in 1931 and additions were made in 1973.

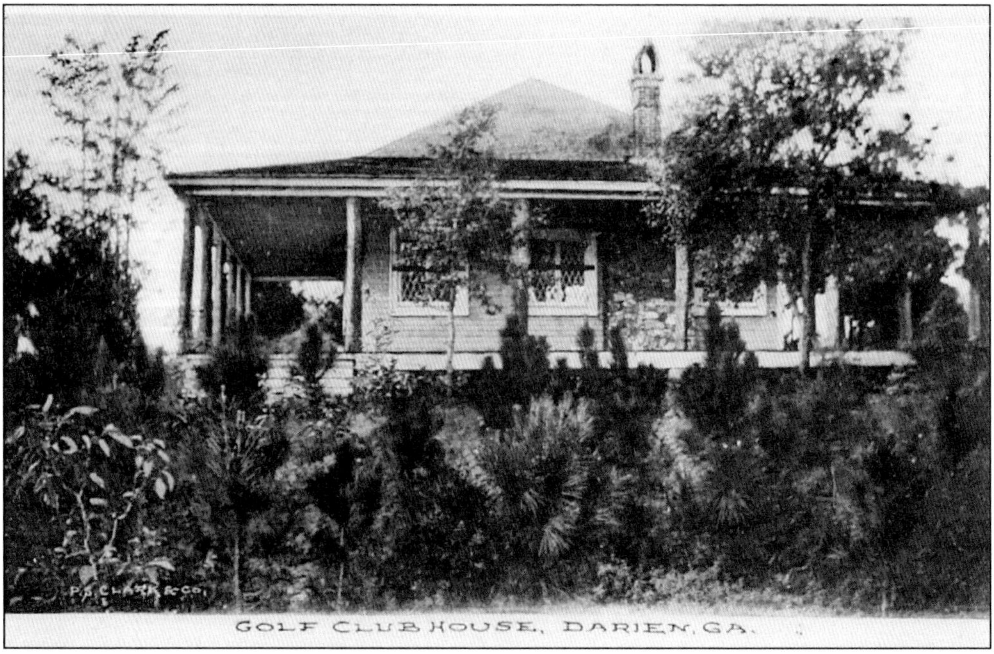

THE GOLF CLUB HOUSE AT DARIEN.

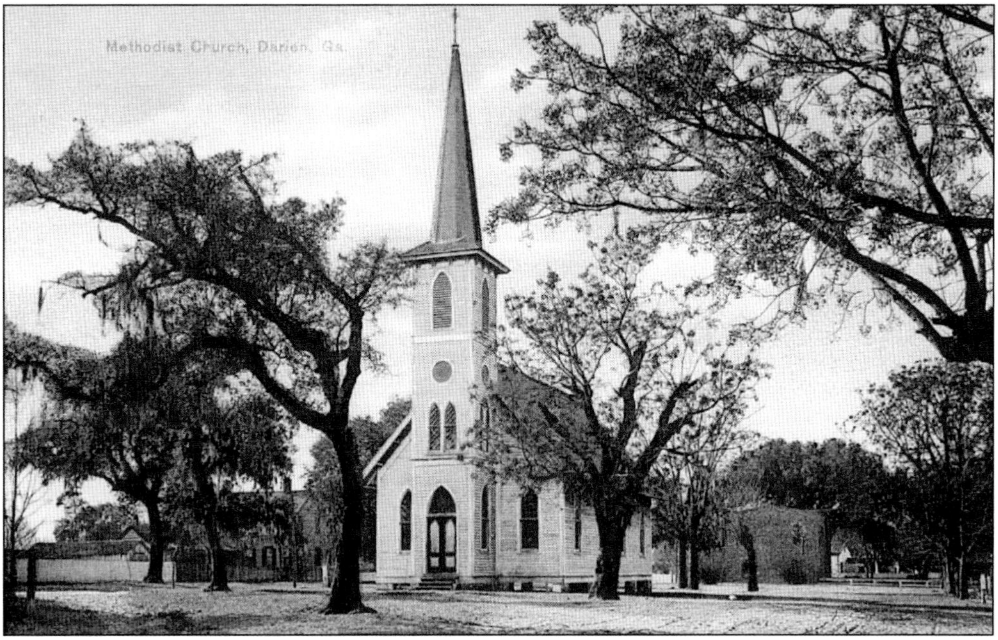

THE METHODIST CHURCH AT DARIEN.

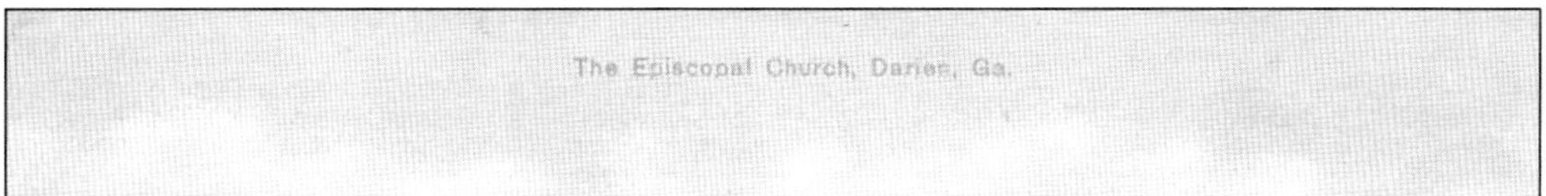

THE EPISCOPAL CHURCH AT DARIEN.

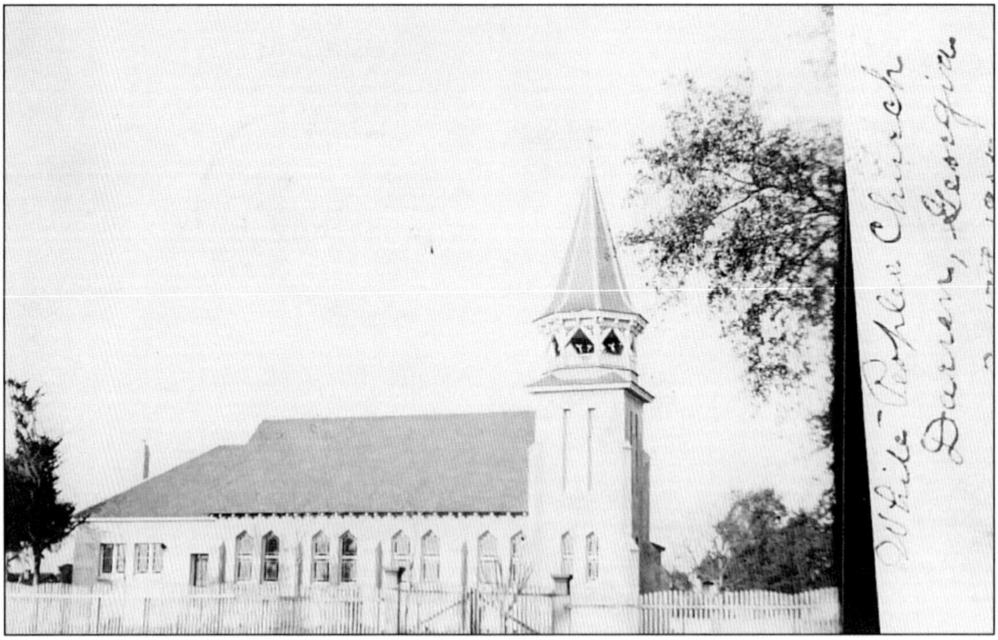

The Presbyterian Church for White Members at Darien in 1905.

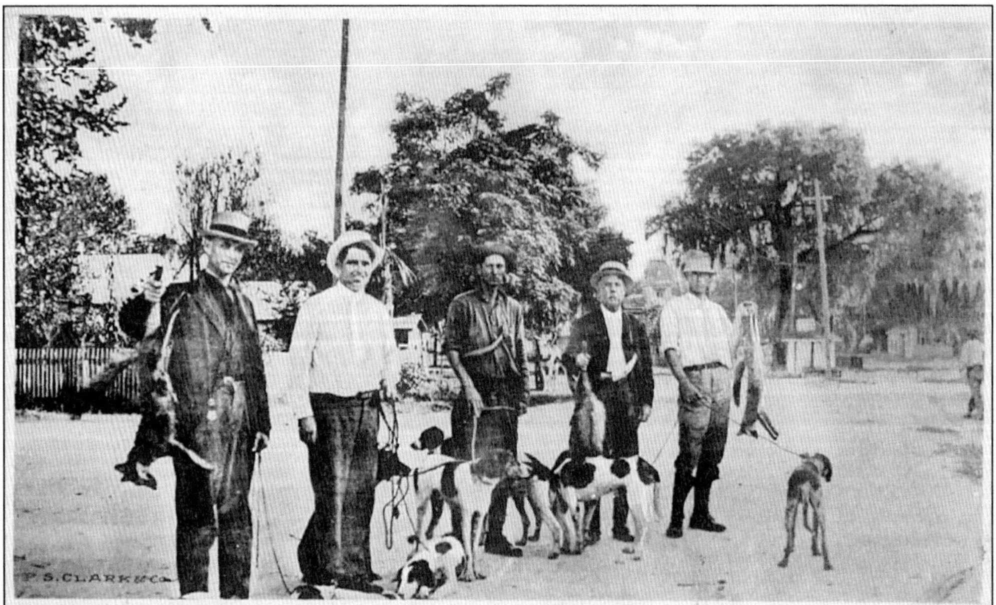

The Results of a Fox Hunt. A three-hour fox chase near Darien in the mid-1910s yielded three foxes.

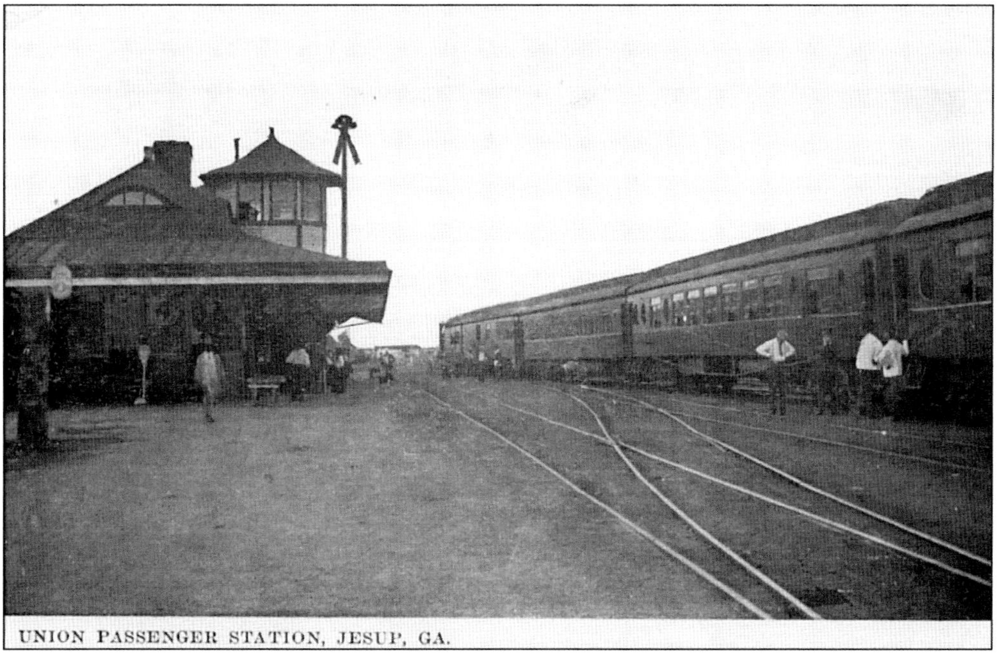

The Union Passenger Depot in Jesup in 1912. This post card was sent to Philadelphia and the sender was all business and to the point. The message read like a telegram: "Will be in Phila on Wednesday morn at 11:35 will meet you at office at 1:00 oclock. will go to Pottstown on 1:25 P&R. Clifford."

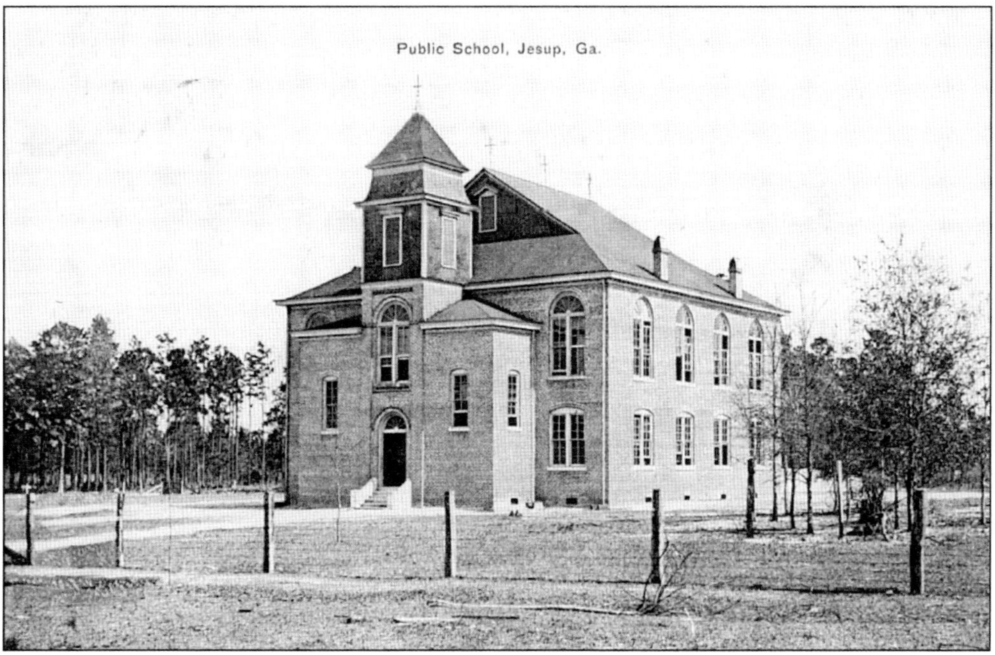

The Public School at Jesup, c. 1908. This school was typical of other small-town schools across the state.

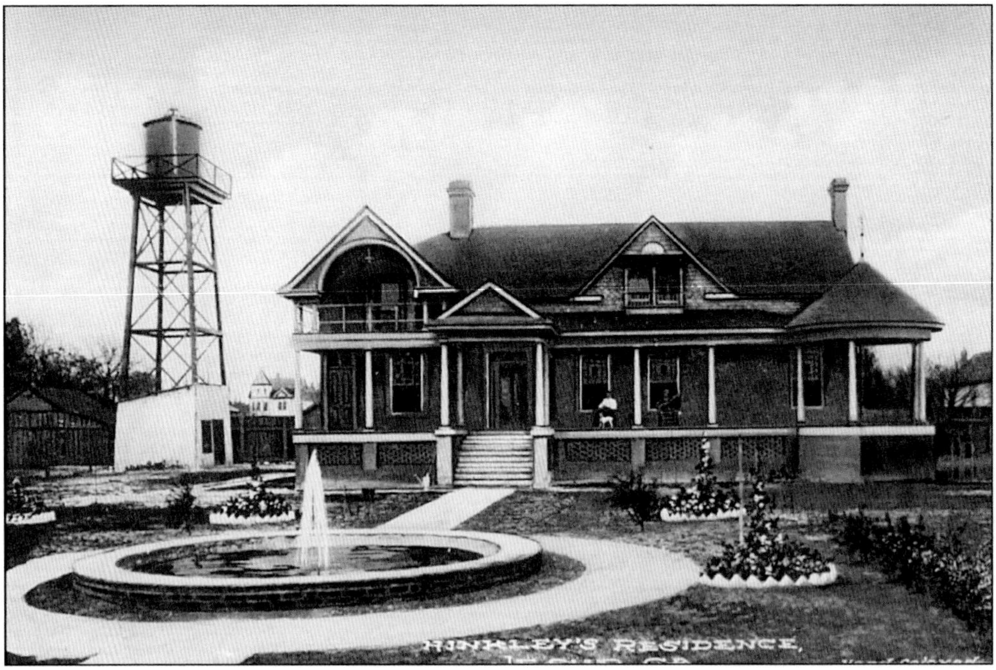

The Residence of a Mr. Hinkley at Jesup, c. 1912. This was certainly a fine home with its own water tower and a very unusual fountain in the front yard.

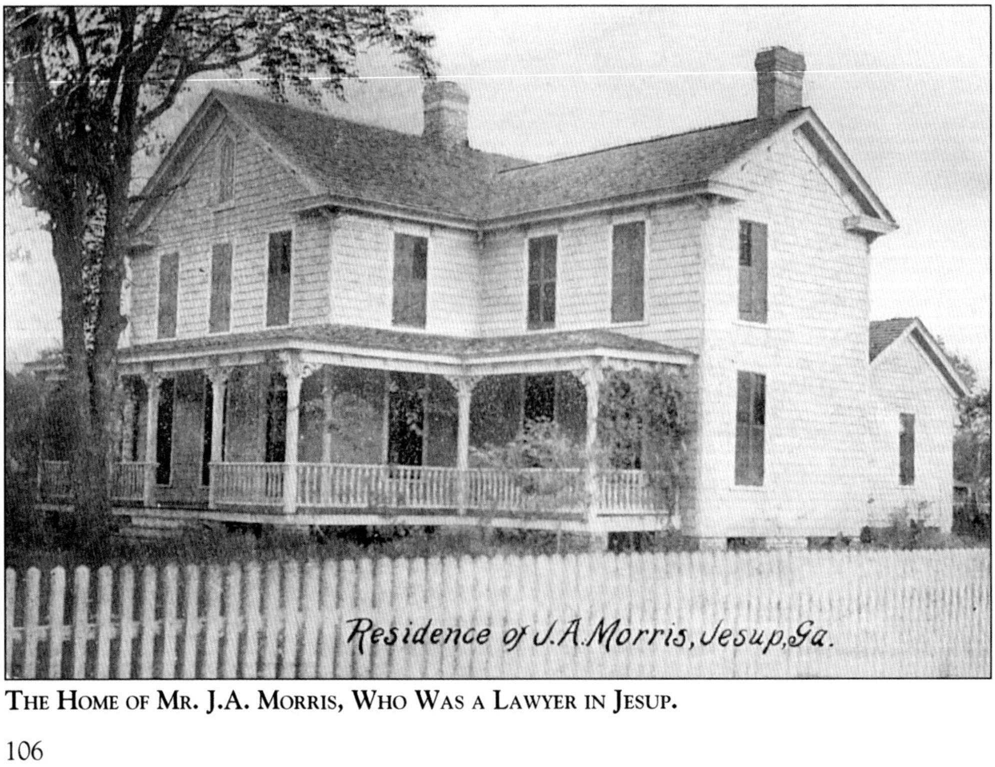

The Home of Mr. J.A. Morris, Who Was a Lawyer in Jesup.

Six

SAVANNAH AND ENVIRONS

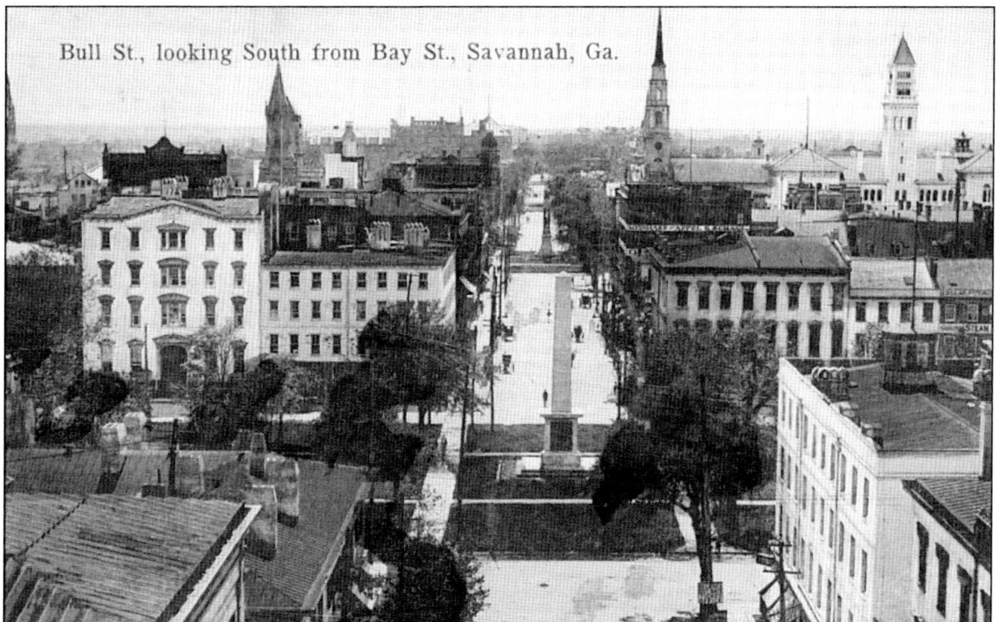

A DELIGHTFUL BIRD'S-EYE VIEW OF BULL STREET LOOKING SOUTH FROM BAY STREET IN SAVANNAH, C. 1906.

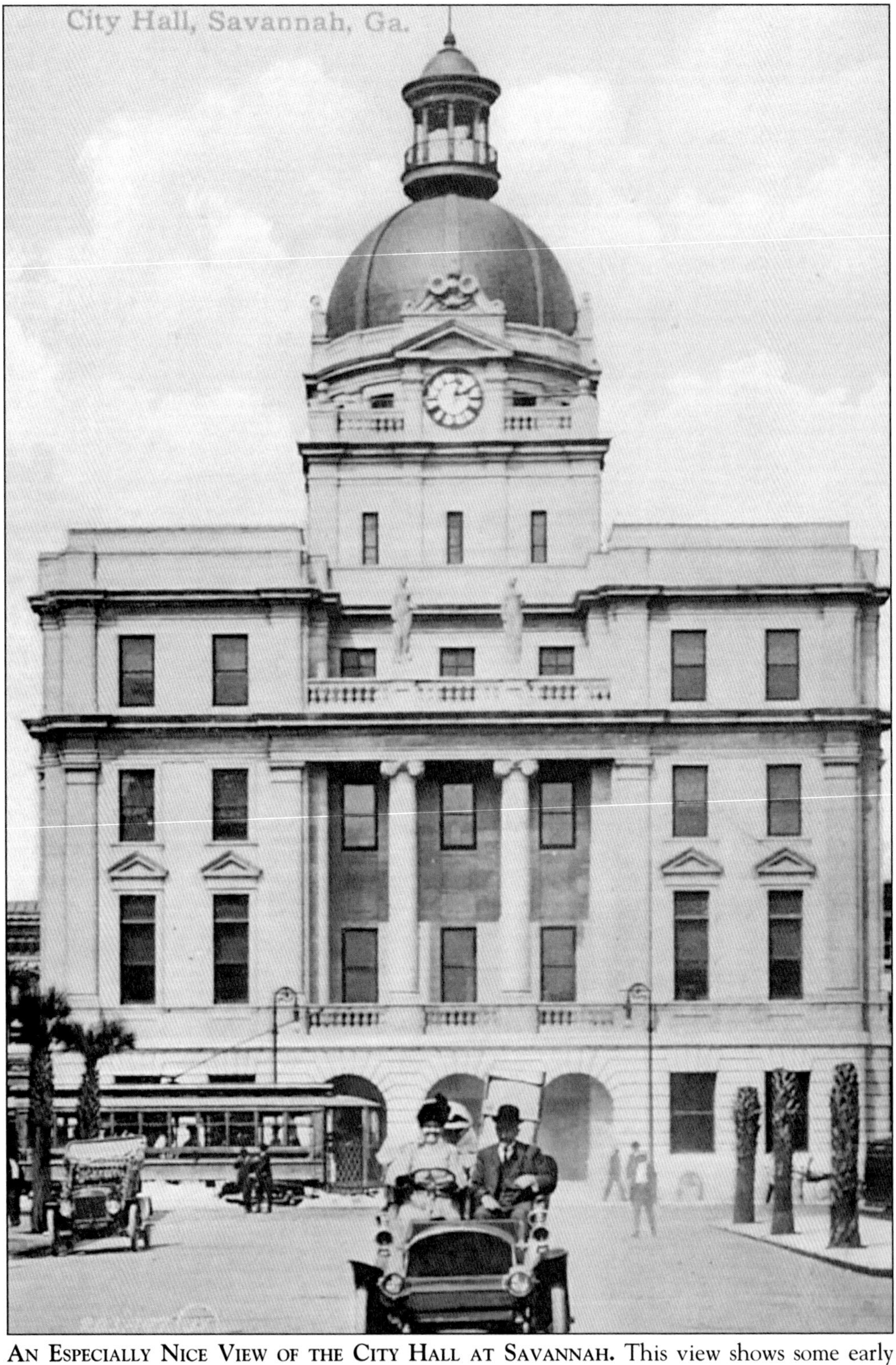

AN ESPECIALLY NICE VIEW OF THE CITY HALL AT SAVANNAH. This view shows some early motorists out with their "horseless carriages."

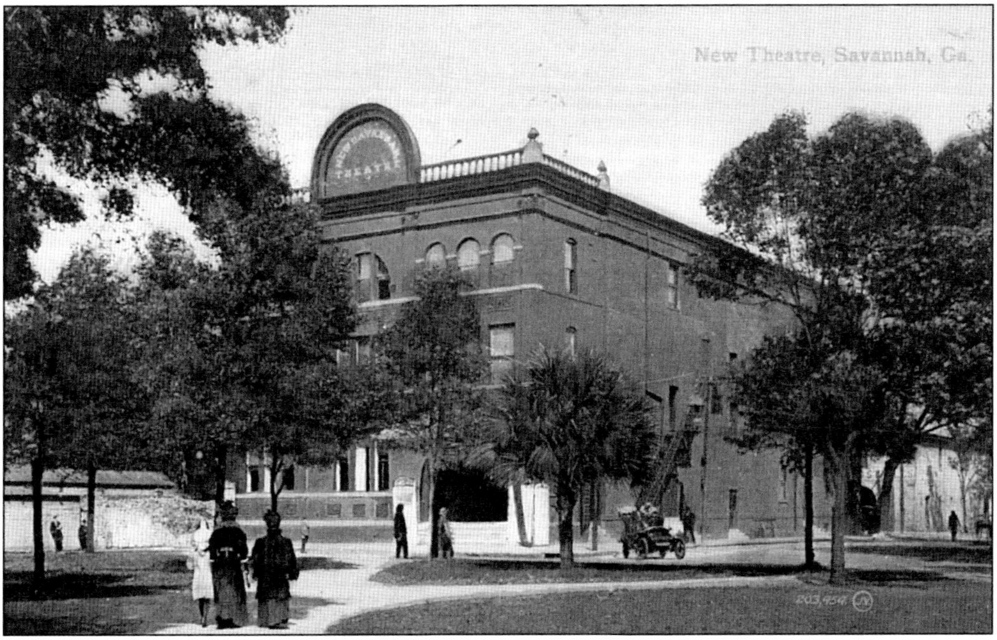

THE NEW SAVANNAH THEATER IN SAVANNAH IN 1910.

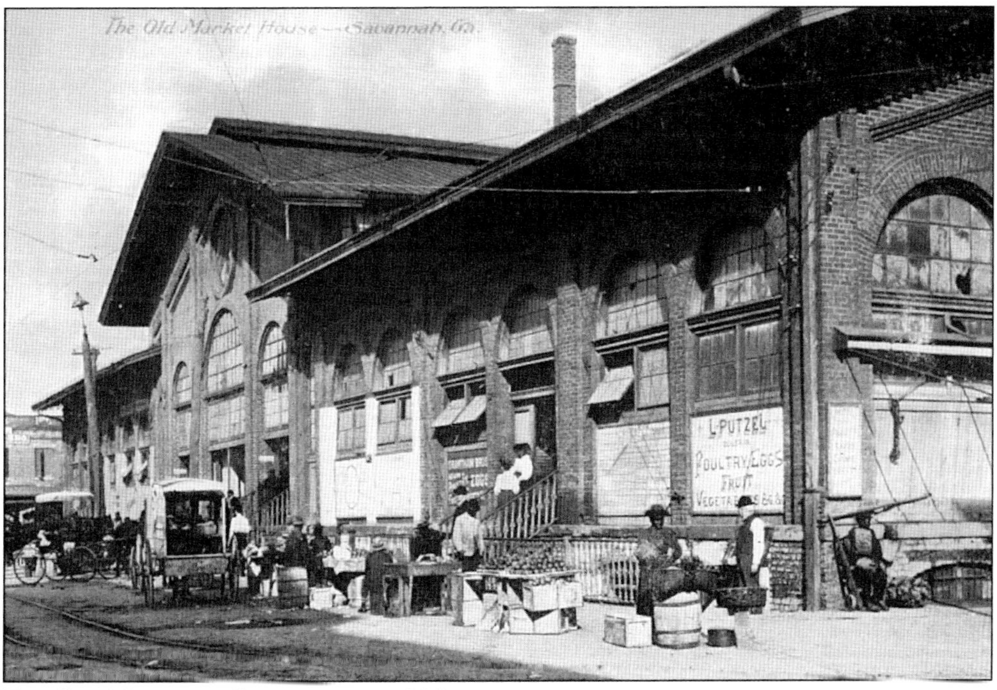

THE OLD MARKET IN SAVANNAH, C. 1908.

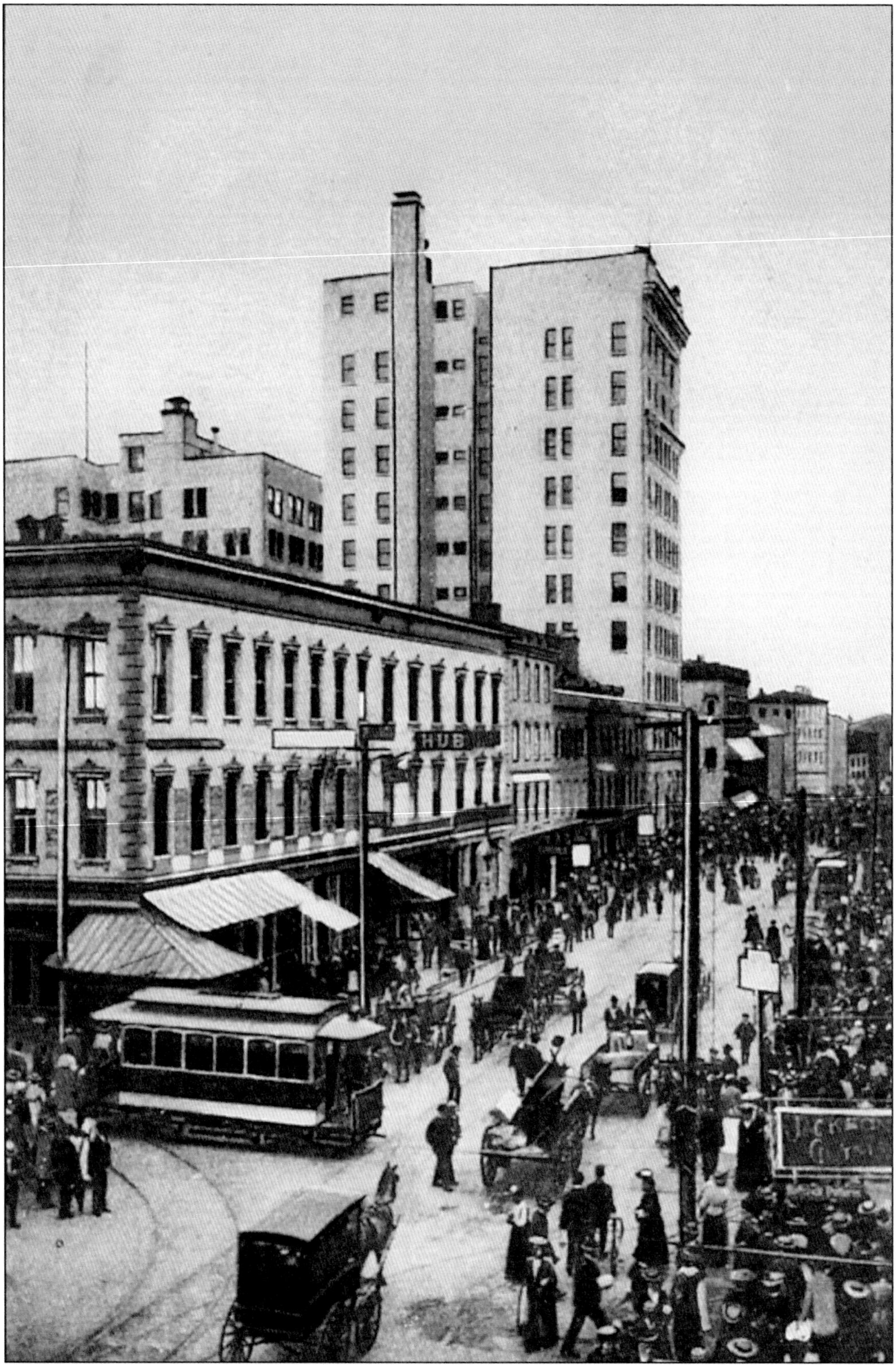

A CROWDED INTERSECTION ON BROUGHTON STREET IN SAVANNAH, C. 1910.

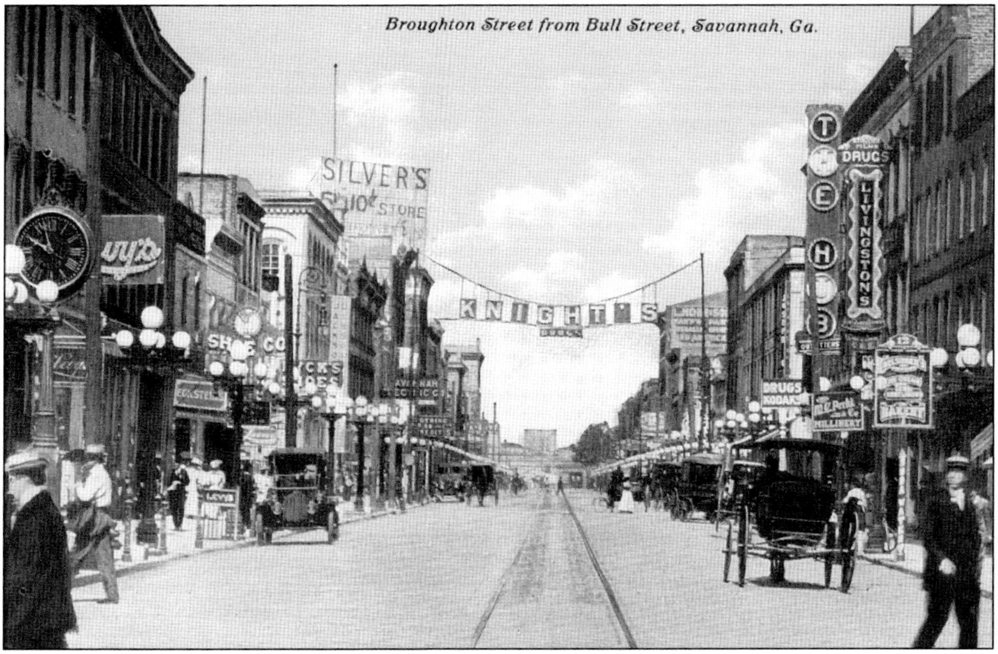

A VIEW OF BROUGHTON STREET LOOKING FROM THE INTERSECTION WITH BULL STREET IN SAVANNAH. Numerous businesses can be identified from the many signs.

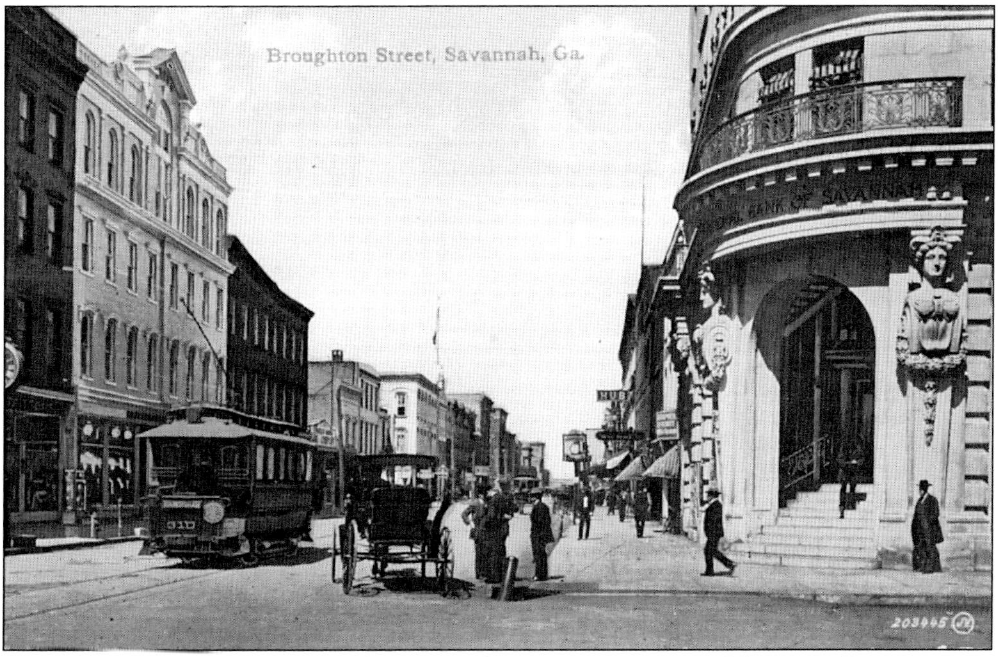

ANOTHER VIEW OF BROUGHTON STREET IN SAVANNAH WITH THE NATIONAL BANK ON THE CORNER, AT THE INTERSECTION WITH BULL STREET.

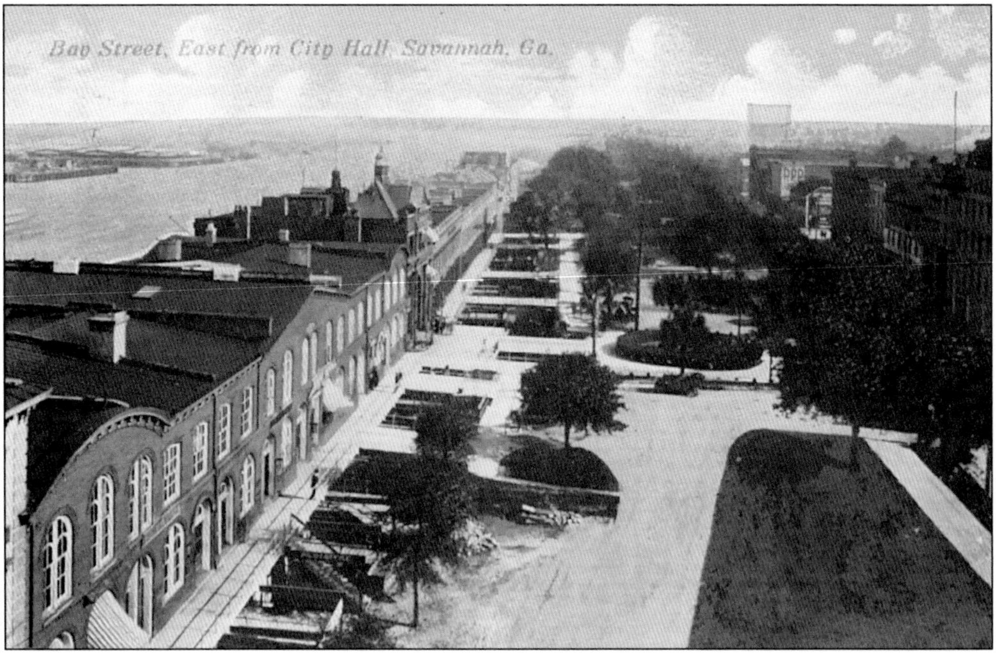

A Bird's-eye View Taken from atop City Hall, Showing East Bay Street in Savannah.

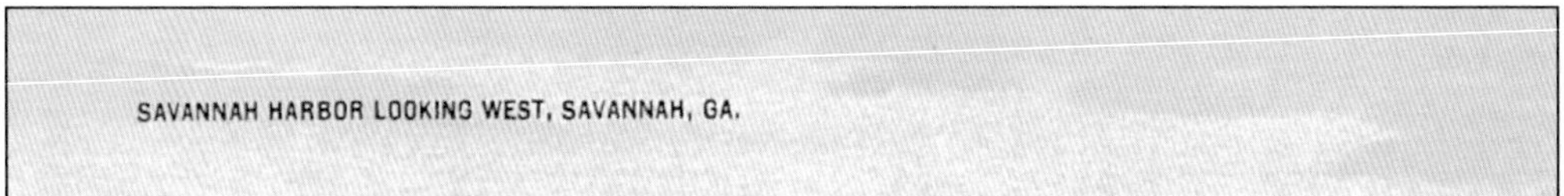

A Bird's-eye View of the other End of Bay Street in Savannah.

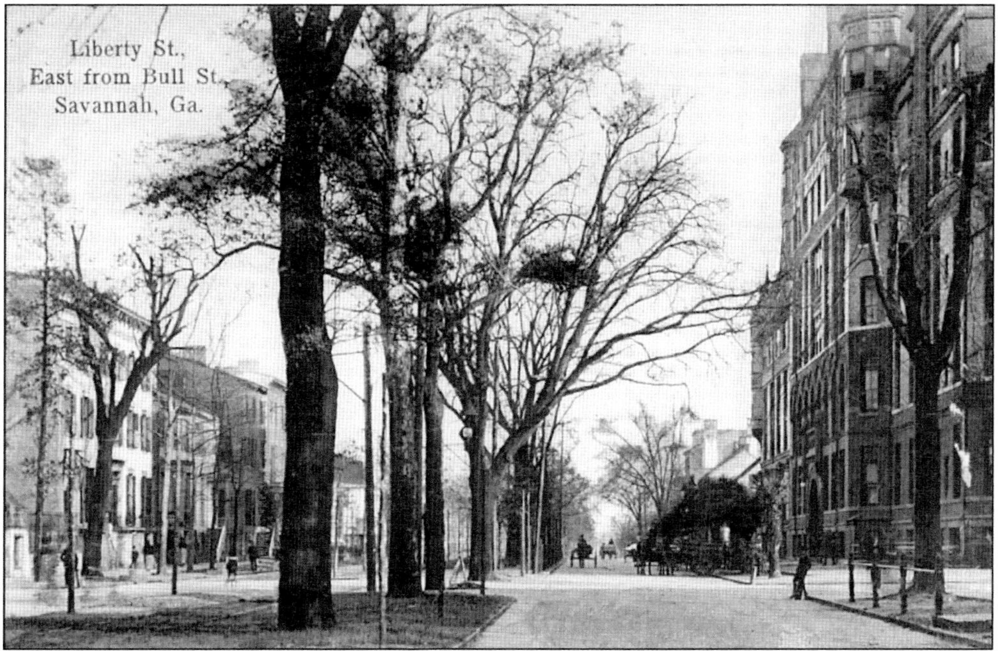

LIBERTY STREET IN SAVANNAH, LOOKING EAST FROM BULL STREET.

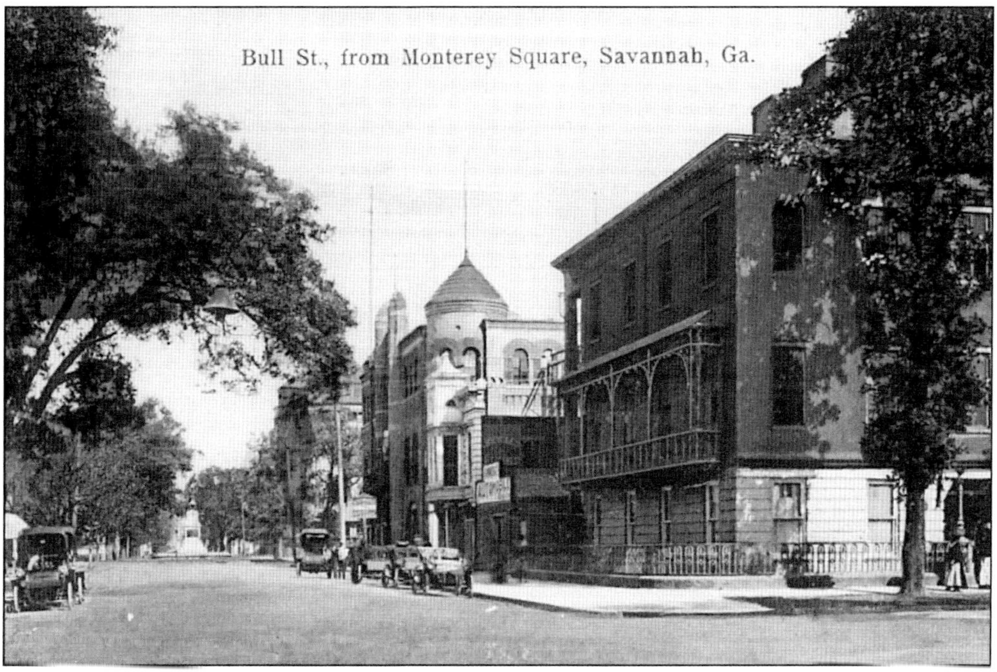

BULL STREET IN SAVANNAH, AS SEEN FROM MONTEREY SQUARE.

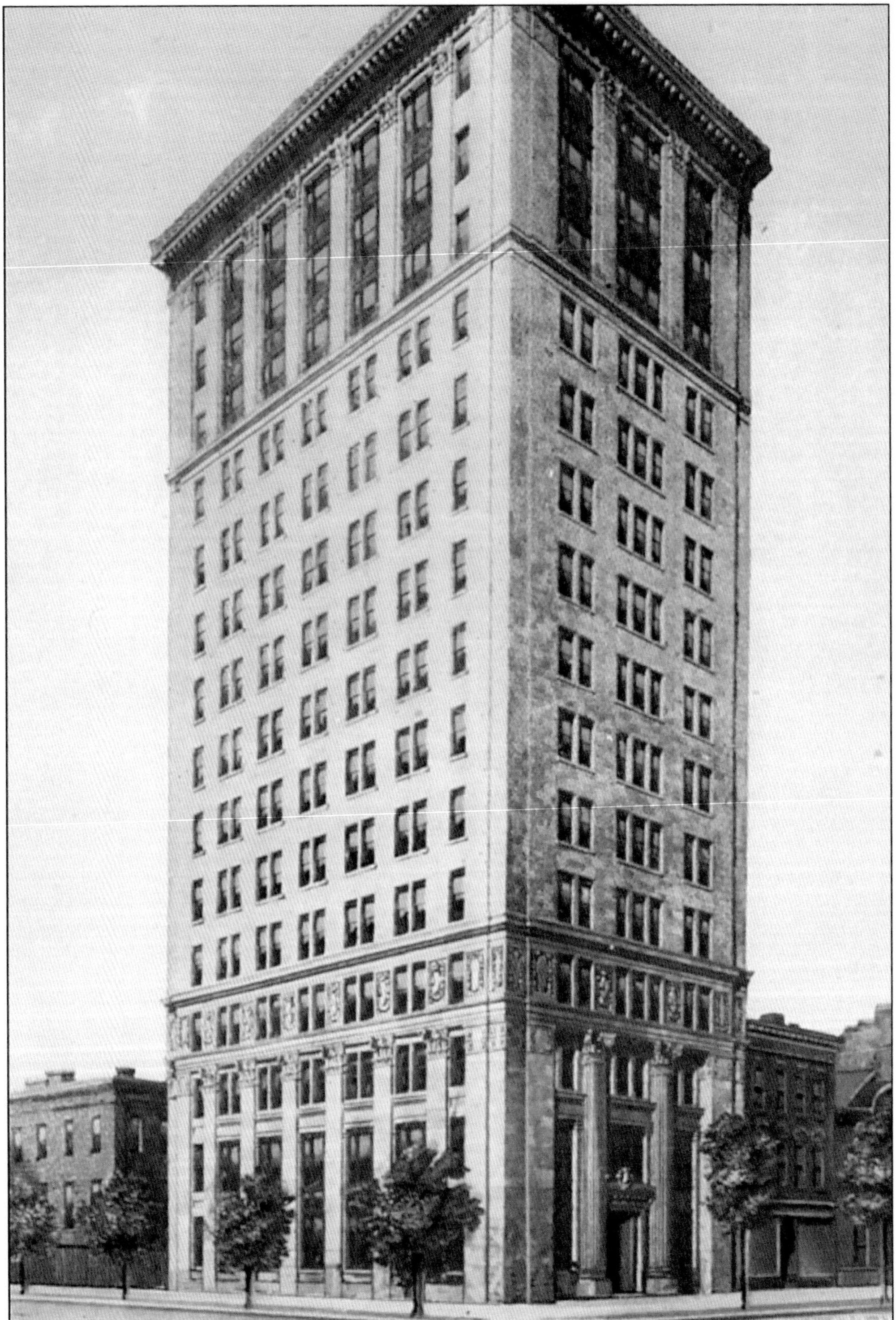

THE SAVANNAH BANK AND TRUST COMPANY, ON THE CORNER OF BAY AND DRAYTON STREETS IN SAVANNAH.

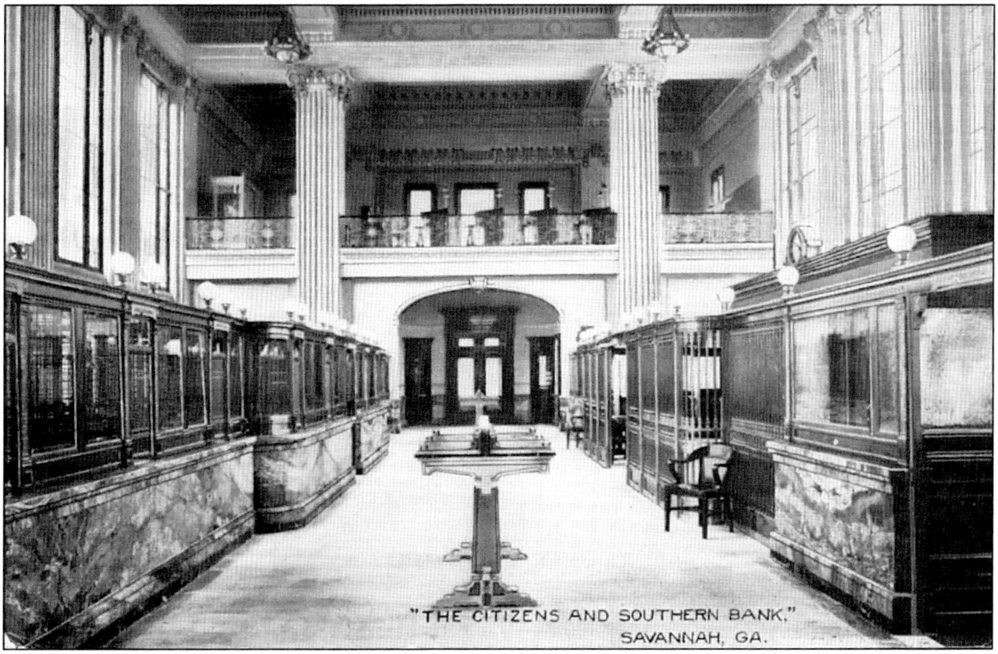

AN INTERIOR VIEW OF THE CITIZEN'S AND SOUTHERN BANK, LOCATED AT THE CORNER OF BRYAN AND DRAYTON STREETS IN SAVANNAH.

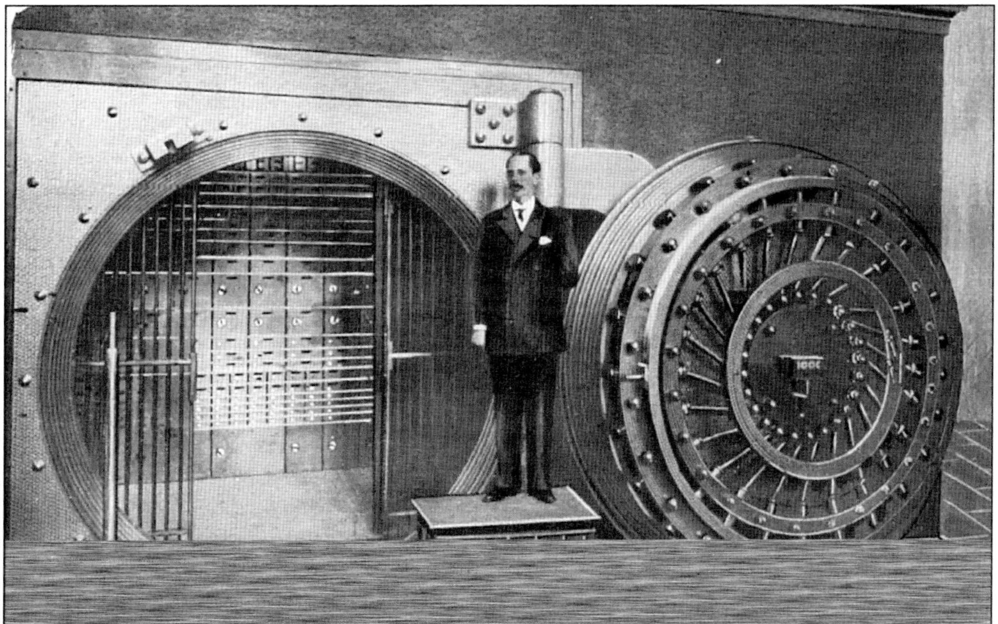

A LOOK INSIDE THE HUGE SAFE DEPOSIT VAULT OF THE CITIZEN'S AND SOUTHERN BANK IN SAVANNAH.

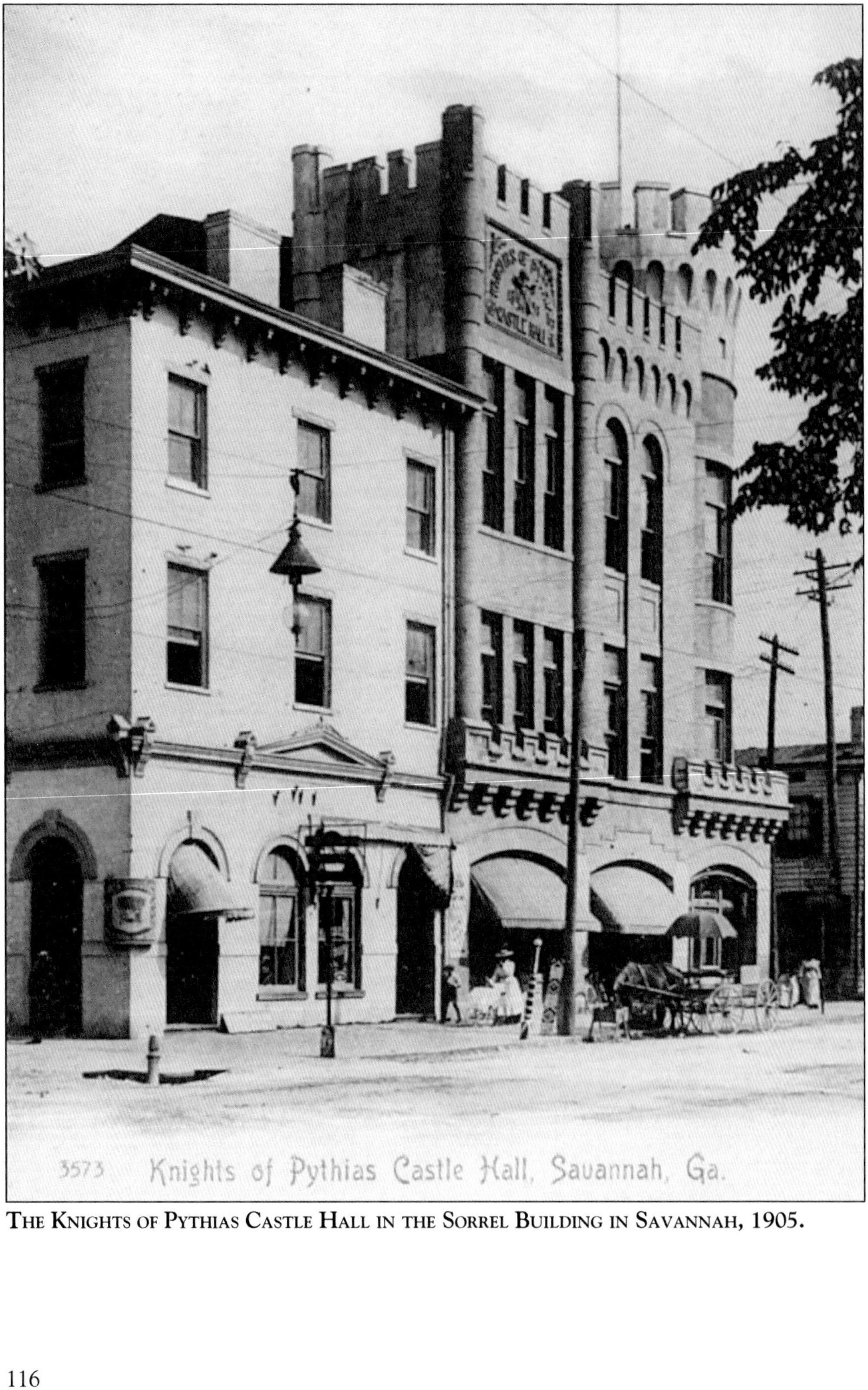

The Knights of Pythias Castle Hall in the Sorrel Building in Savannah, 1905.

THE MASONIC TEMPLE IN SAVANNAH, c. 1910.

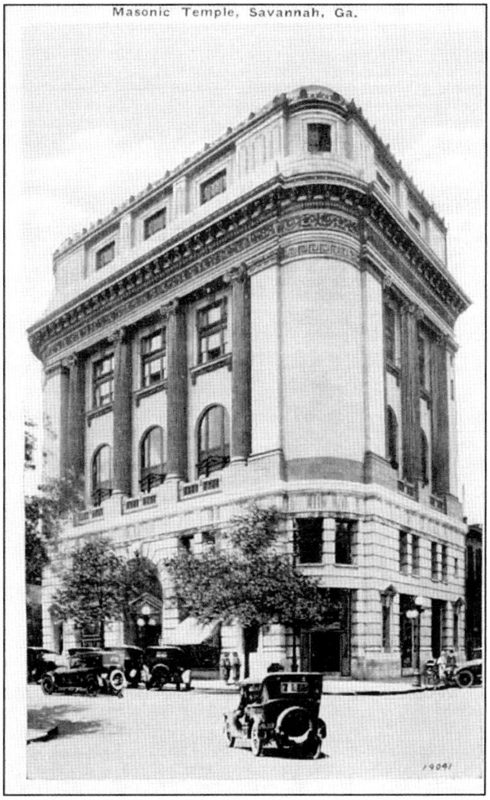

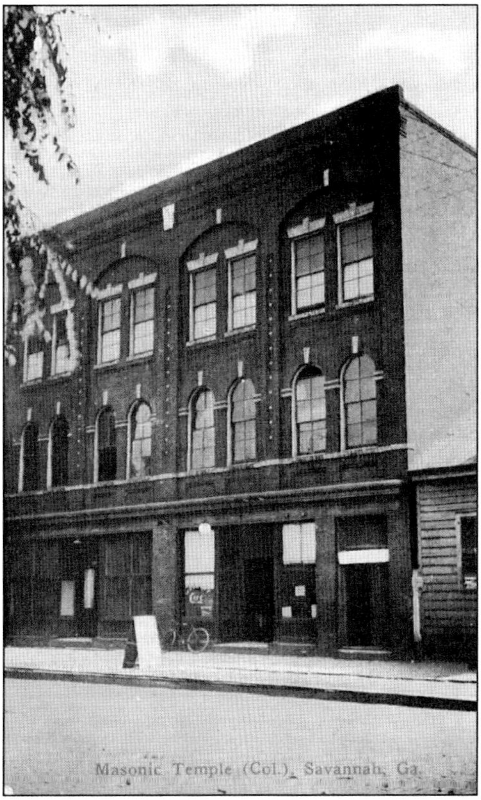

THE MASONIC TEMPLE FOR BLACK MEMBERS IN SAVANNAH, c. 1912.

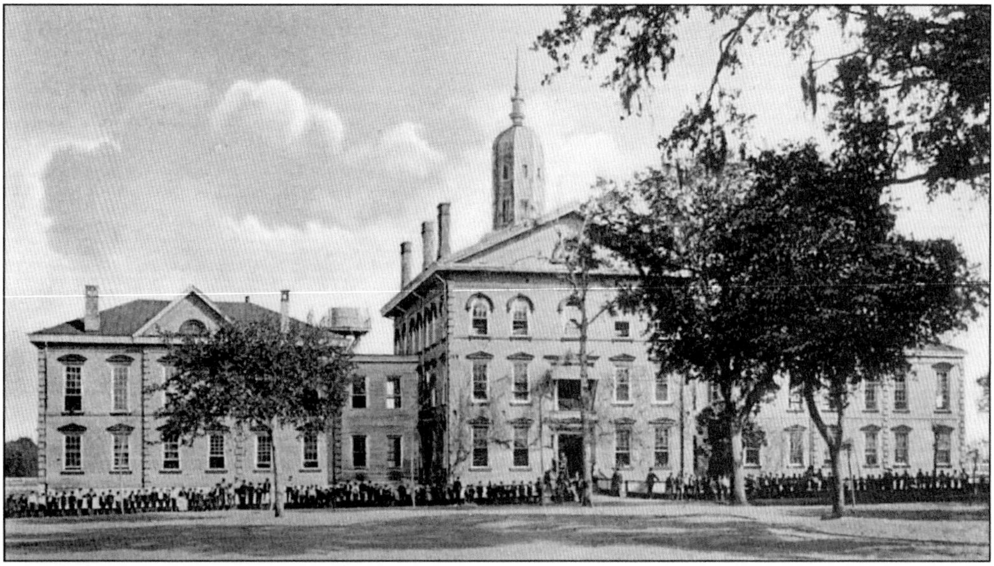

The Bethesda Orphanage in Savannah in 1905. Although the printed message on this card credits its founding to John Wesley, it was in fact begun by George Whitefield and James Habersham in the late 1730s.

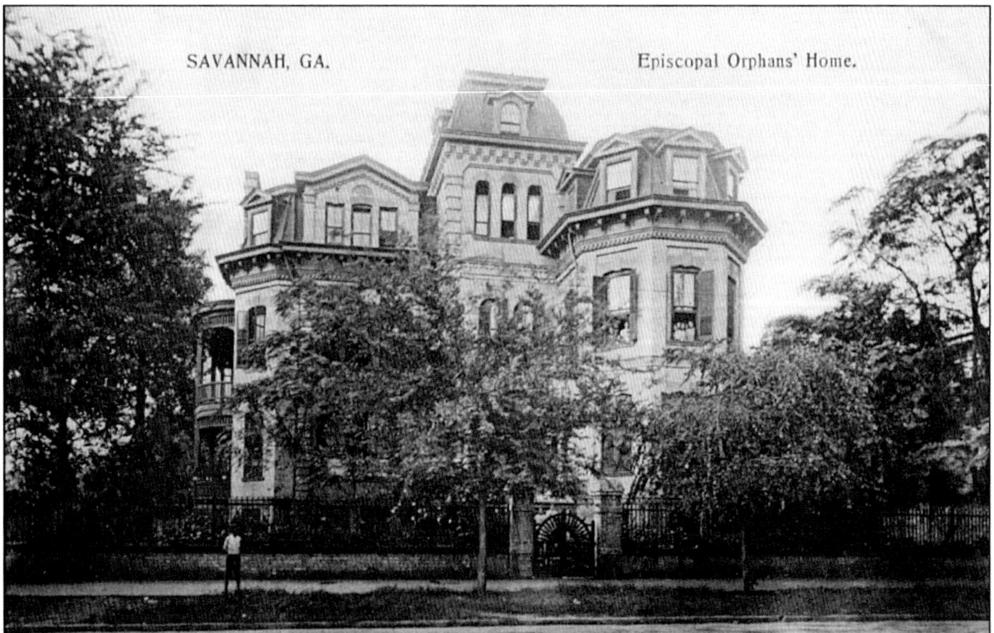

Another Orphanage. The Episcopal Church also sponsored an orphanage in Savannah, seen here.

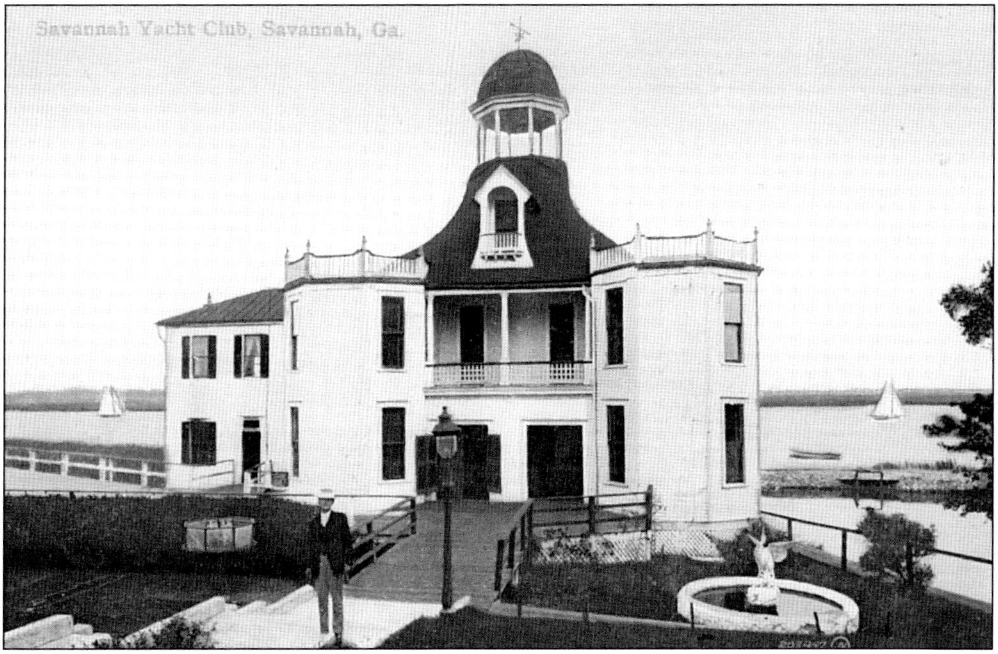

THE SAVANNAH YACHT CLUB AT SAVANNAH, C. 1908.

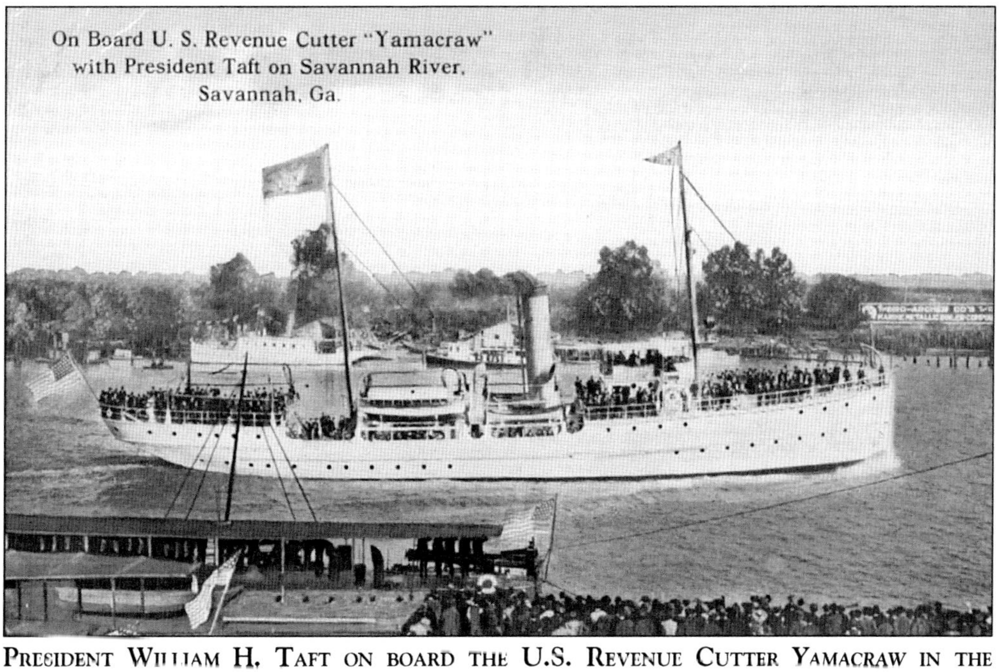

PRESIDENT WILLIAM H. TAFT ON BOARD THE U.S. REVENUE CUTTER YAMACRAW IN THE SAVANNAH RIVER, DURING A VISIT ABOUT 1910.

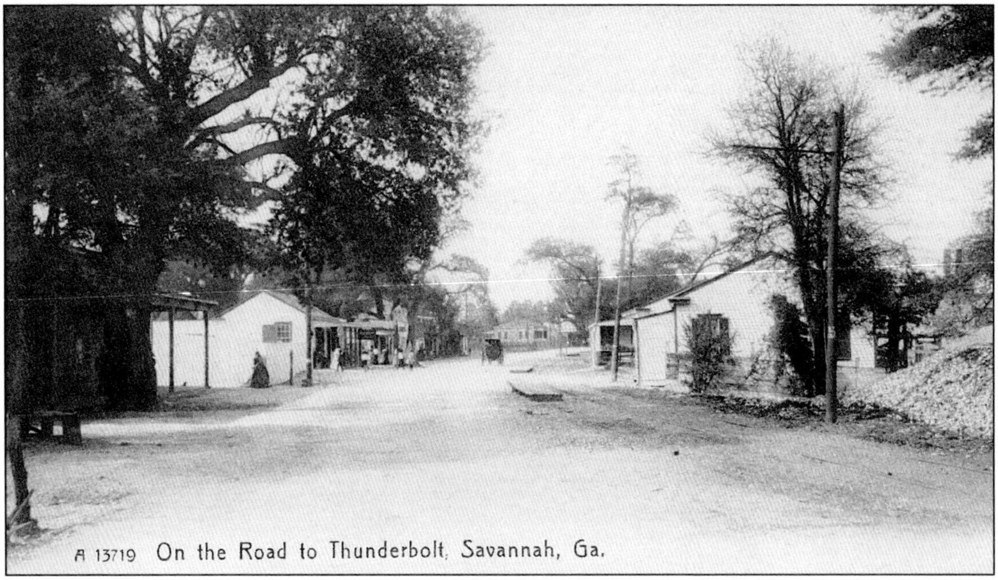

A VIEW OF THE ROAD FROM SAVANNAH TO THUNDERBOLT ABOUT 1905.

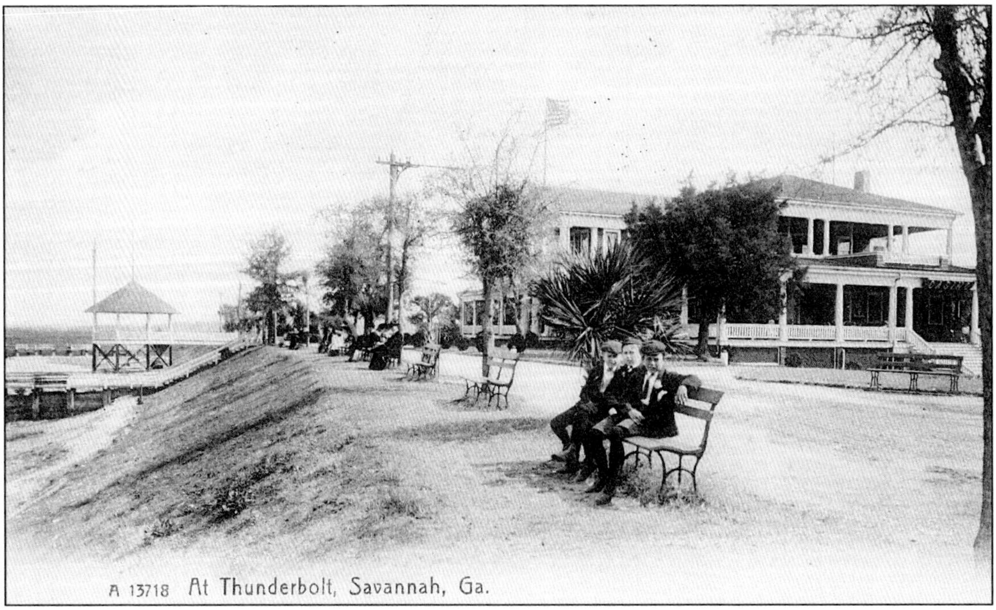

A VIEW OF THUNDERBOLT ABOUT 1905.

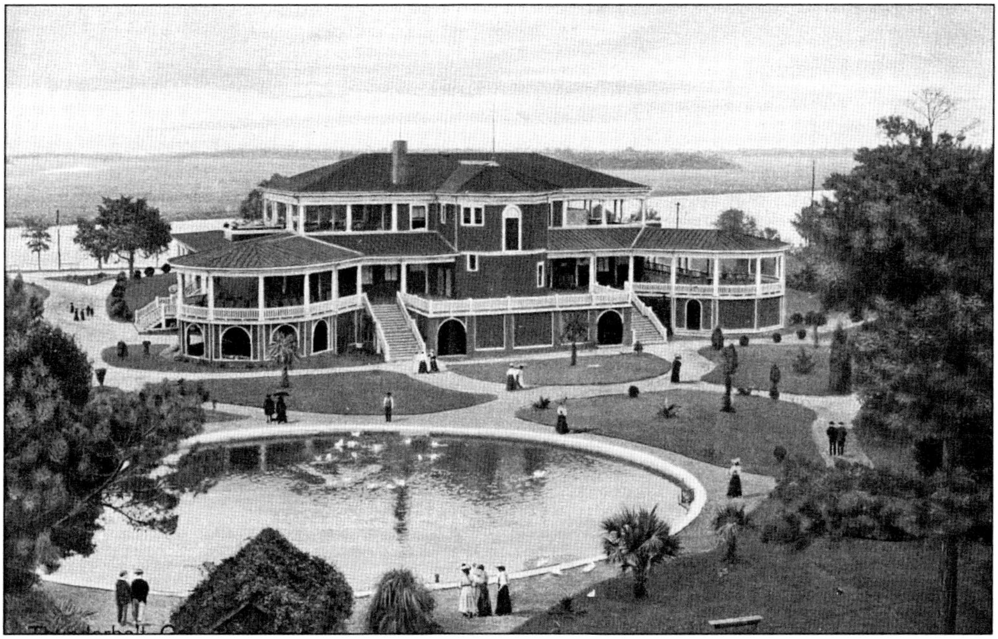

THE CASINO RESORT AND HOTEL AT THUNDERBOLT. This was quite a popular tourist attraction around the turn of the century.

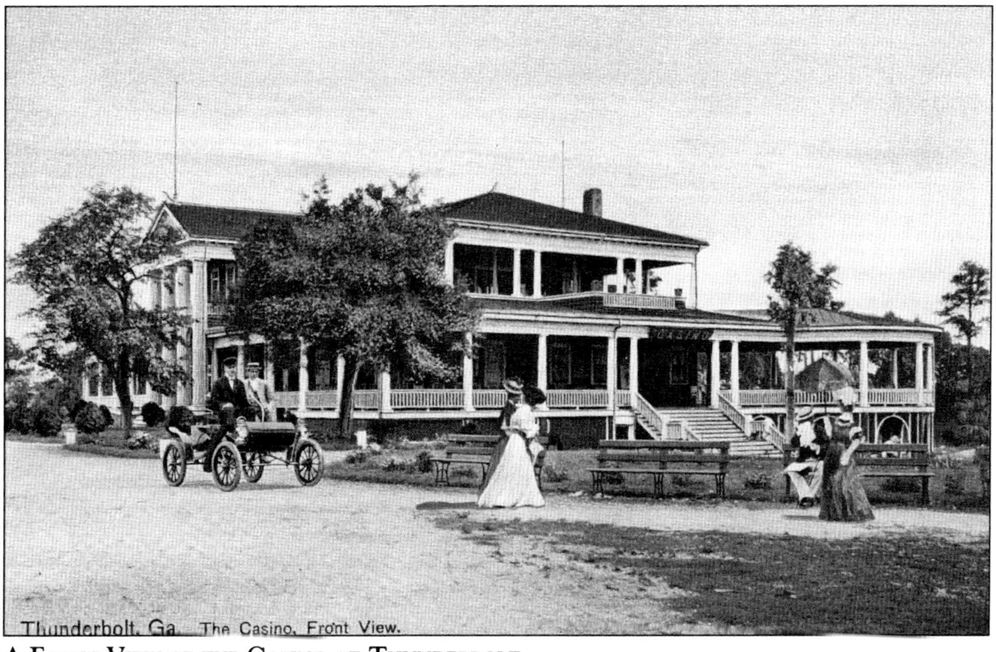

A FRONT VIEW OF THE CASINO AT THUNDERBOLT.

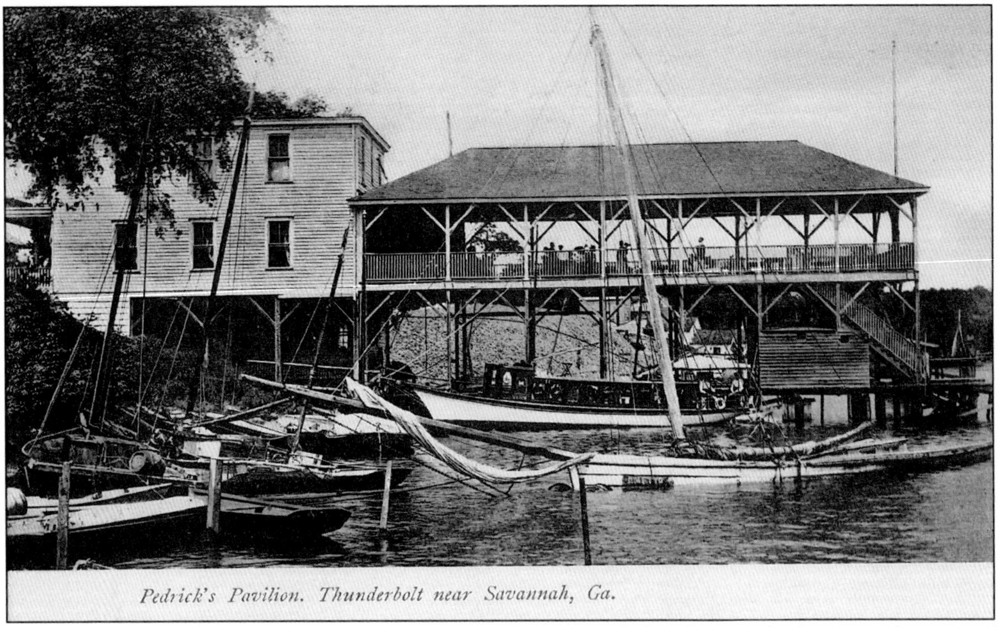

PEDRICK'S PAVILION AT THUNDERBOLT. The pavilion provided a place to dock private boats and to gain access to the water.

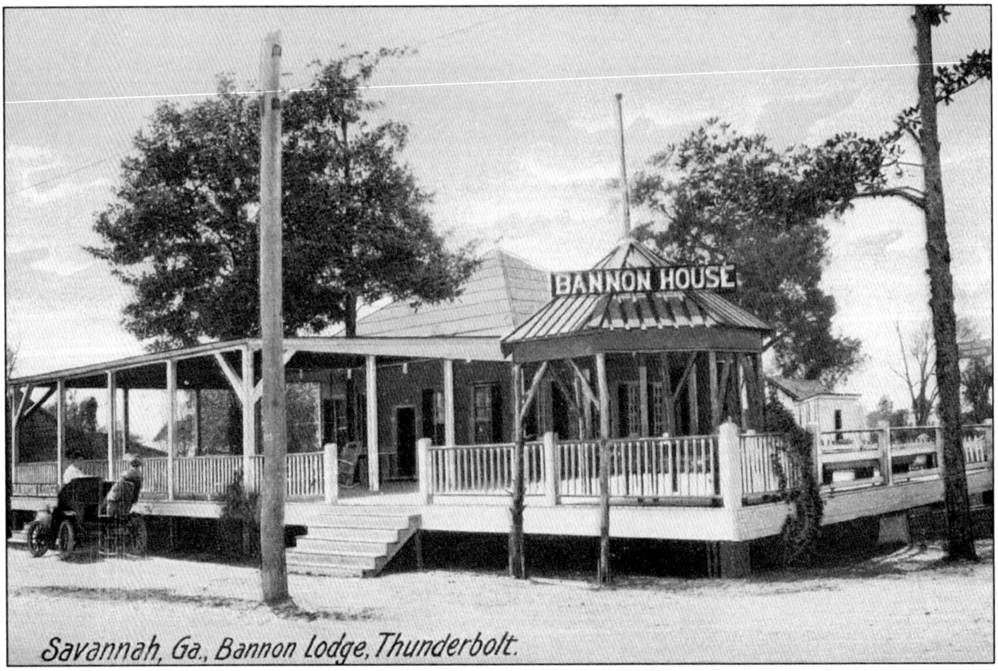

BANNON LODGE AT THUNDERBOLT. The lodge offered visitors a shady, sand-free spot to enjoy a snack or drink.

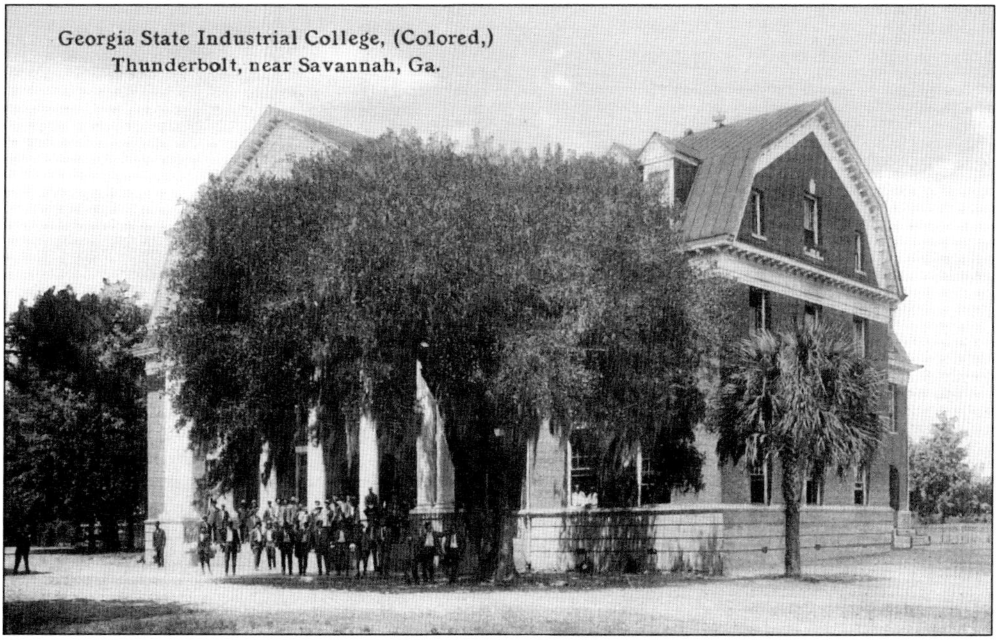

THE GEORGIA STATE INDUSTRIAL COLLEGE FOR BLACKS AT THUNDERBOLT, NEAR SAVANNAH.

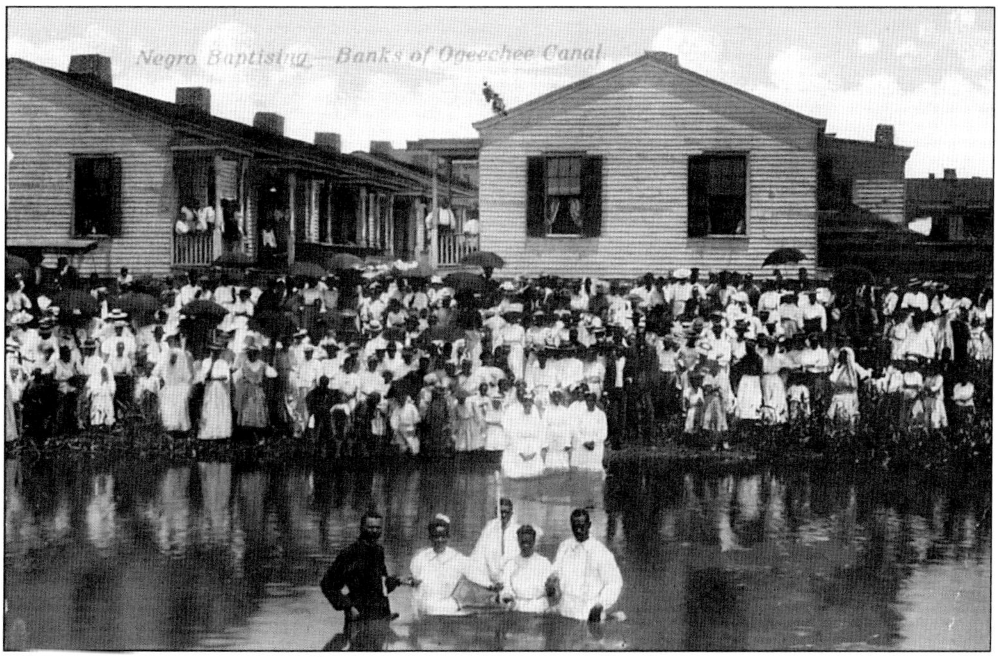

AN OPEN WATER BAPTISM. Friends and relatives congregated on the banks of the Ogechee Canal in Savannah *c.* 1912 to witness the baptizing of several church members.

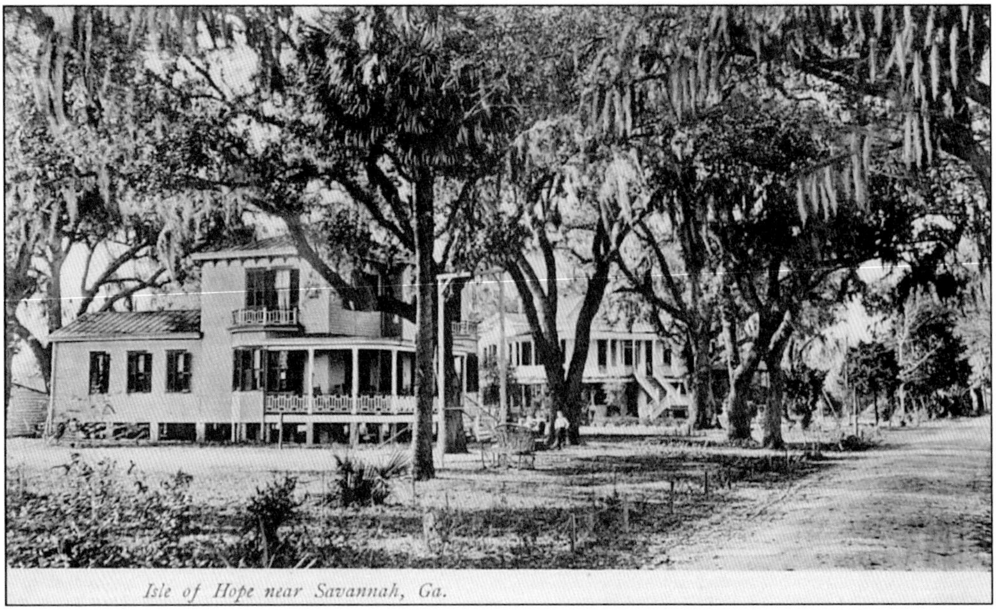

Isle of Hope, near Savannah. This area could boast of some beautiful homes along the waterfront.

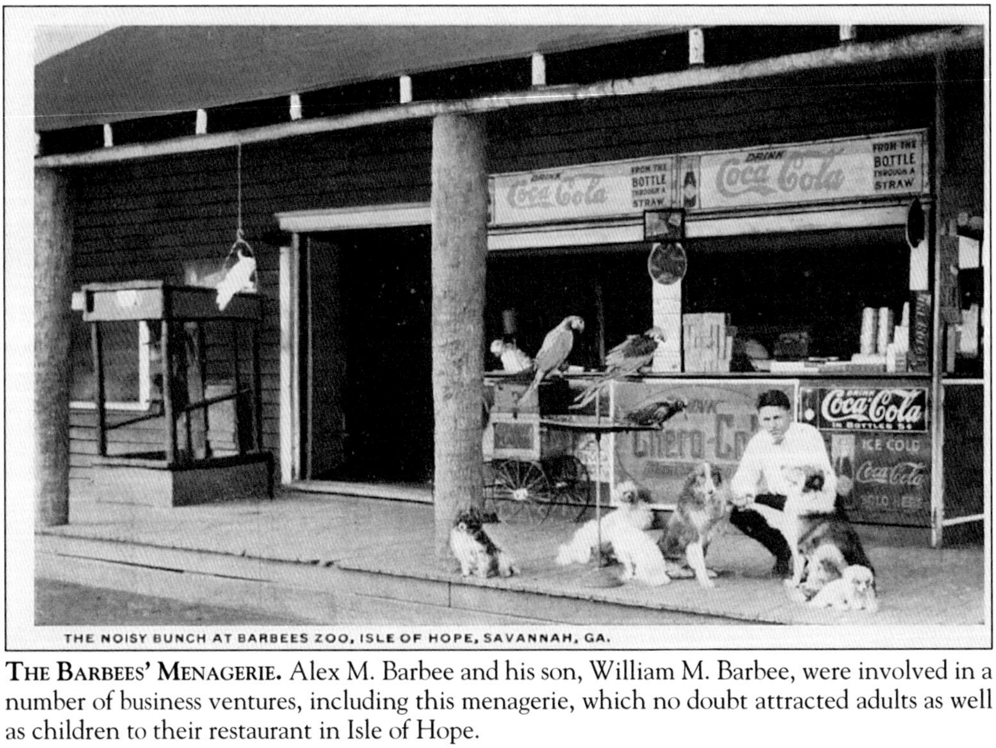

The Barbees' Menagerie. Alex M. Barbee and his son, William M. Barbee, were involved in a number of business ventures, including this menagerie, which no doubt attracted adults as well as children to their restaurant in Isle of Hope.

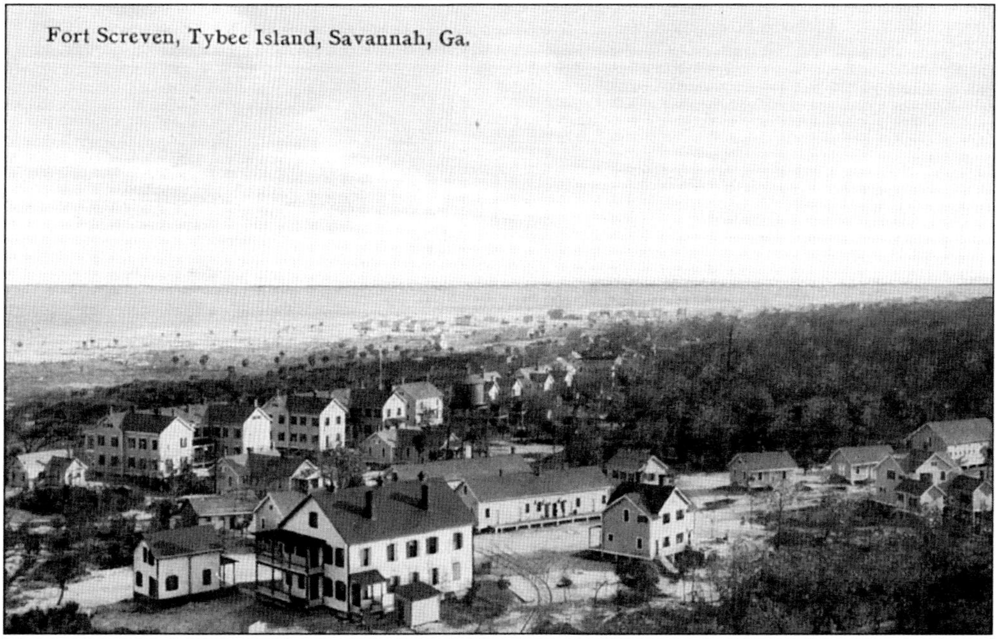

A BIRD'S-EYE VIEW OF FORT SCREVEN AT TYBEE ISLAND.

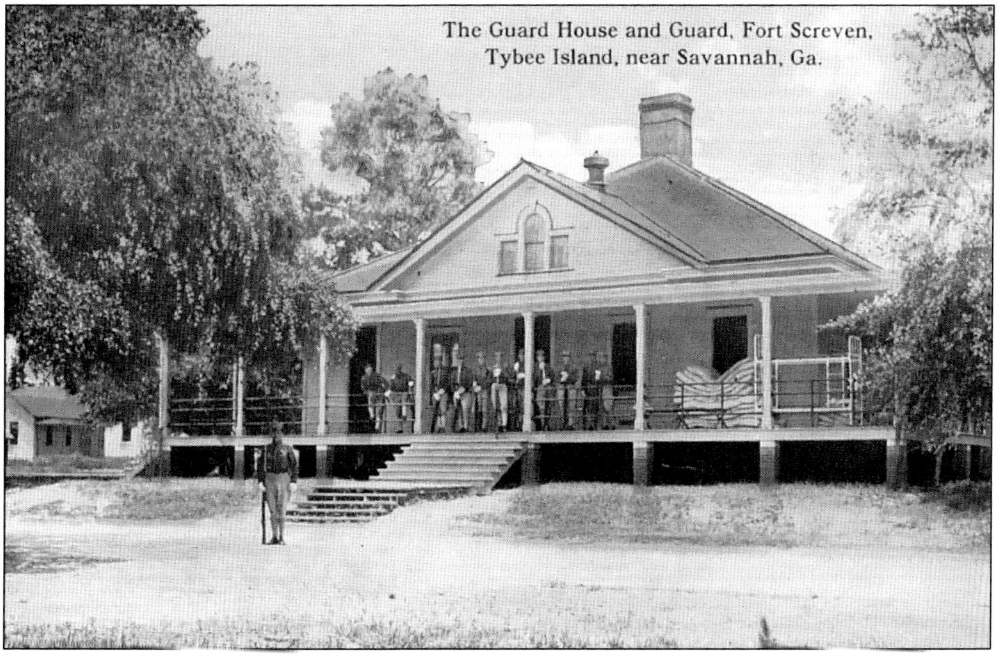

THE GUARD HOUSE AND SOLDIERS AT FORT SCREVEN ON TYBEE ISLAND.

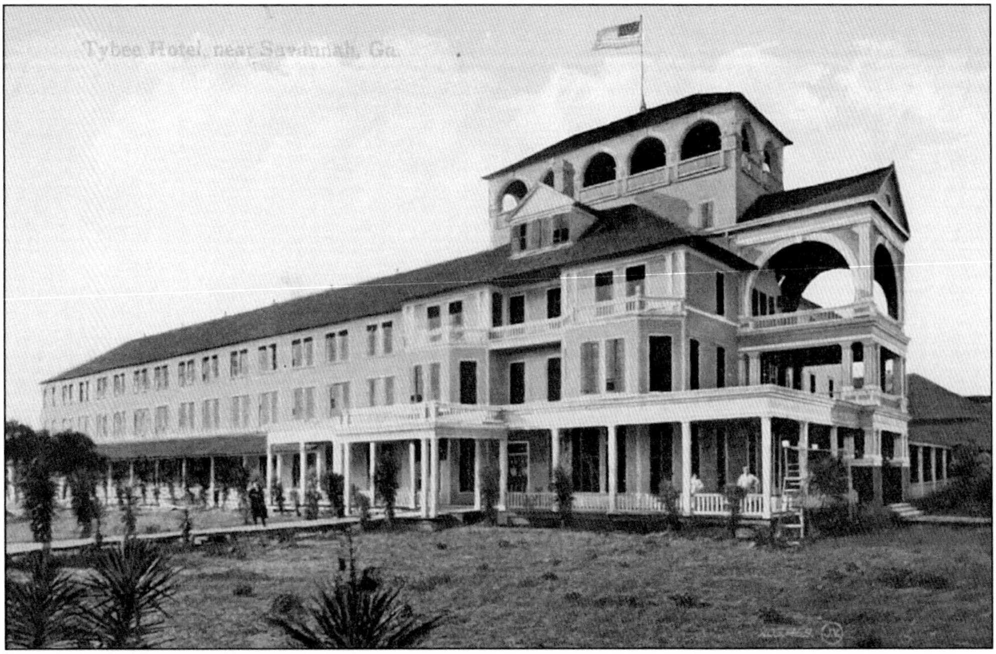

THE TYBEE HOTEL ON TYBEE ISLAND.

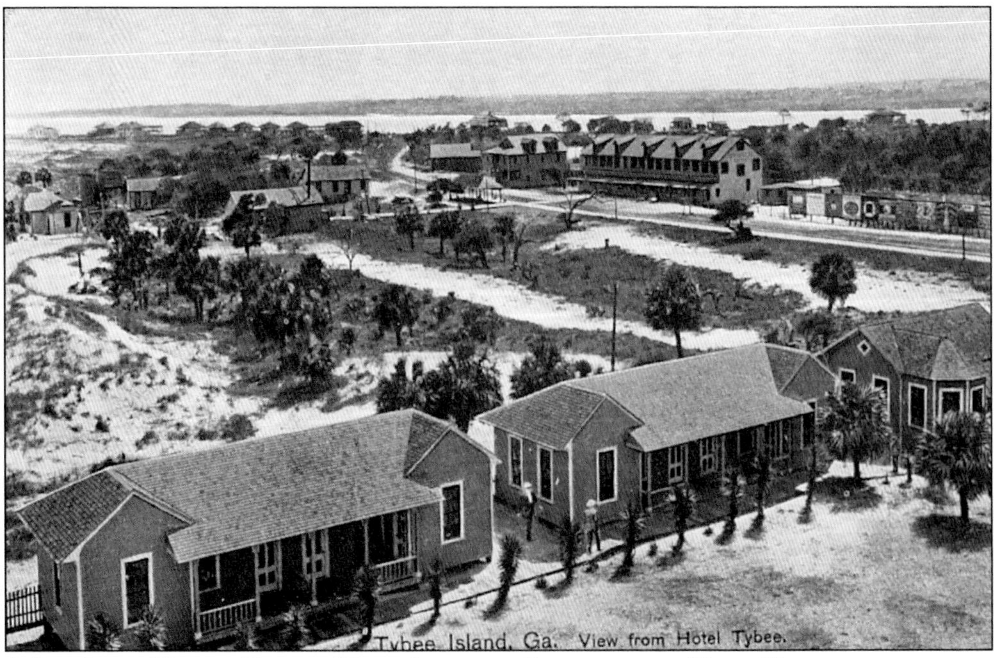

A BIRD'S-EYE VIEW OF PART OF TYBEE ISLAND AS SEEN FROM THE TYBEE HOTEL.

BIBLIOGRAPHY

Anonymous. *1909–1910 Business and Professional Directory of the Cities and Towns of Georgia*. Atlanta, Georgia: Young and Company, 1910.

Jordan, Robert H. and J. Gregg Puster. *Courthouses in Georgia*. Editing and design by Patti Anderson and Mary Jackson. Norcross, Georgia: The Harrison Company, 1984.

Krackow, Kenneth K. *Georgia Place-Names*. Macon, Georgia: Winship Press, 1975.

McKenny, Frank M. *The Standing Army: History of Georgia's County Confederate Monuments*. Alpharetta, Georgia: W.H. Wolfe Associates, 1993.

Winn, Les R. *Ghost Trains & Depots of Georgia (1833–1933)*. Chamblee, Georgia: Big Shanty Publishing Company, 1995.

INDEX